New Security Challenges Series

General Editor: **Stuart Croft**, Professor of International Security in the Department of Politics and International Studies at the University of Warwick, UK, and Director of the ESRC's New Security Challenges Programme.

The last decade demonstrated that threats to security vary greatly in their causes and manifestations, and that they invite interest and demand responses from the social sciences, civil society and a very broad policy community. In the past, the avoidance of war was the primary objective, but with the end of the Cold War the retention of military defence as the centrepiece of international security agenda became untenable. There has been, therefore, a significant shift in emphasis away from traditional approaches to security to a new agenda that talks of the softer side of security, in terms of human security, economic security and environmental security. The topical *New Security Challenges series* reflects this pressing political and research agenda.

Titles include:

Janne Haaland Matlary
EUROPEAN UNION SECURITY DYNAMICS
In the New National Interest

Michael Pugh, Neil Cooper and Mandy Turner (*editors*)
CRITICAL PERSPECTIVES ON THE POLITICAL ECONOMY OF
PEACEBUILDING

Brian Rappert and Chandré Gould (*editors*)
BIOSECURITY
Origins, Transformations and Practices

Brian Rappert
BIOTECHNOLOGY, SECURITY AND THE SEARCH FOR LIMITS
An Inquiry into Research and Methods

Brian Rappert (*editor*)
TECHNOLOGY AND SECURITY
Governing Threats in the New Millenium

Ali Tekin and Paul Andrew Williams
GEO-POLITICS OF THE EURO-ASIA ENERGY NEXUS
The European Union, Russia and Turkey

Lisa Watanabe
SECURING EUROPE

New Security Challenges Series
Series Standing Order ISBN 978–0–230–00216–6 (hardback) and
ISBN 978–0–230–00217–3 (paperback)
(*outside North America only*)

You can receive future titles in this series as they are published by placing a
standing order. Please contact your bookseller or, in case of difficulty, write to
us at the address below with your name and address, the title of the series and
the ISBN quoted above.

Customer Services Department, Macmillan Distribution Ltd, Houndmills,
Basingstoke, Hampshire RG21 6XS, England

Geo-Politics of the Euro-Asia Energy Nexus

The European Union, Russia and Turkey

Ali Tekin

Assistant Professor of International Relations,
Department of International Relations,
Bilkent University, Turkey

Paul Andrew Williams

Assistant Professor of International Relations,
Department of International Relations,
Bilkent University, Turkey

palgrave
macmillan

First published 2011 by
PALGRAVE MACMILLAN

Palgrave Macmillan in the UK is an imprint of Macmillan Publishers Limited, registered in England, company number 785998, of Houndmills, Basingstoke, Hampshire RG21 6XS.

Palgrave Macmillan in the US is a division of St Martin's Press LLC, 175 Fifth Avenue, New York, NY 10010.

Palgrave Macmillan is the global academic imprint of the above companies and has companies and representatives throughout the world.

Palgrave® and Macmillan® are registered trademarks in the United States, the United Kingdom, Europe and other countries.

ISBN 978-0-230-25261-5 hardback

This book is printed on paper suitable for recycling and made from fully managed and sustained forest sources. Logging, pulping and manufacturing processes are expected to conform to the environmental regulations of the country of origin.

A catalogue record for this book is available from the British Library.

A catalog record for this book is available from the Library of Congress.

10   9   8   7   6   5   4   3   2   1
20   19   18   17   16   15   14   13   12   11

Printed and bound in Great Britain by
CPI Antony Rowe, Chippenham and Eastbourne

Contents

Part II The European Union, Russia and Other Actors

Part III Turkey as a Transit and Candidate Country

List of Maps, Tables and Figures

Maps

Tables

Figures

Acknowledgements

Both of us are extremely grateful to Alexandra Webster and Liz Blackmore at Palgrave Macmillan for their unstinting support and patience through all stages of the publication process. We also wish to thank Turkish Petroleum Pipeline Corporation (Botas) and Nabucco Gas Pipeline International GmbH for allowing us permission to use their Nabucco map as Figure 7.1 in the book.

Ali Tekin

Several people were crucial in helping me on this project, especially Duygu Sever and Gizem Kumas, who performed excellent research assistance on various chapters. The graduate students in my various EU courses participated in lively discussions of the topic, providing me with additional motivation to complete the manuscript. I also wish to thank the Jean Monnet Chair Programme of the European Commission for supporting my attendance at numerous conferences, where I had the opportunity to share some of the ideas contained in the book. In addition, the Minda de Gunzburg Center for European Studies at Harvard University kindly provided me with a 6-month visiting fellowship in 2008–09, which allowed me to work on the topic of the book.

Paul Andrew Williams

I would like to thank Bilkent University for supporting my sabbatical leave in 2009–10 and Woodrow Wilson International Center for Scholars for the complementary offer of a visiting scholarship position during that time. My student interns at the Wilson Center, Jakub Olszowiec and Arda Bilgen, provided invaluable research assistance on my part of this joint book project. Finally, I would be negligent to the utmost in not expressing my sincerest gratitude to my wife Zeynep for all her sacrifice and support throughout this entire process as well as to my parents Melvin and Mary for their innumerable and indispensable words of reassurance and encouragement.

List of Abbreviations and Acronyms

ACG	Azeri–Chirag–Guneshli oil field
AIOC	Azerbaijan International Oil Consortium
APD	Accession Partnership Document
bcm	billion cubic metres
bcma	billion cubic metres per annum
BG	British Gas
BOTAS	Turkish Petroleum Pipeline Corporation
BP	British Petroleum (previous name)
BPS	Baltic Pipeline System
BSEC	Organization of the Black Sea Economic Cooperation
BTC	Baku–Tbilisi–Ceyhan oil pipeline
BTE	Baku–Tbilisi–Erzurum natural gas pipeline
CAC	Central Asia-Centre natural gas pipeline
CAGP	Central Asian Gas Pipeline
CBC	Cross-Border Cooperation
CEER	Council of European Energy Regulators
CEO	Chief Executive Officer
CFSP	Common Foreign and Security Policy
CNPC	China National Petroleum Corporation
CO_2	Carbon Dioxide
CPC	Caspian Pipeline Consortium
DEPA	Greek Public Gas Corporation
EAURATOM	European Atomic Energy Community
EBRD	European Bank for Reconstruction and Development
EC	European Community
ECSC	European Coal and Steel Community
ECT	Energy Charter Treaty
EEA	European Economic Area
EEC	European Economic Community
EIA	Energy Information Administration
EIB	European Investment Bank
EIF	European Investment Fund
ENP	European Neighbourhood Policy
ENPI	European Neighbourhood and Partnership Instrument

a growing source of its energy consumption requirements that origi-
nates in and transits the Former Soviet Union (FSU) territories of Russia,
Belarus and Ukraine, countries lying outside the ambit of EU regulatory
control and increasingly embroiled in contentious energy disputes that
have demonstrated a strong potential to generate negative 'spillover' for
the security of European energy supplies. Reflecting major differences in
respective levels of dependency (on Russia) and capacities for respond-
ing to unequal degrees of 'sensitivity' and 'vulnerability' (Keohane and
Nye, 2001, pp. 3–32) to disruptions in Russian energy supplies, member
states have addressed the EU economy's prominent dependence on the
latter in sometimes embarrassingly divergent and incompatible ways.
On the one hand, relevant authorities in the largest economies in the
EU27 – notably France, Germany and Italy – have implied, by endors-
ing or condoning joint undertakings between incumbent energy firms
headquartered there and those based in Russia, that the 'problem' of
Russian gas cut-offs can be resolved by building new pipelines bypassing
Belarus and Ukraine. Conversely, given their historical legacy of economic dependency on Russia, states that joined the EU in the 2004 and
2007 enlargements have been more receptive to the view that European
'energy crises' stem from Moscow's unfriendly stance towards the efforts
of ex-Soviet bloc countries to move closer to Europe. Thus, they back
stronger European Commission efforts to diversify the EU27's overall energy portfolio further away from Russia. Trying to accommodate
EU constituencies' competing perspectives, the Commission has largely
cobbled EU-wide energy policy out of a series of ad hoc compromises
(Andoura et al., 2010, pp. 51–60).

In the same five-decade period during which collective European institutions could either afford to ignore energy security matters or fail to
muster the collective vision to tackle this issue, Turkey, starting with
the 1963 Ankara Association Agreement, embarked on a similarly gradual and equally fitful campaign to join the EU. While accepted into the
Customs Union in 1995 and formally invited to commence accession
talks in 2005, Turkey has continued to encounter a sturdy opposition to its full-membership bid by various EU member states that have
effectively blocked negotiations on many separate chapters, including
energy (by new member state Cyprus in exchange for Turkey's refusal,
under provisos related to its membership in the Customs Union, to
open up its trade portals to *all* EU27 member states). Officials of key
member states, notably France and Germany, have become increasingly
adamant that Turkey, which in certain ways already attained this status by signing the 1995 agreement, accept an ambiguously defined and

1
Introduction

Europe's security, Russian energy and Turkey's EU accession bid

In many ways, energy and security issues were embodied in the European Union's (EU) seminal origins – the treaties establishing the 1951 European Coal and Steel Community (ECSC) and the 1957 European Atomic Energy Community (EURATOM). Oddly enough, however, during the half-century spanning the 1957 Treaty of Rome and the 2007 Treaty of Lisbon, the EU and its predecessor organisations largely decoupled these two issues from each other. All but relegating common security architecture to the remit of the North Atlantic Treaty Organization (NATO), an omission that did not seem particularly glaring after the collapse of the Soviet Union seemed to corroborate the triumph of global free-market liberalism (Fukuyama, 2006) and the concurrent creation of the European Community in the 1992 Maastricht Treaty gave added impetus and saliency to the single market project, Brussels turned its primary institutional attention to the gradual implementation of an *internal* energy market that would be an integral and compatible component of the single market. Even this latter objective has proceeded at best rather fitfully, though, with many member states failing to meet the various domestic market-opening stipulations contained in the EU's *acquis communautaire* – notably the first and second packages of Electricity and Gas Directives (Andoura et al., 2010, pp. 21–2).

However, the *external* security dimensions of EU energy policy barely appeared on the radar screen until the first cut-off of Russian gas supplies to Europe in January 2006. This incident opened a formidable Pandora's box of anxieties and apprehensions concerning European reliance on

SCP	South Caucasus Pipeline
SEEECT	South-East Europe Energy Community Treaty
SEEREM	South-East Europe Regional Energy Market
SGI	Sour Gas Injection
SOCAR	State Oil Company of Azerbaijan Republic
TAP	Trans Adriatic Pipeline
TCO	Tengizchevroil
TEN-E	Trans-European Networks-Energy
TGII	Turkey–Greece–Italy Interconnector
TPAO	Turkish Petroleum Corporation
UK	United Kingdom
UN	United Nations
UNSC	United Nations Security Council
US	United States
USSR	Union of Soviet Socialist Republics
WTO	World Trade Organization

ERDF	European Regional Development Fund
ERGEG	European Regulators' Group for Electricity and Gas
ESPO	East Siberia–Pacific Ocean oil pipeline
EU	European Union
FDI	foreign direct investment
FSU	Former Soviet Union
G8	Group of Eight
GATT	General Agreement on Trade and Tariffs
GCC	Gulf Cooperation Council
GDP	Gross Domestic Product
GECF	Gas Exporting Countries Forum
GHG	Greenhouse Gas
GUEU	Georgia–Ukraine–European Union pipeline
IEA	International Energy Agency
IGA	Intergovernmental Agreement
IMF	International Monetary Fund
INOGATE	Interstate Oil and Gas Transport to Europe
IT	Iraq–Turkey oil pipeline
kgoe	kilograms of oil equivalent
km	kilometre
KPO	Karachaganak Petroleum
KRG	Kurdish Regional Government
LNG	liquefied natural gas
mcm	million cubic metres
mcma	million cubic metres per annum
MoU	Memorandum of Understanding
mt	metric tonne
mmt	million metric tonnes
mmta	million metric tonnes per annum
mtoe	million tonnes of oil equivalent
NATO	North Atlantic Treaty Organization
NEGP	Northern European Gas Pipeline
NG3	natural gas route 3
NG6	natural gas route 6
NIF	Neighbourhood Investment Facility
OPEC	Organization of Petroleum Exporting Countries
PCA	Partnership and Cooperation Agreement
PEOP	Pan-European Oil Pipeline
PKK	Kurdish Workers' Party
PRC	People's Republic of China
PSA	Production Sharing Agreement

mutably benchmarked 'privileged partnership' with the EU in lieu of full membership.

Turkey's open scorn for and rejection of a 'privileged partnership' might seem merely righteous, yet irrelevant, but for the existence of certain potential bargaining counterweights in its possession. The intergovernmentalist approach (Moravcsik, 1998) exemplifies the bottom-up view of national economic interests in member states rationally bargaining over the adoption or preservation of competing preferences at the EU level, a process of aggregate policy formation in which Turkish interests have become entangled, from the vantage point of the rest of Europe, in both beneficial and adverse ways. Energy is at the crux of this entanglement. EU energy consumption and importation profiles have evolved since the end of the Cold War in ways that increase Turkey's significance to the EU. While the immediate post-Cold War boost to neo-liberal globalisation dovetailed with a gradual widening of supplier bases, which reduced its collective importation-relative (but not consumption-denominated) dependency on Russian natural gas, the EU's *absolute* consumption of gas from Russia and elsewhere continued to grow. Moreover, the 2004 and 2007 enlargements of the Union, which presupposed the unanimous approval of the EU15, incorporated 12 new member states that added less to the overall size of the EU economy than to its dependence on Russian energy. In some cases, however, especially among the older EU15 member states, diversification of EU-area crude oil imports may have actually entailed *increased* reliance on Russia (versus their traditionally dominant Middle East and North African suppliers) in both absolute and relative terms.

As various tables in Chapter 4 and explication in Chapter 7 show, Turkey experienced considerably higher rates of growth in overall energy consumption between 1992 and 2007 and vastly exceeded the EU27's average rate of growth in imports of non-EU and Russian gas supplies. Therefore, it would seem to occupy a rather weak position from which to assist in adding *independent* Europe-bound transit routes for Russian or non-Russian gas. Nonetheless, given its evident willingness to ratify the EU's preferred Energy Charter Treaty (ECT) and legislate and implement some EU-approved energy-market liberalisation measures, as well as the advantageous interposition of its territory between major non-Russian supply regions and Europe, Turkey serves as a potential *acquis*-compatible 'Southern Energy Corridor' (Meister, 2010, p. 24). Nevertheless, fuller fruition of the latter status, elements of which have already materialised in the inchoate form of the construction of the Baku–Tbilisi–Erzurum (or South Caucasus) pipeline taking Azeri gas to

Turkey and the complementary Turkey–Greece Interconnector piping a fraction of this gas to Greece, has become inextricably linked to further progress on Turkey's EU accession negotiations.

Nonetheless, a dual political risk emerges with the coupling of this membership issue to European security-of-supply concerns. On the one hand, the EU may overestimate Ankara's interest in 'energy corridor'-centric cooperation, especially in terms of aligning the Turkish energy infrastructure with EU standards and purposes, without reciprocal assurances on Turkey's membership chances, the precariousness of which has been signalled by the Cyprus-spearheaded suspension of the energy-chapter negotiations. That is, the EU, the larger strategic aims of which can all too easily be operationally derailed by the parochial interests and prejudices of its individual member states, risks alienating Turkey, which has already been nurturing a parallel track of economic and political cooperation with Russia (and may be doing the same with various other non-European countries), as manifested in its extant and burgeoning energy trade relationship with Russia, one that matches EU–Russian energy relations in robustness (Linke and Viëtor, 2010, pp. 3–4). Turkey, on the other hand, may overstretch its energy 'hand' to try to win more than larger transit fees and privileged access to energy supplies, for which it has already been criticised vis-à-vis the Nabucco Gas Pipeline undertaking (Yigitguden, 2010, p. 17) – it may also grab for the highest-hanging fruit of full membership in the premier league of European states. While Turkey has other non-energy-related benefits to offer the EU (Ibid., p. 18), the latter has evolved considerably since the 1950s to embody a larger number of ideational values (and members) that have raised the membership bar that Turkey must clear.

Our purpose

After they first occurred in late 2005 to early 2006, periodic cut-offs of Europe-bound supplies of Russian gas to key transit state Ukraine dramatically elevated the concern for energy security on the EU's policy agenda. Thus, one key aspect of our focus here does concern the motivations and nature of the European Commission-led response to these crises as encapsulated in the European Energy Policy and one of its key planks, diversifying external energy suppliers and transit routes. For the sake of situating our own examination of the subject matter, the reader of this book will necessarily encounter discussion of EU energy security (which often incorporates considerations of the respective roles that Russia and Turkey play) and Turkey–EU relations, with the former's EU membership bid lying at the centre of this long and characteristically arduous interaction. While analyses of these issues have typically proceeded in mutual isolation, we prefer to provide a distinctively detailed treatment of Turkey's strategy of linking its 'energy corridor' role, centrally for non-Russian supplies of natural gas, to real and discernible progress on its EU accession. Thus, our book offers a unique perspective on the implied and expressed connections that have been drawn between Europe's energy security, the external dimensions of which have become as prominent on the agenda as its internal market integration aspects, the emergence as a new 'Southern Energy Corridor' to convey various supplies through Turkey, and the latter country's prospects of joining the EU.

The line of logic contained in the following discussion similarly underscores our interest in analysing the dualistic linkages that have emerged to connect EU energy security, Turkey's 'energy corridor' (the exact nature and terms of which have not been precisely defined) status and Turkey's EU accession campaign. Reflecting its roots in the now-expired Coal and Steel Community (Andoura et al., 2010, p. 23), European Energy Policy has been inwardly focused – that is, on stronger integration and liberalisation of domestic electricity and gas markets, with infrastructural ramifications extending mainly to greater storage capacity and augmented interconnectivity (i.e., reversible flow) within the intra-EU grid networks. To the extent that the EU has looked beyond its borders in the energy domain, it has largely done so by joining in stronger multilateral efforts, such as International Energy Agency (IEA) precautionary oil stockpiling and emergency sharing provisions (Ibid., pp. 18–19), or by trying to 'externalise' its energy *acquis* – that is, the packages of EU electricity and gas market directives – to neighbouring non-EU territories, especially primary and secondary transit countries. Over the past 15 years, the EU has fervently advocated adoption of the ECT and its ancillary Transit Protocol by Moscow and other FSU countries, key non-member states that produce and export crucial supplies of energy (some oil, but primarily gas). However, Russia has 'un-signed' itself from a scheme (Meister, 2010, p. 24) that had always aimed to liberalise its crucial upstream and transit sectors in line with General Agreement on Tariff and Trade/World Trade Organization (GATT/WTO) rules. The EU did externalise the energy *acquis* to the non-EU signatories of the Energy Community of Southeast Europe Treaty (Andoura et al., 2010, pp. 56–7), but other key transit partners, notably Turkey and Ukraine, remain observers only.

Only in more recent years did the European Commission, struggling simultaneously to incorporate environmental sustainability goals into the mix of energy-related objectives, finally endorse concerted and directed efforts to secure the EU's external supply base, especially in oil and natural gas. It has sought to address this issue via 'dialogue' with existing extra-EU suppliers and, more critically, via diversification of suppliers. As Turkey is poised to play a major 'energy hub' role with regard to the latter objective (Yigitguden, 2010, pp. 13–14), its accession aspirations have encroached upon the EU's energy security picture as well. Turkey began to liberalise its energy market in accordance with EU law in 2001, thereby signalling that the country's energy infrastructure might be enlisted into EU networks without any implied necessity to promise full accession. Though Turkey's continued willingness to apply EU reforms without reciprocal assurances on accession is not a novel issue, it is specifically relevant in terms of our analysis to the extent that the EU decides to base its diversification plans on completion of the centrepiece Nabucco Pipeline Project, which will cross Turkey and then four EU countries in succession. A five-state intergovernmental agreement (IGA) containing favourable gas off-take rights and transit-tariff concessions for Turkey was signed in July 2009 in Ankara, imparting fresh political impetus to this project. Yet, it remains uncertain whether the Nabucco Project's 'clear and transparent' transit framework, as envisaged by the EU energy commissioner, will guarantee Turkey's adherence to EU energy regulations, especially when Moscow, which also signed a raft of important agreements with Ankara in 2009, is strenuously competing to secure Ankara's energy-related allegiance.

As diagrammed in Figure 1.1, our central argument holds that the extent and endurance of the EU's need to diversify supply routes for *any* source of gas around extant transit territories *or* supplies away from Russian sources (the bold-font line of logical analysis) should enhance Turkey's EU membership prospects.

Our book consists of several objectives. First, we assess which policy tools and types of power – for example, 'soft', 'hard' or a 'smart' melding of the two (Nye, 2009) – the EU holds and has employed to bolster and maintain its energy security. This is a matter with crucial moral and political importance not only for the most relevantly vulnerable EU member states, especially those in the ex-Soviet bloc, but also for all members' willingness to act, not according to the *realpolitik* dictates of unilateral expediency, but with more serious regard for the ideal of the EU as flagbearer for a more solidaristic Europe that safeguards the interests of both the weakest as well as the strongest of its members

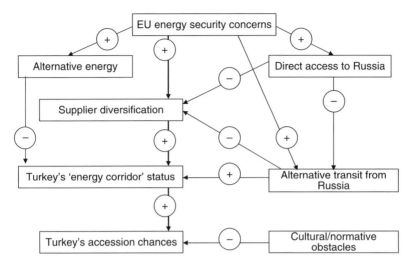

Figure 1.1 The energy logic of Turkey's EU accession bid.

alike. Second, we explore the degree to which European energy security, as articulated by key EU institutions, has actually crystallised around limiting or mitigating dependency on Russian energy supplies. We then examine how Turkey has become more crucial to EU energy security in terms conveying non-Russian supplies from the Caspian and Middle East regions. In this context, we seek to appraise the EU's relative success in extending the panoply of its energy regulations to potentially critical transit state Turkey without offering commensurable reciprocity on accession. By contrast, we analyse how Turkey has capitalised on EU concerns for widening diversity of external suppliers and supply routes in order to pinpoint how Turkey's linkage strategy has had a positive or negative influence on its EU accession chances.

As expressed in Figure 1.1, we acknowledge the most likely qualifications to our argument in our relevant chapters, the plan of which is laid out in the next section. The first key caveat is that the EU possesses a wide array of methods for ensuring its energy security, including conservation, ramping up renewables production, and, even within the narrower scope of securing gas imports, creating direct access routes to *Russian* gas. Thus, although the fact that the external dimension of European Energy Policy still falls largely into the remit of individual member states – even after Lisbon (Andoura et al., 2010, pp. 11–13) – may discomfit some member states and the EU as a collective, others may not even see much need to make Turkey a 'Southern energy corridor' at all, let alone a fellow member in order to ensure the *acquis*-guided functioning of this corridor. As a country that uses no gas from Russia or anywhere else and has had stronger countervailing motivations to block Turkey's energy-chapter accession talks, Cyprus exemplifies this case. Moreover, Turkey's growing importance as a gas corridor may still not be enough to overcome the plethora of countervailing cultural or normative obstacles to its EU membership. As implied above, Turkish officials might even overplay the energy card to the point of further alienating European public opinion. Our main purpose in this scholarly endeavour is not to proffer crudely defensive assertions (for example, that the EU has no other choice but to admit Turkey on the basis of its importance as an energy corridor), but to analyse the causal logic and empirical validity of the nexus between Turkey's ascribed significance as a conduit for extra-EU27 supplies of oil and gas to Europe and its EU accession chances.

Plan of the book

Part I of this book focuses on the EU as a coherent energy actor (or a less coherent collection of energy actors) in its own right, in order to obtain a better understanding of how its central institutions has chosen to craft collective policies to address what has been an often uneasy trinity of objectives defining its pursuit of energy security – integrating its internal electricity and gas markets according to liberal economic principles, incorporating environmental sustainability criteria into its energy-related agenda and securing supplies of energy imported from outside the EU27.

Chapter 2 launches into an examination of the evolution of EU energy policy. Here we explore how the Union's conceptualisation and implementation of energy security have evolved over the years and even decades, as reflected in the EU's ongoing effort, which dramatically accelerated in 2006, to advance a European Energy Policy. It examines the contents of this policy to determine how much concerns for physical security and diversity of external supplies have taken on a more urgent emphasis in relation to internal energy market integration and mitigation of carbon emissions from fossil fuel production and consumption. The last section of this chapter addresses the question of why the EU faces difficulties in coming up with a common energy policy by focusing on competing preferences among member states, uncertainties in the nature of a European energy regulator, and finally, what 'storyline' (market or geo-politics) the EU seems to be gravitating towards as the rule of global energy game.

Building on the preceding chapter's discussion, Chapter 3 delves into the outward-orientated facets of the EU's energy security profile. After providing an introductory overview of the EU's pattern of hydrocarbon importation and consumption, the chapter discusses what the EU has developed and put forward in terms of external policy through a variety of 'green papers', strategic energy reviews and so on. It also surveys the institutionalised approaches and policy instruments that the EU has applied towards each set of its major energy producing partners. This chapter also dwells on the issue of how to theorise European (external) energy policy. It expands the previous chapter's discussion on the energy policy 'storylines' as subsets of broader liberal and realist schools of thought in the fields of international political economy and integration theory.

The chapters in Part II offer a fully detailed examination of how the EU and its separate member states are attempting to manage as well as mitigate, either separately or concertedly, the pronounced dependence on Russia, which supplies the plurality shares of European oil and gas imports. Chapter 4 analyses EU dependence on imports of Russian energy supplies (mainly gas), how this dependence has made it vulnerable to gas cut-offs to Belarus and Ukraine and the tools that the EU has used to mitigate this vulnerability, especially the use of its vast market power to extend the energy *acquis* to its relevant neighbourhood. It also addresses how member-state company efforts to gain access to the Russian upstream sector and build direct pipeline connections to Russian gas (i.e., bypassing Belarus and Ukraine) have affected the EU's capacity to influence a broad array of energy trade and investment issues involving Russia.

Chapter 5 inverts the thrust of the analysis to explore how Europe, without much realistic hope of achieving self-sufficiency in energy, has tried to broaden its dependence on imports of a variety of non-Russian oil and gas supplies and to what extent this has achieved a sufficient diversity of supplies and suppliers for most EU member states. It then considers Russian counteractions – part of a larger policy of 'wide-area rent-seeking', especially in gas (hence, gas 'w-a-r-s'), consisting of what we call 'near encirclement' and 'far encirclement' – to consolidate relationships with states and their firms in the EU's key non-Russian source countries and regions.

The following chapter concentrates even further on various EU efforts to obtain more oil and gas from the Caspian and Middle East regions, which have increasingly become key to fulfilling the goal of supply diversification, in light of competition with other major importers like China. Our analysis covers efforts by various EU member states to do this without involvement of the Turkish land mass and how Turkey has emerged as increasingly crucial to EU plans to diversify imports.

In Part III, the book switches tracks to examine EU energy security requirements from the perspective of many official and unofficial actors in Turkey, which appears headed to becoming a major transit country, or so-called energy corridor, while maintaining its bid to accede to the EU. Continuing in the vein of the previous chapter, Chapter 7 analyses in greater detail how Turkey could serve as an energy corridor in the context of the European Energy Policy. It focuses on Turkey's existing, but limited, role in transporting non-Russian gas to Greece (and in the near future to Italy) as well as on the prospects for completion of the EU-backed Nabucco Pipeline, which is slated to convey even larger volumes of non-Russian gas from the Caspian and Middle East. Here we also consider the counterscenario of a Pyrrhic victory for Nabucco, wherein the project is built but becomes subverted into a conduit for *Russian* gas that is more reliable than Ukrainian or Belarusian assets.

The last main chapter of the text, Chapter 8, constitutes in many respects the cornerstone of the book's analytical focus. It addresses the larger political implications of Turkey's role as an alternative pipeline-based energy corridor for bundled gas supplies to Europe, notably the prospects for Turkey's successful linking of its energy corridor status with EU membership. We attempt to demonstrate that, regardless of whether Turkey becomes simply an alternative transit route bypassing the Ukraine (for all sources of gas, including Russian supplies) or the ideally envisaged route for supplies not controlled by Russia, the EU will need to ensure Turkey's implementation of the energy *acquis* one way or another, as evidenced in recent attempts with Ukraine. This chapter also considers the possibility that the EU extends its energy regulatory influence over Turkey and Ukraine by means of guaranteed financial support, thus recognising Turkey's geopolitical importance to Europe without granting accession and making it riskier for Turkey to overplay its energy card with respect to expediting progress on this process.

Part I
EU Energy Policy

2
Evolution of EU Energy Policy

Introduction: the energisation of European Energy Policy

Energy is a fundamental factor in the construction of European Union (EU) project. The deep interaction and cooperation among the founding members of the Union crystallised around energy considerations. The European Coal and Steel Community (ECSC) and European Atomic Energy Community (EURATOM) treaties not only established the roots of the European Community but also ensured regular supply of coal and coordination in nuclear energy. However, despite the importance of energy in daily lives, the European Energy Policy ultimately proved to be an unsuccessful example of integration (Pointvogl, 2009, p. 5704). In developments following ECSC and EURATOM, member states remained reluctant to create a common energy policy. To illustrate, the Maastricht and Amsterdam Treaties did not include chapters on energy and, instead, only mentioned this issue in passing (European Commission, 2000, p. 9). In the Treaty on EU, 'measures in the spheres of energy, civil protection and tourism' were lumped together and only Article 129b referred to energy infrastructures together with transport and telecommunication in the discussion of trans-European networks (European Union, 1992). The new Lisbon Treaty also included weak language on energy cooperation, but introduced a new legal basis for EU legislation in the field of energy as well as provisions for qualified majority voting in some areas of energy policy. The Treaty also brought forward an energy solidarity clause – namely, that EU energy policy needed to resonate with a spirit of solidarity between member states (Youngs, 2009, p. 26). In many ways, this weak form of integration is surprising, especially when considering the potential benefits of integration towards a common energy policy (Pointvogl, 2009, p. 5704).

Since the mid-1980s, the EU's demand for energy has been increasing at a rate of 1–2 per cent per year, with the EU increasingly consuming more energy than it can produce. If the current trends continue unchecked, in the next 20–30 years non-EU products will constitute 70 per cent of the EU's energy consumption – a situation that could lead to dependence on oil, gas and coal imports at levels of 90 per cent, 70 per cent and 100 per cent, respectively. This would leave all economic sectors from transport to industry vulnerable to variations in international markets (European Commission, 2000, pp. 2, 12, 20). Consequently, many issues revolving around energy-supply security have risen higher on the EU agenda. These include military and political conflicts in producer regions, diplomatic confrontations with supplier states, secure transportation of energy products and protecting investments in oil and gas production (Bahgat, 2006, p. 961). The energy issue has itself become further entwined with additional concerns over global warming and other environmental damage from energy production, transportation and consumption as well as the hazardous effects of certain energy types on health. Thus, addressing these health and environmental issues requires that the EU secure more than raw access to energy – it needs clean and efficient energy.

Member states are highly interconnected and operate in an interdependent energy market not only among themselves but also in international terms. Consequently, national approaches to the energy issue, as well as unilateral energy policy decisions to meet the aforementioned challenges, automatically affect other EU members. Uncoordinated national decisions concerning energy policy seem to have aggravated the Union's overall vulnerability in energy. Yet, EU-level coordination and harmonisation of energy policies merely represent initial steps towards greater energy security. Self-sufficiency in energy is not a feasible option for the EU given the limited availability of domestic energy resources to meet the demand of its highly industrialised economy at its current standard of living (Ibid., p. 975). Hence, rising energy import dependency appears to be an ineluctable reality of the EU economy. The Union has tried to address its energy security via several policies, including encouragement of investments in renewable energy and broader diversification of its energy mix and repertoire of energy suppliers. However, the EU's most successful attempts at dealing with its energy situation have occurred mainly as part of larger international efforts – either via multilateral regulatory institutions or on a bilateral basis with other producer states, transit countries and energy-importing nations – to address global energy and environmental trends.

Accordingly, EU policy makers have had to account for increasing consumption both in Europe and in abroad. In recent decades, energy demand has skyrocketed globally, within the world market, due to rapid increases in population combined with economic growth. This situation has become saliently pronounced in China and India, where increasing consumption suggests future scenarios of sharper rivalry over access to scarce oil and gas reserves. To put it bluntly, oil demand in China is expected to increase by nearly 3 per cent per year until 2030 as opposed to the 0.3 per cent annual increase in EU oil demand. From the perspective of Middle Eastern oil producers especially, the EU's relative importance as a future customer is thereby projected to diminish (Hoogeveen and Perlot, 2007, p. 494). As a result, the capacity of these developing countries to address energy-supply emergencies and curb their growing demand directly impinges on the EU (International Energy Agency, 2007b, p. 159).

With these challenges still largely confined to the background until recently, the EU was almost myopically focused on issues of climate change and energy efficiency to the extent of neglecting its own supply security. However, the Russo-Ukrainian gas conflict of 2006 served as an unpleasant reminder to member states that they had theretofore largely ignored supply security at their own peril. This conflict also highlighted the fact that dependency on imports made member states vulnerable to external events, including the sometimes capricious decisions of non-EU member states (Geden et al., 2006, p. 14). This 'wake-up call' in 2006 revealed that, for the EU to be able to mitigate the drawbacks of its increasing energy dependence, it quickly had to craft a proactive energy policy. This task has proven easier to proclaim than to accomplish, as energy policy is a multifaceted one with national, EU-level and international requirements. It entails a complex set of issues related to climate change, energy efficiency, investment in renewables, physical security of supply, transparency of energy markets, diversification of the energy mix and so on. With the EU facing such a complicated agenda, energy security has become a critical test of the strength and integrity of EU institutional policy.

European Energy Policy: a crystallising concept

Although the European Commission (2006b, p. 17) recognised that member state energy policies reflect particular national preferences, it admonishes that, 'in a world of global interdependence, energy policy necessarily has a European dimension.' According to its communication entitled 'An Energy Policy for Europe', which actually comprised the EU's first coherent strategic energy review, 'European Energy Policy needs to be ambitious, competitive and long term – and to the benefit of all Europeans' (European Commission, 2007a, p. 3). Ideally, Europe would be transformed 'into a highly energy efficient and low CO_2 energy economy' (Ibid., p. 5). This policy has become identified with achieving coherence among the ancillary objectives of sustainability, competitiveness and security of supply. While none of them alone provides the needed foundation for a complete energy policy, together they are regarded as offering the necessary ingredients for policy success (Ibid., pp. 5–6).

Sustainability, the first element of European Energy Policy, is directly linked to climate change. Eighty per cent of greenhouse gas (GHG) emission in the Union is caused by energy-related activities. If present energy and transport policies were to continue unabated, 'EU CO_2 emissions would increase by around 5% by 2030 and global emissions would rise by 55%' (Ibid., p. 3). Aware that current policies are untenable in this regard, the EU has been aiming to lower domestic and international GHG levels closer to pre-industrial levels with the intention of containing global temperature increases (Ibid.). This has imposed the need for a twofold policy at both the EU and international levels. At the global level, European Energy Policy has laudably vaulted into the forefront of international efforts to stop climate change. At the European level, development of renewables, tapping alternative transport fuels with low carbon output and efforts to change consumption habits have constituted the basic modes of addressing sustainability (European Commission, 2006b, pp. 10–12).

The second element of European Energy Policy is competitiveness. The concentration of oil and gas reserves in a few countries and companies, in addition to the volatile prices in international energy markets, impacts the EU adversely. This effect has become more pronounced over time, as the EU has become more dependent on foreign energy resources – a situation that entails a heavy economic burden on EU citizens. 'If, for example, the oil price rose to 100$/barrel in 2030, the EU-27 energy total import bill would increase by around € 170 billion, an annual increase of € 350 for every EU citizen' (European Commission, 2007a, p. 4). An EU-level energy policy could bring the full fruits of market liberalisation to EU citizens, raise the level of investments in the energy sector and undergird an internal energy market based on fair and competitive prices. The goal of European Energy Policy is to establish appropriate policies and legislative frameworks to foster energy liberalisation (Ibid.). This competitiveness orientation aims to open energy markets and generalise their benefit to EU citizens in line with latest technological innovations and investments in clean energy production (European Commission, 2006b, p. 17).

Actually, the European Energy Policy has sought to bring about more than simply market liberalisation. Stimulating investment has served as a social instrument to create jobs and economic growth as well as to accelerate innovation in the fields of energy efficiency and renewable resource development. In short, European Energy Policy constitutes another means of establishing the EU as a global leader in the growing knowledge-based economy. Cited earnings of € 20 billion and employment of 300,000 personnel in this sector have placed the EU in the forefront of advances in renewable technologies. This provides a crucial piece of evidence for suggesting that 'competitiveness', by creating an atmosphere conducive to financial investment while also bolstering the 'sustainability' component of European Energy Policy, may be compatible with the Union's determination to lead on the climate change front (European Commission, 2007a, p. 4).

Security of supply constitutes the last, but not least, element of European Energy Policy. While concerns for energy security and uninterrupted continuity of oil and gas flows to Europe lie at the heart of the creation of a viable common policy, acting upon these concerns has remained stubbornly entrenched in the respective national security understandings of each member state. Increasing dependency on imported hydrocarbons constitutes a potential threat to the EU since it leaves the Union more highly exposed to external dynamics outside its realm of discretionary action. In 2030, reliance on imports of gas and oil – already 57 per cent and 82 per cent in 2007, respectively – is expected to rise to 84 per cent and 93 per cent. When such a level of dependency is compounded by uncertainty about the willingness and capacity of oil and gas exporters to meet rising global demand, risks of supply disruption emerge as one of the major lacuna in the EU's energy security picture (Ibid., pp. 3–4). European Energy Policy suggests tackling the Union's increasing dependency on imported energy resources by limiting demand, varying the energy mix and diversifying 'sources and routes' of supply of imported energy (European Commission, 2006b, p. 18).

Policy evolution

As it largely represents the result of independent developments in different but related issues of energy, today's European Energy Policy resembles an accumulation of disparate proposals, initiatives, regulations and decisions. Although the EU has achieved some important milestones on the way to a common energy policy, developing, implementing and enforcing such a policy has been complicated by the difficulty that the organisation has experienced in trying to reconcile the often incompatible pillars of European Energy Policy – that is, sustainability, competitiveness and supply security. This difficulty makes the evolution of common energy policy a highly *sui generis* case when compared to sectors such as agriculture, where integration has proceeded in a discernibly step-by-step fashion. In this respect, it is problematic to talk about the general evolution of European Energy Policy. Figure 2.1 usefully illustrates this point – that while different policies have originated at different time periods, their purposes are closely related. Each of these policies aims to secure present and future access to clean and sustainable energy at affordable prices in a competitive market. Ongoing market liberalisation dates back to 1996. Even in the early 2000s, the process of liberalising the energy market was not yet finalised. Then, directives on renewable energy sources and biofuels, as well as Energy Efficiency Action Plans, were initiated to curb excess demand, address sustainability and encourage more efficient consumption of energy. Determined to become an active global player, the EU's internal developments vis-à-vis energy policies have been unmistakably influenced by larger international trends like the 1990s Kyoto negotiations.

While this figure provides a general overview of the evolution of European Energy Policy, policies relevant to security of energy supply are absent. The necessity of having to refer to every aspect of the energy

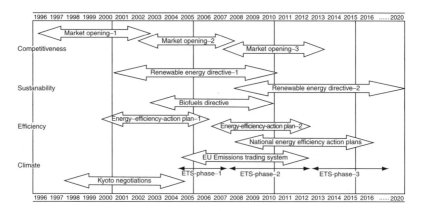

Figure 2.1   Development of EU energy policies over time.
Source: Eurostat (2009b, p. 3).

'trinity' of European Energy Policy and the fact that each of these aspects has evolved in and of itself complicate study of the development of European Energy Policy. To overcome this difficulty, specific policies on market reform, efficiency, solidarity and supply security will be addressed in seriatim below. Nonetheless, general comments and important reference points in the history of European Energy Policy need to be highlighted, as this historical path constitutes a foundation for current policies.

Historical roots of EU energy policy

Post-War European integration began with energy issues, culminating in the ECSC and EURATOM. However, in the evolution of the EU itself, policies concerning energy and energy security remained on the backburner. Left fully to the national discretion of member states, decisions and policies on energy security were initially excluded from the process of EU-level integration. Later, as the international setting transformed, the Union's energy policy began to develop in earnest, following an 'event-driven' path. In other words, European Energy Policy originated in the need to respond more capably and efficiently to international energy supply crises (Hoogeveen and Perlot, 2007, p. 486).

Turbulence in the Middle East

Historically, major social and economic crises originating in producer regions, especially in the Middle East, provided a strong impetus to European Energy Policy. These crises intensified concerns about energy supply security. The 1956 Suez crisis, the 1967 Six-Day War between Egypt and Israel, the 1973–74 Arab oil embargo and the oil crisis following the Iranian Revolution in 1979 all reminded Europeans of their vulnerability to external crises and the criticality of maintaining uninterrupted supplies of energy. Although these specific occasions galvanised the EU to work towards decreasing import dependency, the initiatives in question made little headway towards developing a common European policy (Ibid., p. 487).

Still, policy makers in both energy importer and exporter countries took the crises in the 1970s as significant 'reference points' in the history of the energy trade. From the perspective of the EU, the absence of cooperation and solidarity between member states, combined with sudden oil-price increases engineered by the Organization of the Petroleum Exporting Countries (OPEC) in the 1970s, upset the economic and political stability of both the EU and its individual member states.

This period's events thrust two major concerns into the foreground of the EU energy policy-making agenda, especially in terms of security of supply (Ibid., p. 488). The first concern, arising out of the 1979 oil crisis, originated out of fear that 'political instability in producer countries and regional tensions will lead to a disruption in oil supply' (Ibid.). Accordingly, potential instability became a crucially necessary factor for European policy makers to consider when considering the reliability of energy suppliers. This fear of instability in producer countries materialised as a key challenge as addressed in many European documents. For example, the 2006 green paper emphasises that, in the next 20–30 years, EU's energy needs 'will be met by imported products, some from regions threatened by insecurity' (European Commission, 2006b, p. 3).

The roots of the second major concern for European policy makers date back to the 1973 oil crisis, where exporter countries purposefully wielded oil and natural gas as weapons against foreign consumers and governments. Accordingly, EU and energy-importing consumer countries in general fear that governments may threaten them with politically motivated supply disruptions as tools to achieve their objectives in the international arena. In this respect, the 1973 oil crisis highlighted the vulnerability of European states to Arab politics – a situation that appeared to render the import-dependent and militarily impotent EU open to a myriad of energy-related abuses (Hoogeveen and Perlot, 2007, pp. 488–9).

The seminal energy policies of the Union in response to such crises came with the establishment of emergency oil stocks. Starting in 1968, the European Council issued its Oil Stocks Directives to address the risks of temporary supply disruptions (European Commission, 2008a, p. 10). The Council realised that difficulties – permanent or temporary – that have the potential to reduce the supply of imported oil products from the developing world could wreak havoc on economic activity, as in the 1970s. Thus, on 20 December 1968, the European Council imposed an obligation on member states of the European Economic Community (EEC) to maintain minimum stocks of crude oil and/or petroleum products (68/414/EEC). Member states were expected to adopt necessary laws, regulations and administrative provisions to keep enough petroleum stockpiles to be able to cover internal consumption requirements for 65 days (European Council, 1968). Later, in response to the 1973 oil crisis, the International Energy Agency (IEA) was created to oversee oil supply emergencies. The European Council launched two directives – 73/238/EEC and 77/706/EEC – in 1973 and 1977, respectively, to synchronise its emergency policies with those of the IEA.

The new directives requested the establishment of a consultative body to coordinate measures among member states, especially in terms of rationing consumption in times of shortage and regulating prices to prevent excess volatility (European Council, 1973, 1977).

Post-Cold War challenges

Towards the end of the 1980s, while the EU was busy with the deepening of integration and the absorption of its new Southern members, the Cold War suddenly ended, erasing major ideological, political and economic divisions between Eastern and Western Europe. This introduced new needs and opportunities to cooperate in the energy sector. Increasing interdependence between energy importers and exporters has required a multilateral framework to replace the bilateral agreements that formerly facilitated international cooperation in the energy sector. While the rich hydrocarbon reserves in Russia and its neighbours had not yet been fully explored and extracted, Western European countries and private energy companies had both the financial and technological capacity to make these investments as well as the intention to diversify their energy sources by trading with new suppliers (Bahgat, 2006, p. 968).

With the aim of encouraging economic growth, enhancing the EU's security of supply, and creating a common foundation for energy collaboration in Eurasia, Dutch Prime Minister Ruud Lubbers proposed establishing a European Energy Community at the Dublin European Council in June 1990, which lead to the signing of a political declaration on the Energy Charter in December 1991. Later, in 1994, the Charter was signed in Lisbon. After its first 31 signatories agreed, the Energy Charter Treaty (ECT) and the Protocol on Energy Efficiency and Related Environmental Aspects entered into force in 1998 (European Energy Charter, 2010). To date, 51 states (including Turkey), the European Community and EURATOM have ratified the ECT, although major energy producers and/or transit states – namely Australia, Belarus, Iceland, Norway and Russia – have signed but not yet ratified the treaty. Emerging as an important milestone in the external efforts of the EU to ensure supply security, the ECT advanced provisions on the proper functioning of free trade in energy materials in line with World Trade Organization (WTO) rules on the protection and promotion of investments, energy transit, energy efficiency and dispute settlement. Signatories committed to eliminating anti-competitive market distortions in the trade of energy products and in the procedures concerning investments.

Notably, parties agreed the facilitation of 'free transit without distinction made on the origin, destination or ownership' of energy materials, 'without imposing delays, restrictions or unreasonable taxation' (Ibid.). The ECT also included conditions to ensure that the contracting parties retained their respective sovereign rights to 'choose the geographical areas in their territory to be made available for exploration and exploitation' and that efforts were made for the reduction of environmentally harmful effects of energy-related activities and for the increase of energy efficiency (Ibid.).

The 'green paper'ing of EU energy security

In the interim between the ECT's signing and entry into force (crucially but fatally without Russia), efforts within the Union to synchronise national energy policies and develop a common internal European Energy Policy continued apace. In the decade between 1990 and 2000, three green papers on energy were launched by the European Commission that partially established baseline references for a common energy policy. Starting with the European Commission's (1994a) first green paper – entitled 'For A European Union Energy Policy' – the EU began to embrace sustainability, security of supply and the need to establish an internal market. In this manifesto, the Union put forward the necessity to increase its role in the energy sector. Based on the potential challenges that the Union could face in coming years due to its rising import dependency, the Commission identified a number of main objectives for common policy. The most outstanding feature of this report was its emphasis on the necessity to harmonise national- and community-level energy policies in order to generate a common position on transnational energy challenges. A common position on energy was presumed to require cooperation between decision makers of energy policy and private actors in the energy sector. It also called for clear identification of the Community's responsibilities on the environment, air pollution and climate change due to CO_2 emissions.

The European Commission (1996) launched its second green paper – entitled 'Energy for the Future: Renewable Sources of Energy' – in 1996. As its name suggests, this document introduced targets for the incorporation of renewable energy sources into the future Community strategy on energy as well as for more widespread use of wind, solar energy, hydropower and biomass. Apart from what would become a somewhat tired reiteration of the need to strengthen cooperation among member countries, the paper differed from its predecessor in that it moved one step further and offered concrete strategies for the specific issue of renewable resources. Accordingly, the Commission called for mobilisation of national and Community instruments for developing these resources in order to increase the percentage of renewable energy available in EU's energy mix. Taking into account high startup costs of renewable energy, the 1996 report also recommended emphasising the real competitiveness of renewable resources in juxtaposition to the external costs of other energy sources. It also recommended increased research and development activities that would highlight how the contribution of renewable energy could help achieve the Union's energy security, climate change, air pollution, employment and regional development goals.

The European Commission's next (2000) green paper – 'Towards a European Strategy for the Security of Energy Supply' – became not only one of the most significant of this series, but also one of the most important documents in the EU energy literature itself. As in previous papers, the 2000 report reaffirmed environmental concerns and interdependence between the member states. It once again stressed that a community dimension was required in order for new strategies dealing with energy-related challenges to be effectively created and implemented. Nevertheless, this green paper placed a sharper emphasis on the Union's increasing import dependence. The Commission declared that one of the main purposes of European Energy Policy should be to reduce the Union's vulnerability stemming from its dependence on a narrow plurality of external energy suppliers, rather than maximising energy self-sufficiency. The report centrally recommended developing a strategy for security of energy supply. It aimed to 'rebalance its [EU] supply policy by clear action in favor of a demand policy' through taxation measures and energy-saving policies. This report also had an awareness-building effect in that it projected EU oil and gas consumption, CO_2 emissions and import dependence out to the years 2010, 2020 and 2030. The Commission forecast that energy import dependency would reach around 70 per cent in 2030 unless current policies were supplanted by more efficient mechanisms of demand and supply dependence management (European Commission, 2000).

Five years later, the Commission (2005b) released another green paper devoted to 'Energy Efficiency or Doing More with Less'. It aimed to 'identify bottlenecks preventing the capture of cost-effective efficiencies', such as the 'lack of appropriate incentives, lack of information and lack of available financing mechanisms' (Ibid., p. 5). The Commission suggested the establishment of energy efficiency Action Plan, which would bring together national, regional, community and international levels in a multi-level initiative. The report was also significant in that it proposed stepping up international cooperation in energy efficiency and integrating energy efficiency into its inchoate neighbourhood and development policies. Of course, conservation and greater efficiency of energy usage in industry, transportation and household consumption hold synergistic implications for the Union's efforts on the environment and managing import dependency.

Despite a glaring lack of political consensus among member states concerning the implementation of energy strategies, with its successive green papers, the Commission had already started to depict European Energy Policy and the elements it would include. However, in the interim, another important event accelerated the process towards a common energy strategy for the EU. In January 2006, the Russo-Ukrainian gas crisis (discussed more fully in Chapter 4) further awakened Europe to its vulnerability to supply disruptions. This event, which imparted a faster momentum to the evolution of European Energy Policy, was not only instrumental in shaping EU's current energy policies but also became a critical defining moment in the EU–Russia relationship. As Ukraine has been the transit country hosting most of the pipelines transferring natural gas from Russia to Western Europe, this new energy crisis aggravated anxieties that Europe would face energy shortages and other vulnerabilities due to its dependence on a limited number of suppliers and transit routes. It hearkened EU decision makers, as well as European countries, back to the energy fears of the 1970s. In short, EU officials and their constituencies feared the renewed possibility of major oil and gas suppliers using energy resources for political leverage. Although the 2000 green paper had already issued a seminal warning on this matter, member states then devalued the importance of community-level collective action in favour of maintaining national regulations and guarding their sovereignty over energy policies. Yet, as events have implied, supply security depends on a complex relationship among energy exporters, transit countries and EU members as importers, making energy not only a matter of economics but also of foreign policy and national security strategies (Geden et al., 2006, p. 9).

Following this shot across the bow in 2006, European efforts to strengthen energy security and create a common EU policy picked up their pace. Two months after the January 2006 gas crisis, the European Commission (2006b) issued yet another green paper on 'A European Strategy for Sustainable, Competitive and Secure Energy'. This final green paper on energy combined all aspects (as opposed to focusing on one specific dimension of energy) in order to put forth an energy strategy that balanced the three dimensions of energy – sustainable development, competitiveness and security of supply. This 'trinity' of objectives officially became the main feature of European Energy Policy. Throughout the report, the Commission identified six key areas requiring urgent cooperation and action: competitiveness and the creation of an internal market, diversification of the energy mix, solidarity between member states, sustainable development in response to climate change, innovation and technology to increase energy efficiency and fuel diversity through renewable resources and an integrated external policy. Moreover it proposed concrete measures addressing each of the dimensions. These six key areas constituted the skeleton of today's European Energy Policy.

Upon fixing these key areas of European Energy Policy, the European Commission (2007a) issued a 'Communication from Commission to the European Council: An Energy Policy for Europe'. This document, released on 10 January 2007, reinforced the message contained in the 2006 green paper on the centrality of sustainability, security of supply and competitiveness as the Union's main challenges. Moreover, the communication also introduced the 20/20 Package, aimed at reducing GHG emission by 20 per cent, improving energy efficiency by 20 per cent, achieving a 20 per cent share of renewable energy and attaining a 10 per cent share of biofuels by 2020 (Ibid.). This target definitively identified 'the role of the EU in leading the effort to create a climate-compatible energy system' (Eurostat, 2009b, p. 4). In addition to the ambitious targets that it put forth, this document also offered a concrete action plan for reaching them. Consequentially, it emerged as a proposal to the European Parliament and, ultimately, became the basis and essence of European Energy Policy (European Commission, 2007a, p. 5).

The European Council realised that 'An Energy Policy for Europe', along with plans to set new targets for renewables and energy efficiency, only met the EU's energy objectives to a limited degree. Therefore, the Council asked the Commission to prepare a wider action plan on the Union's energy security. On 13 November 2008, the Commission (2008a) responded to the Council's request with the introduction of the Second Strategic Energy Review, 'An EU Energy Security and Solidarity Action Plan'. The Commission highlighted five main points, which its President Jose Manuel Barroso (2008, p. 2) summarised as 'infrastructure needs and the diversification of energy supplies, external energy relations, oil and gas stocks and crisis response mechanisms, energy efficiency, [and] making the best use of the EU's indigenous energy resources'. Unlike previous reports, this action plan emphasised the Union's infrastructure needs and on diversification of both energy suppliers and transit routes. Accordingly, the Commission prioritised realisation of the Southern gas corridor, a diverse and adequate liquefied natural gas (LNG) supply for Europe, effective interconnection of the Baltic region, the Mediterranean Energy Ring, adequate North–South gas and electricity interconnections within Central and South-East Europe, and the North Sea and North West Offshore Grid (European Commission, 2008a, pp. 3–17).

The Second Strategic Energy Review also underlined the importance of international energy linkages and multilateral dimensions of climate-oriented strategies. This was the carrying over of the emphasis, in EU documents especially after 2006, on the external dimension of diversification to increase supply security. However, despite an ambitious international energy policy agenda, integrative efforts in energy have not succeeded. For the EU, energy has remained among issue areas that function along the lines of the subsidiary principle, since member states highlight the national characteristics of energy policies. In addition, member states still cling to their possession of responsibility for launching initiatives on energy. When it comes to a 'common' policy, major progress has been achieved only on the competitiveness element of the European Energy Policy, with chapters on competition rules duly inserted into the *acquis communautaire*. Although the Commission has urged the taking of concrete steps towards creation of a common policy in its green papers and affiliated documents, the reluctance of some member states to countenance further integration weakens the possibility of common energy policy in the near future (Hoogeveen and Perlot, 2007, p. 487).

Stumbling blocks to common energy policy

The Commission's 2000 green paper indicated why the EU has limited power to influence future world markets. Indeed, the fact that the EU failed to create a coherent common energy policy has diminished the Union's bargaining power and worsened its mounting energy-related geopolitical and economic challenges (European Commission, 2000). Six years later, the 2006 report captured the main gap in EU Energy Policy: 'The EU leads the world in demand management, in promoting new and renewable forms of energy, and in the development of low carbon technologies. If the EU backs up a new common policy with a common voice on energy questions, Europe can lead the global search for energy solutions' (European Commission, 2006b, p. 4). However, for European policy makers, the creation of European Energy Policy involves multiple issues, both internally and externally, and different players. Member-state views on the appropriate nature of policies frequently diverge: Should it be integrated, national or detached from state intervention (Pointvogl, 2009, p. 5705)? How responsibility for energy policies is to be divided between 'EU-level actors, governments, energy companies and consumers' has also emerged as one of the central challenges facing EU Energy Policy (Benford, 2006, p. 45).

Despite the release of many directives, statements, reviews and action plans, certain challenges continue to hinder a common European Energy Policy. On the internal dimension of the EU's energy policy, different preferences of member states and uncertainty about the potential European regulatory body for energy issues have blocked member states from reaching agreements over energy policies. On the external dimension, the Union's unclear strategy, which nods towards both market norms and geopolitical considerations, generates sometimes embarrassing policy inconsistencies and uncertainties. As a result, evolution of a common external energy policy has been somewhat glacial.

Competing preferences among member states

The EU is undergoing a dual integration process. The internal deepening of integration, resulting from a range of policies including market to agriculture, goes hand in hand with enlargement and integration of new members into the EU system. Member states' different preferences speed up or slow down these processes. As detailed in Chapter 4 to a greater extent, the creation of a common energy policy is also greatly affected by these disparate preferences, since member states have distinctive energy supply and consumption patterns in line with the demands of their industry and citizens. These patterns determine the extent of member state support for common energy policies (Correljé and van der Linde, 2006, p. 532). In 2006, Commission President Jose Manuel Barroso affirmed that 'The Union has the required size (surface area and population) and required instruments (legislation, budget etc.) but it lacks the political will to forge a common European energy policy' (quoted in Geden et al., 2006, p. 11).

In theory, European Energy Policy aims to increase energy security and to offer feasible solutions to energy-related problems. Some member states have acknowledged the efficiency of dealing with these problems at the EU level (Ibid., p. 14). However, as various green papers have emphasised, European Energy Policy has also aimed to achieve representation of the EU with a 'single voice'. In energy forums, in relations with producer and transit countries or in international agreements concerning energy issues, speaking with a single voice seems crucial for enhancing the bargaining credibility of the Union (Andoura and Vegh, 2009, p. 5). In principle, member states approve the notion of speaking with single voice, but hesitate to transfer real sovereignty to EU-level institutions (Geden et al., 2006, p. 2). As Benford (2006, p. 40) points out, 'Member states still retain the final say over key decisions, such as national energy mixes and relations with supplier states'. The EU exercises serious efforts to represent a single European voice in the international arena. However, '[t]he European Commission is not the government of the EU and Brussels is not its capital' (Hoogeveen and Perlot, 2007, p. 490). In other words, even though the Union represents all 27 members in its bilateral relations, it is not a 'state' as such. While the EU should be a body that can enforce binding policies upon its members, in practice, it can enforce policies only to the extent that its members allow (Ibid., p. 503). This is especially true in energy policy.

The interesting categorisation of the EU as a single voice but not a unified state renders decisions over common energy policies very difficult to achieve. This situation can be explained by reference to intergovernmentalist arguments. Moravcsik argues that nation states tend to cooperate when coordination increases their control on the domestic policies and eliminates negative policy externalities (1993, p. 485). Governments aim to coordinate, thereby reducing the costs of non-cooperation. At the same time, nation states operate in a system characterised by frequent and marked disharmony of interests. In some cases, even if agreements are mutually beneficial to the relevant parties, negotiations can still lead to conflicts. Conflicts arise out of government disagreements over distribution of benefits. In such cases, liberal intergovernmentalism assumes that states make concessions, settling the problem by the 'lowest common denominator' solution. Thus, states select results closest to the national preference or the status quo (Ibid., pp. 487, 501). On the other hand, cooperation or integration fails when member states observe that their individual interests will not be met by the outcome (Rosamond, 2000).

Another liberal intergovernmentalist argument, which would explain member states' attitudes on energy policy making, contends that institutions can ameliorate the international interaction of states.

Institutions are formed for the purposes of reducing transaction costs, providing necessary information that will help states in decision-making, establishing necessary rules, monitoring free-riding, sanctioning non-complying parties and reducing uncertainty (Schimmelfennig, 2004, p. 78). National governments also favour institutions because they strengthen their control over domestic groups (Moravcsik, 1993, pp. 507, 515). The related 'two-level games' concept means that the bargain has two faces – domestic and international. Hence, power-seeking elites form and support coalitions and interest groups at the domestic level. At the international level, considering the demands of domestic groups, the same actors bargain to enhance their domestic position (Rosamond, 2000, p. 136). This process can be directly linked to the relationship of member states with the EU on one hand and to the relationship of member states to their national energy companies on the other hand.

Widely uneven contribution to EU risk exposure has had profoundly debilitating effects on the formation of a common energy policy, even as the latter would presumably mitigate these risks. Member states' vulnerability to import dependence differs in terms of the volumes that they purchase from outside the EU. States with higher energy-import rates generally represent higher shares of the Union's overall risk. Larger EU countries also represent more of a risk due to their high absolute levels of energy consumption relative to those in the rest of the Union (Le Coq and Paltseva, 2009, pp. 4475–6). In terms of natural gas, countries like Austria, Bulgaria, the Czech Republic, Hungary, Latvia, Lithuania, Romania and Slovakia emerge with high-risk indexes since the gas they consume is imported from a relatively undiversified group of non-EU/Norway suppliers. In the same risk index, due to their trade with a greater diversity of gas suppliers, Estonia, Finland, Germany, Greece, Italy, Ireland, Poland, Portugal, Slovenia and Spain represent a 'medium-level' risk group, though the dependence of some of them on Russia remains high. Finally, certain member states, such as the Netherlands and the UK, face lower risks since they benefit from indigenous production or European gas suppliers. However, the picture changes when the main criterion is each country's contribution to EU import dependence. If this is the case, Germany, Italy and Spain appear as the biggest contributors due to their high gas consumptions compared with EU's general consumption trends. Hungary and Slovakia, despite being smaller countries, also contribute significantly to EU import dependence due to their high reliance on non-EU gas exporters (Ibid., p. 4479). Similar risk indexes can also be generated for oil.

Thus, one can conclude that exposure to risk linked to external energy supply not only differs across the member states but also across energy types. Disparate risk levels undoubtedly lead to different preferences among the member states. Unequal measures on risk indexes for oil and gas oblige Europeans to expect non-uniform national policies with regard to the common European Energy Policy. Hence an objective analysis of EU countries' energy profiles is crucial, since assessed energy patterns directly affects the position of each country in energy policy making (Ibid., p. 4480).

A common European Energy Policy would require the member states to share the risks of being vulnerable to external factors due to their dependence on oil and gas imports. Nevertheless, it is evident that the members do not contribute equally or even proportionately to the overall energy supply risks that the Union has to face. Accordingly, a common energy policy creates a different form of the classical 'free-riding' problem. Countries facing higher risks tend to benefit more from common energy security policies, at the expense of relatively less import-dependent countries or at the expense of the members whose foreign suppliers outside the EU are relatively more diversified. As a result, the motivation of some members to support common energy policy may decrease. Due in part to the free-rider problem, energy integration policies remain unsuccessful; therefore, the policies that compensate disadvantaged members and take different energy patterns into account emerge as the most feasible solution to overcome the problem of delayed energy integration (Ibid., p. 4481).

Nevertheless, the member countries' different preferences reflect not only their distinct energy profiles and degrees of risk exposure. Varied perceptions of 'security risks' and market structures also determine countries' respective attitudes towards a common policy. To illustrate, for many years, the context of events occurring in the 1970s stimulated some member states to diversify their energy suppliers away from the Middle East and towards Russia. On the contrary, for the countries that acceded to the Union in the 2000s, dependence on Russia, which they had recently delinked from, represented the bigger potential threat to their security (Hoogeveen and Perlot, 2007, p. 503).

Varied market structures can also play a role. For example, certain states, such as the Netherlands and UK, have liberalised their electricity markets, while certain others, such as France and Germany, have been 'slow' in liberalisation in an effort to maintain the place of their 'national champions' that could become 'European champions' once the single energy market is consolidated. The latter countries' preference indicates that their national interests outweigh EU interests. This attitude is especially the case with strategically important issues such as energy (Ibid.). To sum up, if the target is to create a common European Energy Policy, the member states must permit EU-level interests to trump purely national ones. For this, a new supranational institution in energy field may help.

European energy regulator

Another complexity that renders common European Energy Policy difficult to achieve is the matter of creating a regulatory body. As energy policies become more and more integrated, the EU will be in need of a regulatory body to properly implement energy-related laws and procedures. Such an institution is of course subject to questions concerning the transfer of authority to the EU level. In addition, the creation of an EU regulatory body has implications for those nation states that hesitate to deepen EU integration.

Nevertheless, further than the dilemma over the transfer of sovereignty, the real question contributing to the slow pace of EU energy integration concerns the kind of body that would be both appropriate and feasible. In terms of energy issues, the Commission stands out as an influential actor both in the development of European Energy Policy and in the implementation of related policies. The Commission's green papers, action plans and reports have represented a serious effort towards the creation of common energy policy. In this respect, the Commission does not only influence European energy market but also intervenes into 'national energy sectors by applying single market instruments, such as technical harmonization and competition law' (Benford, 2006, p. 40). The Commission already possesses formal powers over the decisions affecting energy-related implementation. In this capacity, the Commission has been charged with ensuring 'community competences on the development of infrastructure in EU regions, granting aid to developing energy infrastructure in such regions and a mandate to merge environmental policies with energy policies' (Ibid., p. 39). Therefore, one option for the EU is to increase the discretion of the Commission over energy matters. It is important to note that such a decision would be again subject to objections by the member states that think energy issues belong to national security considerations (Ibid., pp. 39–41).

Other than empowering the Commission, European energy regulation can also be achieved by creation of a new actor. With the 2006 green paper, the Commission suggested further discussion regarding the 'adequacy of existing forms of collaboration' and about 'the need for a European energy regulator which would have decision-making powers for common rules and approaches' (Ibid., p. 41). In this case, an independent regulator could be developed and be subject to the supervision of the Parliament and member states. Additionally, current national regulatory authorities could be united under a 'European system of energy regulators'. However, the same concerns about the transfer of sovereignty over energy issues would persist and hinder members' will for further development of European Energy Policy. Consequently, taking into account member states' reluctance, the EU's central aim is 'cooperation between the Commission and national regulators' through progressive modification of existing structures (Ibid.).

The Council of European Energy Regulators (CEER) and the European Regulators' Group for Electricity and Gas (ERGEG) exemplify existing structures that can be further modified to act as regulatory bodies. Both organisations were established with the objective of increasing cooperation between Europe's independent, national energy regulators, and both operate to facilitate 'the creation of a single, competitive, efficient and sustainable internal market for gas and electricity in Europe'.[1] It is possible to state that the EU is close to establishing a regulatory body, as there have already been some efforts to bring together separate national energy regulators. Still, until a common European Energy Policy is realised, EU policy makers will continue to contemplate and debate the most appropriate form of a regulatory body. As a result, the issue of regulation will remain on the agenda of nation states.

Establishing the rules of the global energy game: market versus geopolitics

The third factor that has thwarted attainment of a common policy relates to the external dimension of European Energy Policy. It is vital for the EU to take both 'market' and 'geopolitical' imperatives into consideration. Long-term development of EU energy security policy greatly depends on the EU's ability to navigate between these two issues.

Relations with developing countries constitute an important part of European Energy Policy, since these countries assure the external dimension of energy security (Youngs, 2007a). The Union has thus given importance to international partnerships in energy, especially with important supplier and transit countries. To this end, several initiatives on integrating energy issues into European foreign policy have been assayed. These include agreements with the Algeria, Azerbaijan, Egypt,

Kazakhstan and Ukraine, and, the signing of the South-East European Energy Community Treaty (SEEECT) between Europe and the Balkan states, and the development of partnerships between the EU and Africa, the Black Sea and the Caspian Sea countries (Youngs, 2007b, p. 1).

The tendency of EU, in terms of its external energy policies, is to 'spread eastwards and southwards of internal European market rules' (Ibid.). The EU's means towards this end include the European Neighbourhood Policy (ENP), Action Plans, Partnership and Cooperation Agreements (PCAs) and Association Agreements. As the European Commission's (2006b) green paper states, 'the EU has for some time been engaged in widening its energy market to include its neighbours and to bring them progressively closer to the EU's internal market' (p. 16). Moreover, for the achievement of security of supply, the Union highlights the necessity of a 'common regulatory space' for 'common trade, transit and environment rules, market harmonization and integration' in energy issues (Ibid.).

The above-mentioned panorama does not seem to be problematic on paper. However, different preferences of member states not only slow down the evolution of European Energy Policy's internal dimension but also hinder external policies. While some members support the spillover effect, which in the case of energy refers to the expansion of the internal market to the international level, others hesitate to link energy security with the norms of the internal market. Within the Union, certain states still support only partial liberalisation of energy markets, so the internal market is still not fully unified. In this milieu, it is unclear how the EU can launch an external policy based on market rules. Far from creating a common external energy policy, the Union even fails to respond as 'a single entity' to 'external energy shocks' due to 'the absence of both pan-European market mechanisms and sufficient physical interconnections' (Youngs, 2007b, p. 6).

Some member states argue that, instead of aiming for a liberalised, free market, a more 'government-led, geopolitical approach' should be adopted by the Commission. While countries such as France, Germany and Italy do not reject free market rules, they indicate that 'negotiated reciprocity in producer states' is a prerequisite for the proper functioning of liberalisation efforts. When this is the case, member states resort to bilateral agreements and, in order to maximise their national interests, some go as far as denying the application of transparency and information-sharing principles even in interactions with fellow members. Youngs (Ibid., p. 7) argues that, 'In private many member state diplomats opine that while they feel bound to go along with the EU's market rhetoric, such an approach is in practice increasingly unrealistic, in light of a more difficult geopolitical context.'

However, European policy makers have not only indicated their willingness to create an 'international energy market' but have also emphasised the significance of promoting shared rules and principles as well as transparent legal frameworks in producer and transit countries. This means that the market structure that the Union tries to promote is not only a means to trade oil and gas, but also a way to export and extend the Union's political and economic principles in the field of energy. Accordingly, 'the development of inter-connecting energy systems between different geographical areas, based on EU regulatory norms and the acquis', and the widening of the ECT's sphere of influence are part of EU's external energy policy (Ibid., p. 2). To complete a common energy policy, the ECT is a crucial consideration with respect to that policy's external dimension. This document's requirements on 'rule of law and the role of governments' are essential, notably in regards to foreign direct investment (FDI) in the energy sector (Ibid.). As Commissioner Benita Ferrero-Waldner (2006, pp. 139–42) has indicated, good governance, respect for human rights and other market norms aligned with the European ones 'improve conditions for EU investment in producer states'.

In fact, in order to achieve energy security in terms of uninterrupted supplies at affordable prices and also in terms of environmentally safe production, the EU has felt compelled to extend its rules-based principles to its periphery. This can be accomplished through 'enhanced legal frameworks' that control market regulations, safety and environmental standards. Policy makers have stressed that an international energy regime with common rules and norms would also be helpful in containing rising demand in countries like China and India. The creation of an international energy regime would also secure future supplies to a certain extent, as the latter countries would be included in the same system. Countries would also adopt many of the same energy policies, active demand management being a crucial one (Youngs, 2007b, p. 5).

Consequently, energy security today requires more than simple supply diversification policies and market liberalisation. Since the energy market consists of a complex and global connection of several actors as producer, consumer or transit countries, 'a wider approach is now required. This approach should take into account the rapid evolution of the global energy trade, supply-chain vulnerabilities, terrorism, and the integration of major new economies into the world market' (Yergin, 2006, p. 70). States still consider energy security as a part of their responsibility, and in many of them oil and gas extraction, as well as transit infrastructures, are controlled by national governments through state companies. Therefore, 'this wider approach' becomes heavily controlled by national interests; instead of the market's invisible hand, diplomatic negotiations determine the agenda (Geden et al., 2006, p. 10).

Taking all of these facts into account, the Commission indicates that European dependence on external supplies can be managed through the development of an energy community in the periphery of Europe, consisting of neighbours and major energy partners. Scholars agree with this 'regional' strategy. The Union's integrated structure, the existence of a common currency, common interest in energy security and common concern for Russia's non-aligned policies suggest that the EU has many available avenues for realising its regional aims. Ultimately, the EU seeks a 'pan-European geo-energy space' that would accomplish voluntary integration of trade partners in energy with accepted common multilateral rules (Mane-Estrada, 2006, pp. 3780–5).

It is clear that while the Union finds the expansion of its internal market rules a feasible option, it cannot neglect that some member states feel the need to override this unity. Some member states have sought to conclude bilateral agreements based on geopolitical conditions in these regions that are crucial for energy extraction. This process of conducting bilateral agreements, while practical, is not appropriate for market liberalisation. This dilemma of certain member states leads to an inconsistency in external energy policy.

Conclusion

Despite the fact that the energy issues, such as coal and nuclear sectors, treated as of vital importance to the European project in its initial decade, the Union has not been able to develop a common energy policy. There have been a multitude of factors behind this lacuna. The main reason has been that the member states are protective of their sovereign policy-making power in the energy sector. Given their divergent attitudes towards a common EU foreign policy, member states have considered energy policy as a strategically important policy area that they want to keep under their national control. This has paralysed attempts to develop a common EU energy policy. As a result, the Union's energy initiatives have been largely ineffectual.

Yet, there have been significant promising efforts to develop the skeletal outlines of a common energy policy. These efforts followed an event-driven path. They began with the first oil shock in the mid-1970s as member states sought to forge better relations with the Middle Eastern producers and later continued in the 1980s with efforts to utilise a greater diversity of energy suppliers, including Russia. However, truly systematic energy policies and their corollary policy instruments emerged only within the last decade. A series of green papers, since the first one in 1994, have served as a rough roadmap for the Union on the way to reaching the destination of a common approach to internal and external energy issues. Again, the problems with Russian gas transport were of fundamental importance in spurring action in the energy field. In addition, the EU's ambition to become a world leader in environmentally efficient energy policies played a role in identifying and implementing new energy policies.

However, these policies and instruments do not make for a common energy policy per se. The member states retain their policy-making competence over the energy issues. Although it introduced a new legal base for EU legislation in the field of energy, as well as provisions for qualified majority voting in some areas of energy policy, the new Lisbon Treaty retained the EU's feeble language on energy cooperation (Youngs, 2009, p. 26). Considering the potential benefits to be had from a common European Energy Policy, this weak form of integration is surprising (Pointvogl, 2009, p. 5704). Thus, the Lisbon Treaty missed the chance to remedy the EU's weakness in energy policy despite developments that require a strong European leadership within and outside Europe on many significant energy (and environmental) issues.

The European deadlock on common energy policy seems difficult to overcome in the near future. Different energy profiles and preferences of the member states are complemented by competing interpretations of how the EU needs to approach the issue. While certain countries can more or less agree that the EU should base its policies on free-market principles both internally and externally, others remain pessimistic about the full ramifications of such market policies and prefer a geostrategic approach based on bilateral or regional diplomatic initiatives. The EU has to negotiate between these two approaches, a job that would have been facilitated within the framework of a common European policy rather than based on ad hoc choices between the two.

3
External Dimension of European Energy Policy

Introduction: growing EU apprehension of energy vulnerability

European Energy Policy has multiple aspects with complex linkages. Its three main objectives – sustainability, competitiveness and security of supply – form a trinity and concrete achievements on each of these dimensions are vital to this energy policy's overall success. However, despite the empirical artificiality of any barrier separating the internal and external aspects of energy policy, this chapter makes an analytical distinction between these aspects in order to focus on those policy modalities and instruments that have been devised and implemented to secure an uninterrupted flow of foreign energy supplies to European consumers. Thus, as a point of departure from the previous chapter's discussion of general European Union (EU) energy policy, this chapter specifically addresses that policy's external dimension.

Increasingly dependent on imported energy resources, the Union needs a unified approach to external energy policy that would define and clarify its relationships with global energy actors, including producers, consumers, transit countries and major energy companies (European Council, 2007, p. 19). According to the European Commission (2006a, p. 3), it is vital for Europe to develop an external energy policy that is

> coherent (backed up by all Union policies, the Member States and industry), strategic (fully recognizing the geo-political dimensions of energy-related security issues) and focused (geared towards initiatives where Union-level action can have a clear impact in furthering

its interests). It must also be consistent with the EU's broader foreign policy objectives such as conflict prevention and resolution, non-proliferation and promoting human rights.

This chapter first examines the external facets of the EU's energy security profile. It then directs its focus to the external policy that the EU has crafted through a variety of 'green papers', strategic energy reviews and so on, marking the institutionalised approaches and policy instruments that the EU applies towards its major energy producing partners. The last part revisits the previous chapter's discussion of which 'storyline' drives the EU's external energy policy choices by reference to the larger cognate debate between liberal and realist approaches to integration.

The EU as energy consumer *par excellence*

The top three sources in the EU's current energy mix consist of oil, natural gas and coal, although the EU's internal energy policies concerning the usage of nuclear power and renewable resources would undoubtedly impinge on the relative percentages of different sources. The 20/20 Package offered 'An Energy Policy for Europe' that established an ideal target of 20 per cent renewable resources within the EU's overall energy mix by 2020 and rekindled hopes that the EU might be willing to decrease its high dependency on oil and natural gas. Nevertheless, current policy trends and national preferences of separate member states indicate that a radical shift in favour of alternative energy resources is not forthcoming in the near future.

Figure 3.1 illustrates the change between 1991 and 2006 in the respective proportions of different fuels within the Union's overall energy consumption, a subject discussed more extensively in the next chapter. Oil has remained the single largest energy source of the Union. However, despite slight relative changes in hydropower, biomass and nuclear power usage, more significant variations have occurred with respect to consumption of coal and natural gas, with coal losing eight per cent of its previous share and natural gas gaining six per cent. The same source (Eurostat, 2009b, p. 11) indicates that the fraction of imported energy in the total also grew, from 46 per cent of gross inland consumption in 1991 to 55 per cent in 2006. Correspondingly, the Union's respective 2006 dependencies on natural gas and oil imports were approximately 61 per cent and 84 per cent (Directorate General for Energy and Transport, 2009, p. 30). These proportions are projected to rise to 84 per cent

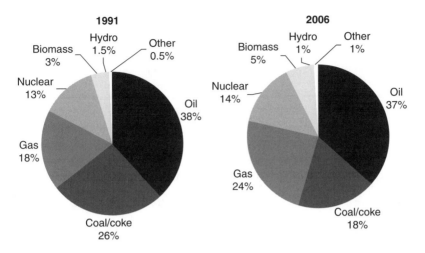

Figure 3.1 Gross inland consumption shares by type of fuel in the EU27.
Source: Eurostat (2009b, p. 21).

for natural gas and 93 per cent for oil by the year 2030 (European Commission, 2007a, p. 26).

As elaborated on below and further in Chapter 4, the Union's relatively high consumption of natural gas and oil and the significant share of net imports within its total energy consumption cannot help but raise the EU's relations with energy-exporting states to the apex of the European Energy Policy agenda. With limited indigenous oil and gas production capacities on the one hand and increasing consumption needs on the other, the EU has a seemingly natural interest in cultivating good relations and favourable trade terms with energy producers. As most of its gas is transported via pipelines, the same perspective applies to relations with its energy transit countries.

The EU and its separate member states do not depend equally on every external energy supplier, although specific producer countries comprise the EU's major energy trade partners. This fixes a critical reference point for the development of external energy policy, since deliberate decisions by these producers vis-à-vis their own energy resources and potentially destabilising internal political and economic dynamics may directly affect the flow of oil and gas to Europe. Concerning oil imports, Table 3.1 shows both the amount and origin of imported oil over the period 2000–06. Russia, Norway, Libya, Saudi Arabia and Iran represent the five major oil exporters to the EU, with Russia holding a large plurality share

Table 3.1 Crude oil imports into the EU

Origin	Crude Oil Imports into the EU-27 (in Mio tonnes)							
	2000	2001	2002	2003	2004	2005	2006	Share 2006 (%)
Russia	112.4	136.8	154.7	170.8	188.9	188.0	189.0	33.5
Norway	115.9	108.1	103.1	106.4	108.6	97.5	89.1	15.8
Libya	45.5	43.8	39.2	45.9	50.0	50.6	53.2	9.4
Saudi Arabia	65.1	57.5	53.1	61.5	64.5	60.7	50.9	9.0
Iran	35.5	31.4	25.9	34.7	35.9	35.4	36.4	6.4
Other, Middle East	54.7	48.3	43.2	27.8	28.5	30.0	32.1	5.7
Kazahkhstan	9.9	9.1	13.4	15.9	22.2	26.4	26.8	4.8
Nigeria	22.4	25.7	18.4	23.2	14.9	18.6	20.2	3.6
Other Origin	54.3	54.3	64.2	56.5	56.1	66.1	66.9	11.8
Total Imports	515.8	514.9	515.3	542.9	569.5	573.3	564.6	100.0
In Million barrels	3765	3759	3761	3963	4158	4185	4121	

Source: Directorate General for Energy and Transport (2009, p. 31).

of 33.5 per cent. Over the period in question, supplies from major partners Norway and Saudi Arabia experienced a constant decrease, a fact that may signal a type of diversification that is specifically pertinent to the EU's oil-needs profile.

In terms of natural gas imports, as Table 3.2 indicates, Russia and Norway constituted the major EU trade partners in 2006, supplying respective shares of 42 per cent and 24 per cent. These were followed by Algeria, with a respectable 18.2 per cent of the total. Although their shares within overall EU imports remained relatively minuscule, Libya, Egypt and Qatar nonetheless made some inroads into the EU market, indicating some fervency in the EU's search for alternative natural gas suppliers over the last decade. The table also indicates the growing importance of gas as a whole in the EU energy market.

This brief overview of the EU's energy profile and its dependency on external sources, especially Russian gas, highlights the significant need for serious focus on the external aspects of EU energy policy.

Europe's external energy policies: groping towards coherency

In the EU's view, many policy areas link up to the issue of energy. The EU also recognises the interdependent character of energy relations among

Table 3.2 Natural gas imports into the EU

Origin	Gas Imports into the EU-27 (in TJ, terajoules)							
	2000	2001	2002	2003	2004	2005	2006	Share 2006 (%)
Russia	4,539,709	4,421,515	4,554,744	4,895,252	4,951,044	4,952,879	4,927,552	42.0
Norway	1,985,231	2,136,379	2,601,569	2,699,473	2,801,723	2,671,779	2,844,269	24.2
Algeria	2,203,075	1,957,181	2,132,477	2,158,803	2,042,137	2,256,826	2,134,886	18.2
Nigeria	172,020	216,120	217,882	335,929	410,260	436,319	560,986	4.8
Libya	33,442	33,216	25,536	30,390	47,809	209,499	321,562	2.7
Egypt						202,419	317,420	2.7
Qatar	12,443	27,463	87,952	80,414	160,170	195,713	245,158	2.1
Trinidad and Tobago	36,334	24,498	19,120	1,365		29,673	154,244	1.3
Other Origin	112,810	199,256	125,425	100,023	313,245	409,387	223,232	1.9
Total Imports	9,095,064	9,015,628	9,764,705	10,301,649	10,726,388	11,364,494	11,729,309	100
In Mio Cubic meters	240,610	238,509	258,326	272,530	283,767	300,648	310,299	

Source: Directorate General for Energy and Transport (2009, p. 31).

countries and the fact that multilateral efforts are needed to tackle global energy challenges. Thus, the EU's ambitious goals of sustainability, renewable resources and preventing irreversible climate change must parallel efforts to cooperate not only with external supplies, but also with transit states and other consumer countries, in order to obtain optimally effective outcomes.

While the EU as a consumer ideally prefers a competitive diversity of supplies and transit routes and greater predictability of flow and price in the international oil and gas markets, producer countries have voiced the need for greater security of demand to guarantee that revenues are substantial enough to cover the necessary investment outlays – estimated by the at \$26 trillion to meet projected 2030 energy demand (International Energy Agency, 2009f, p. 43) – that they themselves may have to make if they otherwise bar sufficient inflows of foreign direct investment (FDI) in their coveted 'upstream' energy sectors. Unfortunately, outside economic access to these sectors has demonstrably tended to narrow when rising energy prices make investment more attractive (Williams, 2008). Nonetheless, the EU has expressed an abiding belief in its ability to consolidate mutual trust among all relevant actors through legally binding, albeit elusive, long-term agreements that can also assure an environment conducive to heavy-duty investment in the capital-intensive activities of extracting and shipping resources (European Commission, 2008a, p. 7).

External energy policy for Europe extends beyond supply security and amicable relations with major producer and transit countries. Accordingly, issues such as climate change, energy efficiency, renewable resources, development of new technologies and investment in clean and sustainable energy production have been incorporated into the holistic scope of EU external energy policy. In this vein, the EU has encouraged bilateral and multilateral cooperation and sought to widen the geographical coverage of its internal policy arrangements, especially with regards to CO_2 emissions and energy efficiency. The EU has also promoted energy cooperation among countries in broad-based arenas such as the UN, International Energy Agency (IEA) and Group of Eight (G8) (European Commission, 2006b, p. 17) and incorporated nuclear safety and security standards as well as sustainable and affordable energy criteria into its development policy, especially with respect to Africa (European Commission, 2002). Moreover, it has cultivated partnerships with key countries, such as Brazil, on alternative energy sources, notably biofuels.

The institutionalisation of cooperation on energy issues is crucially important since the future EU has been projected to consume 'less than

10 per cent of the world's energy' and to 'account for only 15 per cent of new CO_2 emissions' (European Commission, 2007a, p. 18). Accordingly, the EU has stayed in pursuit of its goal of creating an external energy policy based on 'interdependence, cooperation and mutual trust' with its international partners and has thus aimed to expand not only the content but also the geographical scope of its policies, not only for its own energy security but also for global supply security and sustainability (Ibid.).

However, before obtaining greater assurance of international 'mutual trust', the Commission has indicated the importance of progress in the integration of internal market and deepening of internal energy policies as a first step for an effective external energy policy, since this internal coherence between member states would be projected to the international community as a manifestation of Europe speaking 'with the same voice' (the often elusive master objective that is precisely the one being sought after) and thus increase the EU's foreign policy gravitas (European Commission, 2006b, p. 4; Andoura, et al., 2010, pp. 92, 108). The European Commission (2006a, p. 1) has concluded that 'fully developed internal policy is a pre-condition for delivering the EU's external energy interests'. Although the Commission approves 'the legitimate right of individual Member States to pursue their own external relations for ensuring security of energy supplies and to choose their internal energy mix', it has not discarded its emphasis on the invaluable role of collective EU-level policies in enhancing external energy security for the whole of Europe. The whole of Europe includes or should include, by moral and political necessity, those member states least capable of obtaining optimal levels of energy security on their own. In that respect, 'An External Policy to Serve Europe's Energy Interests' that was launched by the Commission discusses how energy security could be embedded in Europe's wider external relations, including the Common Foreign and Security Policy (CFSP). Indeed, energy security has become an integral part of the CFSP, and was, along with climate change, was incorporated into 'European Security Strategy 2003–2008', one of the most significant CFSP documents to date (European Union, 2003; Umbach, 2008, p. 6).

The Commission has proposed several objectives to guide Europe's external energy policy. Promotion of improved governance and transparency, improvement of production and transportation infrastructures, better relations with third countries to promote the necessary environment for European companies to invest in 'upstream' energy activities, promotion of energy efficiency, diversification of suppliers and energy products and encouragement of joint stock holding with energy partners represent those objectives intended to promote secure access to sustainable and competitive energy (European Commission, 2006a, p. 2). The policy strategies and tools associated with EU external energy policy can be classified under several headings. The *first* strategy is the extension of internal energy policies and common energy market to the international arena, which relates to the integration of energy into broader external relations, with the goal of eventually creating a pan-European Energy Community. The *second* major strategy is dialogue with third parties. Policies falling under this category refer to international agreements and energy partnerships with energy supplier and transit countries as well as with other consumer countries that are increasingly dependent on energy imports, like China (see Chapter 6) and India. The *third* main strategy consists of diversification based on instruments that can be used to strengthen extant infrastructures and to construct new ones. As delineated in Chapter 4, prominently featured among these instruments are the financing of feasibility studies for energy projects that are directed towards augmenting EU energy supply security.

Widening the regulatory net of the European energy market

The 2006 'green paper' put forward that, as part of its external energy policy, 'the EU has for some time been engaged in widening its energy market to include its neighbours and to bring them progressively closer to the EU's internal market' (European Commission, 2006b, p. 16). In this regard, the EU has made the Energy Charter Treaty (ECT) a key institutional backbone of its energy security efforts (Haghighi, 2007, p. 189). Specifically, the ECT, which entered into force in 1998, aims to 'strengthen the rule of law on energy issues, by creating a level playing field to be observed by all participating governments' in the areas of 'the protection and promotion of foreign energy investments, based on extension of national treatment, or most-favored nation treatment (whichever is more favorable)', 'free trade in energy materials, products and energy-related equipment, based on WTO rules', 'freedom of energy transit through pipelines and grids' and 'mechanisms for the resolution of State-to-State or Investor-to-State disputes' (Energy Charter Treaty, 2010). The holistic thrust of this treaty provides not only for creating a 'common regulatory space' – in other words, common rules in trade, transit and environment between the member states and the EU's neighbours, paving the way to a 'pan-European Energy Community' (European Commission, 2006b, p. 16), but also freeing access to Eurasian energy, both in terms of production and transit.

The expansion of the EU's own internal market to neighbourhood and 'partnerhood' represents part of a strategy that its policy makers have been pursuing based on the premise that only a well-functioning international market can assure affordable oil and gas supplies and stimulate new investments (European Commission, 2006a, p. 2). As Chapter 2 explained, the extension of the EU's internal market has entailed promulgation of common trade, transit and environment rules by means of bilateral and multilateral agreements. This also means 'reciprocal liberalization of trading conditions and investment in upstream and downstream markets and... grant of access to pipelines by countries situated along transit and transport chains' (European Commission, 2007a, p. 19). Thus, the principle of generalising or externalising shared trade rules and norms, as discussed in further detail below and in Chapter 4 (with respect to Ukraine), constitutes a core element of EU energy security strategy that governs the EU's dialogue efforts towards other consumer, producer and transit countries.

EU efforts take different forms according to the policy partner in question. The EU expects candidate countries and likely candidate countries (in the Western Balkans) to adopt the energy *acquis* outright (Andoura et al., 2010, pp. 56–8). In this regard, although not linked directly to EU membership candidacy, the South-East Europe Energy Community Treaty (SEEECT) has served as a regional instrument for promoting an integrated energy market among the Balkan states – namely, Albania, Bosnia and Herzegovina, Croatia, the Former Yugoslav Republic of Macedonia, Montenegro, Serbia and the UN Interim Administration Mission in Kosovo. The Union has also sought to broaden the membership of this treaty to include Moldova, Norway, Turkey and Ukraine (European Commission, 2007a, p. 24; Energy Community Treaty, 2010). By contrast, the EU has utilised the policy tools of the European Neighbourhood Policy (ENP), Partnership and Cooperation Agreements (PCAs), and Association Agreements to deal with other strategic energy partners (European Commission, 2006b, p. 16).

Dialogue with third parties: compensating for the EU 'hard power' deficit or cultivating 'soft power'?

Another central element of the EU external energy policy includes deepening dialogue and relations with major energy producers, transit countries, neighbours and other major consumers. The Commission's communication to the European Council and European Parliament, entitled 'An Energy Policy for Europe', and the Second Strategic Energy

Review clearly indicate that, in addition to international agreements such as the ECT or multilateral initiatives under the World Trade Organization (WTO) or World Bank, the Union has also concluded numerous memoranda of understanding (MoUs) on energy with several countries in seeking to broaden its geographical diversification of energy supplies and transit routes and make them more secure. Agreements, especially with producer countries, have stressed energy interdependence and noted that success relies on achieving some sort of equilibrium between demand security for producers and supply security for consumers. 'Dialogue' with international partners has not, of course, been devoid of conveying EU preferences for favourable conditions for upstream investment, fewer impediments to fuller market access, reciprocal market liberalisation, arrangements for uninterrupted flows of energy and dispute settlement mechanisms, all reflective of EU supply security concerns (European Commission, 2007a, p. 24; European Commission, 2008a, p. 8).

In this vein, the ENP has been a vital policy framework for the EU. In its ENP Strategy Paper, the European Commission (2004a, p. 17) indicated that, 'Enhancing our strategic energy partnership with neighbouring countries is a major element of the European Neighbourhood Policy.' Hence, the EU27 has sought to institutionalise its external energy dialogues with 'neighbouring' countries, some of which are key players in production (such as Azerbaijan, Algeria, Egypt and Libya) or transit (such as Georgia, Ukraine, Belarus, Morocco and Tunisia). In this context, energy cooperation covers a holistic multitude of issues, including improvement of energy networks, legal and regulatory convergence among energy markets and energy policies, promotion of energy efficiency, innovation of new technologies on renewable resources and mutual business opportunities. To achieve concrete progress in energy cooperation with ENP countries, the EU initiated Action Plans that 'build on existing bilateral or regional initiatives, such as the EU-Russia Energy Dialogue, the Tacis-funded Interstate Oil and Gas Transport to Europe (INOGATE) programme dealing with the Caspian basin (oil and gas pipeline systems)' or the Euro-Mediterranean partnership (Ibid., pp. 17–18).[1]

Promotion of new infrastructure for supply diversification

Promotion of necessary infrastructure to meet the Union's energy needs, together with broader diversification efforts, have been touted in the

EU Energy Security and Solidarity Action Plan. Strengthening existing infrastructure and investing in new physical capacity are crucially important for both internal and external dimensions of energy security, as material access to gas and even a significant supply of oil depends on the existence of pipeline capacity (European Commission, 2008a, p. 6). As such, extension of the Trans-European Networks-Energy (TEN-E) and further promotion of new investments, especially for transportation of oil and gas to Europe, are important parts of the process of fostering the aforementioned pan-European Energy Community. This may require more vigorous but efficient use of financial instruments provided by the European Investment Bank (EIB), the European Bank for Reconstruction and Development (EBRD), the Neighbourhood Investment Fund, and the various twinning programs, as well as loan subsidies to encourage and bring to fruition strategically significant energy projects (European Commission, 2006b, p. 16; European Commission, 2007a, p. 25).

The Second Strategic Energy Review proposes significant energy projects that would contribute to supply security. These include construction of pipelines and the development of legal commitments concerning gas supplies from Azerbaijan, Turkmenistan and Iraq and the development of a southern corridor to pipe gas from the Caspian and Middle East regions. The multinational gas pipelines entailed by these projects have compelled the EU to engage in dialogue and cooperation with transit countries, notably Turkey. Another example of infrastructure projects supported by the Commission consists of the Mediterranean energy ring, which will not only diversify the Union's energy sources away form Iraq, Middle East or Sub-Saharan Africa altogether by connecting the European continent with the southern shores of the Mediterranean but also 'develop the region's vast solar and wind energy potential' by executing projects 'adopted by the December 2007 Euromed Energy Ministerial meeting and the Mediterranean Solar Plan adopted in Paris in July 2008' (European Commission, 2008a, p. 5). These new infrastructure projects and their concomitant supporting international policy dialogues are intended to enhance the Union's energy security via diversification of energy sources in terms of both geographical origins and transit routes. Still, the success of external energy policies is largely dependent on the sometimes fickle and mercurial attitudes and behaviours exhibited by the Union's energy policy partners. The following section examines the EU's relations with its major energy producer partners.

The EU's diverse relations with major energy producers

Since detailed analyses of the EU relations with Russian and non-Russian producers (with the exception of Norway) will be covered extensively in Chapters 4 and 5, this section provides only an introductory outline of the EU strategies, institutional frameworks and policy tools towards its major energy producer regions. As discussed below, it becomes amply clear that the EU has become increasingly reliant on a repertoire of imported supplies that cannot be easily subject to the regulations of the energy *acquis*.

Norway

Norway is the second major natural gas and oil supplier to the EU. It is a significant energy partner not only for Europe but also for the world, as it is the 'third largest exporter of natural gas and the sixth largest exporter of oil' (Energy Information Administration, 2009c, p. 1). Norway differs in a major way from other energy suppliers to the Union because it belongs to the European Economic Area (EEA). Therefore, legislation applying the EU's internal energy market and related policy arrangements, such as competition law, environmental regulations, consumer rights and new technologies, has already been implemented by Norway (European Union Press Release, 2009a). This has fostered an intense energy trade partnership between Norway and the EU, with their total mutual energy trade comprising 61 per cent of their overall trade, which stood at € 92 billion in 2008 (Directorate General for Trade, 2009c). Norway needs the EU as much as vice versa, since its member states buy the majority of Norway's energy exports (Energy Information Administration, 2009c, p. 5).

This high volume of energy trade has arisen partially as a result of a genuinely deep-rooted bilateral energy dialogue between the EU and Norway that started in 2002. Coordination of energy policies, cooperation in research and development of new technologies and collaboration in third-party relations with other energy-exporting countries dominate the agenda of the EU–Norway Energy Dialogue (European Union Press Release, 2009a), perhaps unlike the EU's sometimes more problematic dialogical relationships with other major suppliers. Accordingly, the EU–Norway partnership extends beyond the narrow scope of the hydrocarbons gas trade. In particular, Norway 'shares European Union objectives on climate change and sustainable development and it is particularly committed to the deployment of cost efficient carbon capture and storage technologies' (Market Observatory for Energy, 2009a, p. 2). The European Commission (2008a, p. 7) has underlined the indispensable role of Norway in promoting Europe's energy security and suggested the undertaking of common exploration projects off the Norwegian continental shelf and offshore wind production in the North Sea.

Africa

The EU's energy dialogue with Africa has typically been ensconced in broader development and governance cooperation agendas. The Union has offered financial aid to Africa for poverty reduction projects and improvement of energy delivery systems to rural areas. The EU Initiative for Poverty Eradication and Sustainable Development, launched in 2002, is one such EU effort (Youngs, 2007b, p. 4). However, EU action has often been ineffectual in terms of implementing development projects due to the highs levels of economic and political instability and acute violence that have plagued the region. For example, despite being the EU's fourth largest major natural gas supplier – in the form of liquefied natural gas (LNG) – Nigeria has suffered from its legacy as Africa's 'most under-funded state', where widespread corruption and lack of transparency have limited investment to extremely sub-optimal levels. Instead of paving the economic foundations for instilling rule of law, oil contracts and government positions have been deployed to 'buy off' militants (Youngs, 2007b, p. 14).

As a feasible alternative source region of oil and gas supplies as well as renewables, Africa has a non-negligible role to play in the future of Europe's energy supply security and in meeting its specific objective of greater supply diversity. Despite formidable obstacles to greater levels of inward FDI in the extraction and transportation of resources, Algeria, Egypt, Libya and Nigeria stand out as some of the EU's most important suppliers after Russia and Norway, especially in the natural gas sector. Projects such as the Trans-Sahara Gas Pipeline (see Chapter 5) offer opportunities to enhance the number of routes for getting African supplies to Europe. Accordingly, as the Commission has pointed out in its Second Strategic Energy Review, 'the Africa-EU Energy Partnership with the African Union together with the African Regional Economic Communities will be instrumental in developing a deeper energy dialogue and concrete initiatives' (European Commission, 2008a, p. 9). Aware of this potential, as part of its external energy policy, the EU has approached Africa by means of bilateral cooperation, the European Neighbourhood and Partnership Instrument (ENPI), the European Regional Development Fund and the EIB (Ibid.).

The Middle East

The Middle East has the world's richest proven oil and natural gas reserves. But, as the data for the years 2000–07 indicate, the Middle Eastern producers cannot be defined as Europe's major oil and natural gas suppliers in comparison to Russia or Norway. To illustrate, mineral fuels imported from Iraq and Saudi Arabia account, respectively, for only two per cent and four per cent of total EU fuel imports. However, despite the Union's more intense energy dialogues with Russia or Former Soviet Union (FSU) states in the Caspian region, the Middle East remains a 'critical player in energy policy' for the EU27 due to its rich resources, geographical advantages and its potential to stabilise world market prices in line with its oil supply capacity (Bahgat, 2006, p. 974). As later chapters underscore, it could also play a larger role in filling the EU's natural gas depots. Thus, the EU has had an interest in institutionalising its energy relations with this region as well, as a way of enhancing its external energy security (Ibid.). However, the EU's dialogue reflects not only an international consumer's need to secure its supplies but also perhaps broader and more long-term 'recognition of the fact that producer and consumer countries have common interests in encouraging regular supply at affordable prices' (European Commission, 2008a, p. 9).

The main EU energy cooperation initiatives with the Middle East are located within one of three different frameworks: the Euro-Mediterranean Partnership, policy dialogues with the Gulf Cooperation Council (GCC) and bilateral overtures towards individual states. The Euro-Mediterranean Partnership constitutes the main platform for the EU to pursue its goals of energy security and sustainability in the Middle East. Originally based on the Euro-Mediterranean Conference of Ministers of Foreign Affairs in 1995, the partnership consists of EU member states and their Mediterranean and Middle Eastern partners, namely Algeria, Egypt, Israel, Jordon, Lebanon, Morocco, Palestinian Authority, Syria, Tunisia and Turkey (Directorate General for Energy and Transport, 2008). The Barcelona Declaration adopted at the conference offered three primary spheres of partnership – political and security dialogue, economic and financial partnership and social, cultural and human partnership, all with the aim of creating a common area of peace and stability and a free trade area with economic opportunities where intercultural dialogue and mutual understanding would prevail between religions and people (European Council, 1995).

The Euro-Mediterranean Partnership refers to energy under its Economic and Financial Partnership plank and concentrates on harmonisation of energy markets in the Euromed region; promotion of sustainable development, infrastructure extension and investment financing; and strengthening of research and development programmes (Euro-Mediterranean Ministers of Foreign Affairs, 2008, p. 9). According to the Directorate General for Energy and Transport (2008, p. 5), the priorities of the Euromed Energy Partnership aim to

- Accelerate reform in the countries on the southern shore of the Mediterranean with a view to the gradual integration of the Euromed electricity and gas markets;
- Increase security and safety of energy supplies, infrastructure and oil shipping;
- Strengthen energy interconnections (both South-South and North-South).

On 17 December 2007, at the Euromed Energy Ministerial Conference, in line with the identified objectives, the participants of the Partnership decided on an Energy Action Plan covering the period between the years 2008–13. The process is still ongoing.

The EU's efforts to achieve international cooperation in energy include dialogue with the GCC. The EU's basic challenge here revolves around political dynamics in the GCC. According to European diplomats, despite the Union's emphasis on rule of law and democracy, authoritarian Persian Gulf states and their internal political systems are thought not to threaten European supply security as long as stability prevails and they are 'well run'. However, Gulf countries' internal political dynamics nonetheless directly affect future energy security considerations, since potential regime failures would heighten uncertainty about the uninterrupted flow of oil supplies, as they did in the case of Iran in the late 1970s. For example, in Saudi Arabia, the arbitrary and unpredictable decision-making of the royal family, lack of accountability concerning the flow of oil revenues into the royal budget and consequent public unrest due to popular anger over deteriorating economic conditions have wrought energy related consequences, such as the reversal of market openings or the reluctance to engage in further liberalisation for fear of fomenting further political instability. Hence, for GCC countries, internal social and political trends must be factored into the energy dialogue (Youngs, 2007b, pp. 11–12). Among the bilateral dialogues with individual states in the region, EU–Iranian relations have been noteworthy, although they have been held hostage to Iran's nuclear ambitions and activities, as the EU has clarified that continuation of overall cooperation with Iran is predicated on full suspension of all uranium enrichment activities (Haghighi, 2007, p. 376).

The Caspian region

The Caspian region refers to five Caspian littoral states, namely, Azerbaijan, Iran, Kazakhstan, Turkmenistan and Russia. (The prevailing orientation of Iran's foreign relations places it in the Middle East, while Russia, due to its already critical position in the EU's energy security, is examined in the following section.) The Caspian region's potential to augment the diversification of EU energy supplies is examined more extensively in Chapters 5 and 6, but another aspect of the region's importance from an energy angle is worth discussing here – the legal status of the Caspian Sea. With the disintegration of the Soviet Union, demarcation of official sea boundary lines among the littoral states came into question. No agreement has been reached between these states on whether the body of water resembles a 'lake' or a 'sea'. If the Caspian were not a lake, but a sea, littoral countries would, in accordance with the UN Convention on the Law of the Sea, be able to claim '12 miles from the shore as their territorial waters and beyond that a 200-mile exclusive economic zone', which would lead to an 'uneven distribution of oil and natural gas resources in the basin' (Bahgat, 2006, p. 972). Consequently, without concrete resolution of this matter, a 'de facto regime' has been emerging, with international oil and gas companies engaging in separate deals with littoral countries. Apart from the legal status of the potential undersea reserves, the landlocked position of Azerbaijan, Kazakhstan and Turkmenistan has created further hindrances to the construction of oil and natural gas transit routes (Ibid.).

The institutionalisation of the EU's energy relations with this group of countries began in 1995 in the form of the INOGATE programme. INOGATE was supposed to promote 'European investment in Caspian Sea/Central Asian states in return for their cooperation in supplying energy to the EU member states' (Ibid., p. 971). In February 2001, the INOGATE Umbrella Agreement came into force in order to systematise institutional and legal requirements for 'the development of interstate oil and gas transportation systems' and for the encouragement of 'the investment necessary for their construction and operation' (Ibid.). In 2004, the Baku Initiative was launched in order to develop 'regional energy markets and network interconnections in the Caspian and Central Asia' (Youngs, 2007b, p. 3). The initiative was in fact a bargaining ploy that basically traded European funding and investments in exchange for guaranteed energy supplies to Europe. Similarly, the 2006 Black Sea Initiative addressed a contiguous region, proposing ' "sub regional energy markets" in the Caspian Basin, Caucasus and Central Asia through an EU-Black Sea-Caspian Sea Common Energy House' (Ibid.). With these initiatives, the Union planned to create a region operating on the basis on Europe's internal market principles (Ibid., pp. 3–4).

Additionally, the Union concluded MoUs with Azerbaijan and Kazakhstan in 2006 and with Turkmenistan in 2008 to encourage cooperation in the field of energy. The EU intends to work with these Caspian countries to develop a Caspian Sea–Black Sea–EU energy transport corridor. The MoUs refer to supply–demand balances and common energy security challenges facing the EU and these countries, which are thought capable of being addressed through multiplication of export routes from the latter (which has happened in a de facto sense as part of these countries similar 'multi-vector' foreign policies, although more in terms of branching out to China and Iran than to the EU, a matter discussed more fully in Chapter 6). In this respect 'the deepening of energy market reforms, the development and modernization of energy infrastructures, energy efficiency, energy savings, the use of renewable energy sources' and environment-friendly technologies to combat climate change constitute the key concerns addressed by these MoUs.[2] Consequently, new investments in the region have emerged as increasingly necessary to the mutual economic welfare of both producer and consumer countries, while the creation of attractive, stable, equitable and transparent conditions by means of related legal and financial arrangements have become generally accepted, albeit not always strictly respected, preconditions for this investment.

Energy represents the main EU import from the region and Caspian hydrocarbons have space to grow into an even larger source of EU energy consumption. In 2008, mineral fuels represent 99 per cent of imports from Azerbaijan (Directorate General for Trade, 2009a), 61 per cent from Turkmenistan (Directorate General for Trade, 2009d) and 86 per cent from Kazakhstan (Directorate General for Trade, 2009b), but Azerbaijan, Turkmenistan and Kazakhstan still supply only 2.3 per cent, 0.3 per cent and 3.4 per cent, respectively, of the EU's total mineral fuel imports. Even in light of conservative estimates of the region's oil and gas reserves, these measures indicate that the EU has not fully tapped into this FSU region's true energy potential. As Youngs (2007b, pp. 12–13) has pointed out, unlike agreements concluded under ENP parameters, bilateral energy agreements with Azerbaijan and Kazakhstan have 'delinked' energy from democracy and human rights mandates. EU programmes, with their characteristic foci on governance, security and trafficking issues, remained limited in efficacy (although more so in seller's markets, when more demand is pursuing available supply), so broader EU policies that address the region's political and security needs may be required to achieve more effective future energy security results.

Russia

In 2008, Russia, the world's second major oil producer after Saudi Arabia, accounted for 12.3 per cent of world's total oil output. In natural gas, Russia is the world's number one producer, at 657 billion cubic metres per annum (bcma), amounting to about 21 per cent of world's total production (International Energy Agency, 2009c, pp. 11, 13). Russia also provides the largest volumes of oil and natural gas supplies to Europe. As Tables 3.1 and 3.2 indicated, EU imports from Russia covered 33.5 per cent of total oil imports and 42 per cent of total natural gas imports in 2006 (although these fractions underwent a slight shift in 2007). Although this may be due to earlier successes at reducing *relative* dependence on Russian gas (but not *absolute* dependence, which rose) from much higher baseline levels, the EU's efforts at further diversification away from Russia, if indeed they are sincerely being pursued, may have reached their upper limits and do not seem capable of further reducing Russia's stature in Europe's energy consumption portfolio. Javier Solana (2006, p. 3) has succinctly summed up the matter: 'Russia will be the mainstay of [EU] energy imports.' This has distinguished Russia from other energy partners, thus motivating the Union to hedge its bets on diversification by cultivating a special partnership with Russia.

It is also worth noting that, apart from the EU's high dependency, another related feature that distinguishes Russia from other suppliers has been its pronounced catalysing effect on European Energy Policy. As elaborated on in the following chapter, various cut-offs resulting from Russian disputes with transit countries in recent years have indubitably elevated Russia to a distinct plane of EU external policy. The question of whether Russia's main motivation has been economic or political remains controversial, but these crises noticeably accelerated the EU's efforts to craft a European Energy Policy leading to energy security. As Lynch (2006, p. 5) has argued, 'Crises are salutary moments. They reveal distinct trends that were difficult to highlight beforehand.'

The defining characteristic of the Russian energy sector has been a prominent state control over territorial resources. As most of them exit Russia only after first passing through the country's vast pipeline network, Russia's oil exports are virtually monopolised by state-owned Transneft, with cousin Gazprom controlling almost 90 per cent of Russian natural gas production and all of the country's gas exports. Russia sends almost all of its exported gas to the EU and Turkey, although Japan and China have emerged as rising competitors for Russian supplies. Westward exports pass from Russia to Poland and Germany via Belarus on the Yamal–Europe pipeline and the Blue Stream pipeline delivers gas from Russia to Turkey under the Black Sea (Bahgat, 2006, p. 970). Moreover, as detailed in the following chapter, the new North European Gas Pipeline (NEGP) (or 'Nord Stream') is slated to deliver gas directly to EU customers by the year 2011. It will connect Russia's Baltic Sea coast with that of Germany and may transport gas to the close energy markets of Germany and Denmark and even as far afield as the UK, Netherlands, Belgium, France and the Czech Republic (Nord Stream, 2008).

Institutionalisation of the EU–Russia energy relationship has historically been based on three main legal grounds: PCA, EU–Russia Energy Dialogue and the so-called Four Common Spaces. The initial move which transformed EU–Russia energy relationship into a 'partnership' was the 10-year bilateral PCA which came into force in 1997 (Kausch, 2007, p. 2). The Agreement contained legal arrangements concerning 'political dialogue, trade and cooperation in economic matters, justice and home affairs and bilateral cooperation' (Hadfield, 2008, p. 233). Article 65 of the Agreement directly addressed energy and offered cooperation in issues such as supply security, infrastructure, energy efficiency and formulation of energy policy (European Commission, 1997). However, the EU has generally considered the aforementioned ECT to be the main concrete pillar of its external energy policy and as the key platform from which to institutionalise energy relations with the widest variety of third parties. Its central problem lies in Russia's non-ratification of the treaty, which has largely rendered its provisions inapplicable to the plural proportion of the EU's external energy trade. In August 2009, Russia, which signed the treaty early on, made its lingering distaste official by declaring that it did not intend to become a contracting party to the ECT (Energy Charter Treaty, 2010).

Due to Russia's non-ratification of the ECT, the relationship between the EU and Russia migrated to another platform – the EU–Russia Summits. At the sixth EU–Russia Summit in October 2000 in Paris, the parties agreed on engaging in an energy dialogue to put their energy partnership on a more rule-bound footing. The dialogue has aimed mainly 'to enhance the energy security of the European continent by binding Russia and the EU into a closer relationship'. The EU has aimed via dialogue to convince Russia of the need for greater energy efficiency and conservation, greater energy-market openness, adoption of environmentally sustainable production technologies and improvement of energy production, transportation and investment conditions in Russia. To these ends, the EU–Russia Energy Dialogue has brought in multiple actors, including Russian government representatives, the Commission, EU member states, the EIB, the EBDR and European and Russian energy companies (European Union Press Release, 2009b).

Conversely, compounding its firm opposition to the ECT, Russia has rejected joining the ENP. The EU's effort to bring Russia into the ENP, much like its efforts to bring Turkey into various 'privileged partnership' arrangements that fall short of full membership, was perceived 'as a step that made Russia feel once again like a mere object of the CFSP, whereas it saw its role as that of a proper strategic partner' (Spetschinsky, 2007, p. 157, quoted in Hadfield, 2008, p. 245). This signalled that the EU's strategy of treating Russia like 'just another state' would continue to remain bereft of fruitful results. After the ENP was rejected by Russia, the EU and Russia decided in May 2003 to set up a new framework for cooperation – the 'Road Map of Common Economic Space'. The new framework encompassed 'four common spaces': economy, including energy; foreign and security policy; justice and home affairs; and culture, information and education (Kausch, 2007, pp. 2, 9).

Neither the PCA nor energy dialogue nor 'four common spaces' could fully vanquish the myriad energy-related problems between the EU and Russia. This was amply shown by the two Ukraine–Russian supply crises in 2006 and 2009 that are further detailed in the following chapter. As a consequence, in line with the identified importance of uninterrupted energy supplies and with the need to minimise or mitigate the negative consequences of future supply crises, the participants of the EU–Russia Summit held in Khabarovsk on 21–22 May 2009 broached new forms of crisis management (European Union Press Release, 2009c). Later in the year, on 16 November 2009, the Coordinators of the EU–Russia Energy Dialogue signed a memorandum on creation of an 'early warning mechanism' providing for 'early evaluation of potential risks and problems related to the supply and demand of natural gas, oil and electricity'. The parties also agreed on preventing or rapidly reacting to the threat of emergency situation, officially defined as 'a situation with a significant disruption/physical interruption of supply of natural gas, oil and electricity from the Russian Federation to the Territory of the EU, including supplies transiting through third countries' (European Union, 2009, p. 1).

In short, the Russo–EU energy relationship might be described as a conflict-prone form of cooperative independence among upstream, midstream and downstream parties. On the one hand, as Benford (2006, p. 45) has argued, 'Gazprom's need for revenue from European gas exports constitute the single most important factor in guaranteeing European energy security.' On the other hand, as indicated by the Commission (2008a, p. 8), as part of its external energy policy, the Union has had to retain a concern for deepening legally binding procedures with Russia.

Theoretical reflections on (external) energy policy

As we explored in the preceding chapter, efforts to bring the energy sector into the overall framework of European integration have been ongoing since its launch in the 1950s. However, a common energy policy covering all forms of energy did not materialise until the mid-1990s, when the pressure for the single market began to mount. The reluctance of the member states to pool their competences on this 'strategic sector' was overcome, first in 1996, with the Directive on Common Rules for the Internal Market in Electricity, and then in the form of the Directive on Common Rules for the Internal Market in Natural Gas in 1998 (Haghighi, 2007, p. 4). The main aim of these steps was to secure 'an efficient and well-functioning internal energy market' (Ibid.). However, these efforts did not lead to a serious discussion on *external* aspects of energy security. This particular facet of 'common energy policy' was left to the sovereign foreign policy remit of the individual member states.

Energy issue has multiple facets and thus constitutes a difficult area to be approached in its totality by any single theoretical framework. As is typical in political science, multiple competing perspectives can be employed to conceptualise arguments. Some energy policy experts (Clingendael International Energy Programme, 2004; Corréljé and van der Linde, 2006; Youngs, 2009) have utilised dichotomous metaphors – such as 'Markets and Institutions' versus 'Regions and Empires' – to examine security of energy supply to the EU, although their discussion, while usefully illuminating key divergences in how EU energy policy might take shape, can be located within broader international relations (and integration) theories that are applicable to the EU as a whole. Attempting to do that, we utilise the two best-known opposing theoretical schools of thoughts in international and European political economy – that is, (neo)liberalism and (neo)realism – to explicate a larger set of arguments on energy policy. Table 3.3 sums up the application of liberal and realist schools of thought to European Energy Policy, especially its external aspects. Rooted in the liberal approach, neoliberal institutionalism (Keohane, 1989) and neo-functionalism (Haas, 1958; Schmitter, 2004) have particular relevance for our subject matter. Yet realist-inspired schools of structural realism (Waltz, 1979) and intergovernmentalism (Hoffmann, 1995; Moravcsik, 1998) also prove useful.

Typically, the single market (including energy market) has provided the focal point of debate in integration theory between neo-functionalists and intergovernmentalists. Neo-functionalists points to the high degree of policy entrepreneurship provided by the Commission as well as pressure by European business interests for an integrated

Table 3.3   Theories on EU (external) energy policy

	Liberalism	Realism
Variants	Neo-liberal institutionalism Neo-functionalism	Structural realism Intergovernmentalism
Actors	States as fragmented actors, EU, international organisations and oil companies	States as unitary actors and (economic) blocs
Practitioners	Commission and Parliament	Member states
Goals	Competitiveness, economic security of supply and environmental sustainability	Physical security of energy supply and geostrategic advantage
Policy processes and tools	Spillover, markets, institutions and soft power	Bilateral deals, coercive diplomacy and hard power
Nature of (external) energy policy	Positive-sum	Zero-sum
EU vs. member states' role	Maximum for EU, minimum for member states	Minimum for EU, maximum for member states

single market (Young and Wallace, 2000; Egan, 2007). On the other hand, intergovernmentalists have stressed the significance of the particular period in which political parties that advocated neo-liberal economic policies came to power in important member states that initiated the process of bargaining over the single market (Egan, 2007, p. 266). Neo-functionalism would also place a pronounced emphasis on the spillover effect of the internal energy market on external energy policy. Haghighi (2007) argues that the 'more an activity comes into contact with the most basic principles of the Community, the more probable it is that competence for its formulation and regulation falls to the Community, either as an exclusive power or one shared with Member States' (p. 68). This author goes on to argue that development of an internal energy market would eventually create pressures to increase efficient external energy policies to accompany them (Ibid., pp. 68–70).

Whereas internal energy policy parallels the debate over the single market in general, controversies over external aspects of EU energy policy are comparable to the theoretical debates on the CFSP (Forster and Wallace, 2000; Dover, 2007; Haghighi, 2007). Some suggest that external energy policy be considered as an element of EU external trade and foreign and security policies (Clingendael International Energy Programme, 2004, pp. 15, 17, 26). Like the range of interests in the CFSP, external energy policy interests also diverge widely, fostering a lack of coherence among member states. Member states retain the core competences within the CFSP and divergent, incompatible national interests degrade the efficacy of the policy-making process, producing incoherent or muddled collective action outcomes. This situation could change in a less multilateral international setting, where 'the EU can be expected to change from an economically driven project into a political-strategic driven project' (Ibid., p. 15), but for the time being, '[a] common policy for external energy security is a declaratory expression of the lowest common denominator polices of the Member States' (Haghighi, 2007, p. 427). Of course, it is possible to retain a more optimistic perspective on the CFSP's potential to pool national interests in foreign policy if and when existing individual member states redefine their interests in the EU context. In this case, the CFSP might go beyond mere intergovernmentalism.

In terms of external energy policy, the liberal school of thought highlights the existence of a multiplicity of significant actors, often with cross-cutting agendas and purposes. These actors include not only states (which are not necessarily unitary in nature) and blocs but also international and regional institutions as well as energy companies.

While realists almost universally assert that states strive for survival and are thusly preoccupied with physical security of energy supply, liberals allow for the operation of additional official goals, such as energy affordability and environmental sustainability, and do not assume that these are superseded in importance by physical supply security. It suggests that these policy goals can be best attained through market mechanisms and accompanying institutional structures (regimes) that are constructed on the foundation of multilateral consensus. The liberal approach would consider the 'spillover' of EU internal market rules into the neighbourhood and energy producing countries to be a highly desired policy outcome and supports the proposition that a more advanced system in which energy relations are 'juridified' could lead to more stable exporter–importer relations. This is the idea behind the ECT, to which the Community is a party. This line of thinking assumes that intensification of globalisation and endurance of international institutions could bring Russia and other energy producers into a deeper economic integration with the EU (Clingendael International Energy Programme, 2004, p. 23).

However, diplomatic disputation could trump these 'juridified' relations. Consequently, there is no simple panacea for supply insecurity (Haghighi, 2007, p. 33). As such, the realist approach dismisses the importance of international (regional) energy regimes in relation to the primacy of bilateral deals among energy producers, transit and consumer countries. 'Realist' policy objectives include, but are not limited to, prevention, deterrence, containment and crisis management (Clingendael International Energy Programme, 2004, p. 26), as well as military intervention and occupation. Coercive diplomacy and projection of hard (military) power, membership in power blocs and so on are deemed essential to securing energy supplies. The realist school believe that diplomacy is even more valid especially in the realm of gas, 'due to the inflexibility and rigidity of gas transportation framework and the need to establish and preserve a physical link between two countries or regions' (Luciani, 2004). In sum, realists propose that 'the role of diplomacy in securing gas supply has been the basis in the past and will continue to be so in the future' (Haghighi, 2007, p. 32).

More specifically, the two approaches have clear implications for the relative role and weight of the EU as a supranational institution versus its member states in shaping external energy policy. While liberalism looks positively on EU efforts to develop a common external energy policy, which would institutionalise and impose strict constraints on the member states' policy-making power in the issue area, realism would contend that external energy policy, as part of foreign policy, will be difficult to wrest from the sovereign policy-making domains of individual EU member states. Moreover, as the member states are thought to be more in tune with their own specific needs (Ibid., p. 67), 'intergovernmental' logic is expected to dominate member states' behaviour regarding external energy policy. Indeed, external energy security has typically been seen as the national duty of individual member states rather than the EU. However, in the post-Cold War period, new efforts to gain access to Eurasian energy resources yielded a multilateral energy security framework – the ECT. Though the EU has continued to cultivate bilateral relations with energy-rich neighbours, the 2006 Russo-Ukrainian energy imbroglio galvanised the EU into appealing for greater member-state coordination in external energy policy, including unifying its voice and extending European norms beyond EU borders (Ibid., pp. 63–4).

Liberalism sees the energy issue as an international challenge, consisting of such potentially incompatible elements as sustainability, competitiveness, and supply security. For this approach, this complex challenge can be effectively tackled only if the problem is conceived of as 'global' in nature. Solutions are therefore believed to require a positive-sum approach to the solution, one that will benefit producer, transit and consumer states alike, as well as all citizens of the world. The liberal vision would include 'a Kyoto Protocol agreement driven development' (Clingendael International Energy Programme, 2004, p. 23). On the other hand, the realist approach does not really consider the energy 'crisis' as a global one. Rather it sees the issue as a matter of the distribution of resources among the nations and tends to view energy politics as part of a larger zero-sum struggle for influence among great powers.

Perhaps unsurprisingly, EU institutions, chiefly the Commission, tend to enshrine liberal approaches in their discussions of external energy policy. The Commission in its various documents has emphasised the 'trinity' of sustainability, competitiveness and security of supply and advocated market liberalisation and extension of the EU's energy *acquis*, by various means, to supplier and transit countries. The Commission has taken a strong and noteworthy leadership stand on European and global energy and environmental initiatives, especially global warming. On the other hand, EU27 member states, often with vastly divergent energy profiles and policy preferences, have tended to rely on geopolitical approaches to energy policy. For instance, Germany's high-profile relations with Russia on energy has been an exemplar of energy policy bilateralism in Europe, but others, such as France, Italy, Austria, the Netherlands and Bulgaria, have also fallen into the temptation to pursue their own separate agreements with Gazprom (Youngs, 2007a, p. 1).

Between these two stylised theoretical positions lies a middle ground where the majority of the European practices reside. Indeed, the fullest picture of EU energy policy emerges only when we combine both. Just as the EU is not completely oblivious to the intrusion of uncomfortable geo-political realities into its energy policy-making tableau, member states cannot cavalierly dismiss policy principles envisaged in EU documents (Ibid.). The organisation seems to be acting at the interface of market and geopolitics, or, to put it more clearly, between the 'market-governance nexus' and 'hard-power securitization' in shaping its external energy policy (Youngs, 2009, p. 4).

Conclusion

The majority of the Union's energy consumption is covered by imported oil and natural gas. Moreover, this import dependency is projected to further increase in coming decades, increasing the EU's vulnerability to external dynamics that impinge on the flow of its energy supplies. Accordingly, this chapter analysed the significance of the external dimension of EU energy policy. It discussed the EU's major policies focused on external supply challenges and achieving the objective of supply security. Herein was emphasised that collective EU energy security cannot be attained through purely unilateral efforts. Consequently, special focus was given to the EU's relations with its major energy suppliers.

In the overall evaluation of the EU's external energy policy, the twin endeavours of market liberalisation and extension of the EU's internal market principles to supplier and transit states alike have emerged as crucial policy options on the road to achieving the seemingly incompatible 'trinity' of sustainability, competitiveness and security of supply. The EU has made certain inroads into institutionalising its relations with energy-producing and transit regions and countries, such as Norway, Eastern and South East Europe and the Caucasus. However, as the case of Russia indicated, the EU's promotion of market liberalisation is not easily welcomed by these target states. In response to these 'uncooperative' suppliers, the most feasible move for the EU has been to try to increase its diversity of suppliers and transit routes, which could both decrease the dependency on a single supplier and bypass problematic transit regions.

Russia, the number one oil and gas supplier to the EU and the leading actor in two major gas crises in 2006 and 2009, has been the biggest source of anxiety in Europe's energy security considerations.

Nevertheless, both exporter and importer operate in an international energy market where competition and uncertainty (about supply and demand security) prevail. This has motivated the EU to search for other suppliers and energy suppliers (Hadfield, 2008, p. 243), although the EU's potential as an energy market conversely lowers the incentives of major suppliers to delink themselves from European energy consumers (Spanjer, 2007, p. 2891). In that respect, minimising transit risks by building alternative supply routes are of vital importance for both the EU and those suppliers who want to protect and increase their share of European markets. Diversification of suppliers refers not only to increased cooperation with multiple suppliers and investment in extraction and production activities, but also to obtaining secure uninterrupted transmission of these new oil and natural gas supplies. Consequently, transit countries have become nearly as important as suppliers in efforts to formulate and implement effective energy policies. Taking these into account, one clear conclusion is that Europe remains a large market for new oil and gas supplies. Central Asian and Caspian countries, as well as potential suppliers in the Middle East and North Africa, cannot be precluded from efforts to diversify Europe's energy profile. The picture is clear yet incomplete until there is clearer emergence of a 'bridge' linking demand and supply.

The EU has not yet developed a common energy policy to provide a framework for dealing more efficaciously with energy producers, transit countries, and other consuming countries. Such a weakness has also clouded perceptions of what the Union stands for in terms of its modus operandi on energy security. The EU has too long vacillated between trying to institutionalise market rules while also permitting its powerful member states and their dominant firms to conduct their own private geostrategic approaches, a situation that does little to enhance its international standing or credibility as a global energy policy actor. In terms of theoretical explanations of EU external energy policy, it seems that only a combination of liberal and realist positions provides the fullest picture of EU energy policy. The EU cannot fully ignore uncomfortable geopolitical realities, but member states cannot completely dismiss policy principles envisaged in EU documents. The EU functions at the sharp interface between liberal and realist prescriptive advice in crafting its external energy policy.

Part II

The European Union, Russia and Other Actors

4
EU Dependence on Russian Energy

Introduction: *primus inter pares* – Russia in EU energy security

Goods and influence travel between the Russia and the collective economic area demarcated by the 27 member states of the European Union (EU), so if the latter were asymmetrically and totally dependent on Russia, analysis of the geopolitics of EU–Russian interactions would be simple. However, the particular nature of their mutual energy trade (or their 'money-for-energy' exchange) has clearly advantaged Russia over the EU at saliently critical times, as in January 2006 and 2009, when Russia's dominant gas-producing and exporting firm Gazprom halted the flow of gas to Ukraine, which in turn stopped feeding the Europe-bound transit pipeline. Moreover, a considerable heterogeneity marks EU member states' respective patterns of fuel importation and thus shapes their disparate views on the best way to deal with Russian and other energy exporters. Analysing this heterogeneity is tractable, however, due to a salient divide between the EU15 core, elements of which prefer direct channels of access to Russian gas, and the newer EU10 (now EU12) members, some of which serve as transit states and have thus expressed concern that these projects could elevate the risks of flow manipulation inhering in their near-absolute dependency on Russian fuel sources.

Consequently, while the benefits of using energy more efficiently and exploiting renewable sources, thereby limiting carbon emissions, possibly boosting domestic or intra-EU27 employment and curtailing importation of hydrocarbons, have diffused widely within the EU, member states remain split on the necessity and desirability of reducing dependence on Russia. Key EU15 states could cite the post-Cold War trend of declining relative EU reliance on Russian gas imports to identify the problem as arising not from rent-seeking behaviour by Russia's respective oil and gas pipeline monopolists Transneft and Gazprom (see the following chapter), but from the often disputatious movement of Russian energy supplies across Belarus and Ukraine. Conversely, the EU10, which were unanimously awarded membership by the EU15, have fewer means to mitigate the worst short-term consequences of being more highly dependent on Russian oil and gas. During the 2009 gas cut, for example, Slovakia was reprimanded for moving to ramp up output from a Soviet-era nuclear power plant (NPP), considered one of the three most dangerous in Europe and slated for decommissioning as a condition for EU10 states' 2004 accession (Pancevski, et al., 2009, p. 31; Wagstyl and Ward, 2010, p. 8). Not surprisingly, then, new member states and the European Commission have been decidedly more supportive of measures to broaden the EU's external supplier base, not simply its selection from the menu of supply routes for Russian energy.

Yet, diversification itself has posed a key dilemma for the European Commission and even for the most heavily Russia-dependent member states. As the steep overhead costs and prolonged gestation times associated with diversification projects better allow the monopoly supplier of Russian-controlled gas to obstruct them, the European Commission has had to hedge its bets on major diversification by cultivating various institutional accoutrements of its existing energy 'partnership' with Russia. While it incorporates policies that reflect collective EU27 interests, this partnership seems intended to lend legitimacy to separate and often cross-cutting interests of particular member states. Major energy firms and governments in key EU15 states, namely France, Italy and Germany, by no means the most highly dependent on Russian gas imports, are undertaking joint projects to pipe these imports around extant transit territories, especially as they do not have to incur the largest political costs and risks entailed by this sort of EU–Russian partnership. Moreover, the gathering momentum behind certain of these projects has induced even those EU member states that are more heavily dependent on Russia to jump on the bandwagon for fear of being left out of the pipeline nexus altogether. Consequently, the European Commission has struggled to forge a common energy policy that would establish a 'single reference point' and enable the EU to 'speak with the same voice' (European Commission, 2006b, p. 5) on the need for sufficient diversity of exporters – not just diversion of Russian gas routes – that would ensure against future disruptions in imported energy deliveries.

This chapter addresses, in succession, Russia's role as an EU energy provider, the complications in this energy trade that are posed by the presence of multiple transit territories and the EU's efforts to try to influence the policies and actions of Russia and the transit states in order to ensure its energy security.

A Russo-centric profile of EU energy security

The concept of energy security is closely tied to notions of dependency on foreign suppliers. However, relevant levels and measures of dependency differ. A pivotally significant measure consists of *economic* dependency on energy, as indicated by gross domestic product (GDP) spent by consumers on energy and imports or that earned by producers on energy exports (and rates of growth or decline in those fractions), as well as those volumes of energy required to generate units of GDP (and rates of change in those volumes). Empirically speaking, importing economies have typically decoupled themselves from energy consumption to a greater extent than exporting economies from energy production (Ahrend, 2005, pp. 584–609; Lucas, 2008, p. 90).[1] Notably, according to the European Commission's Eurostat (2010a) database, the energy intensity of the present-day EU27 economy fell by 12 per cent, from 193 kilograms of oil equivalent (kgoe) required to generate € 1000 of GDP in 1999 to 169 kgoe in 2007.

Indeed, economic measures of Russian dependency on their mutual energy trade far exceed those of the EU. In economic terms, though its 2007 trade in mineral fuels with the Russian Federation accounted for over half of the EU27's overall trade deficit, imports of Russian mineral fuels made up less than 7 per cent of the total value of EU imports and an infinitesimal fraction of the EU's overall 2007 GDP of nearly € 13 trillion (Eurostat, 2010b). Conversely, Russia exports one-quarter of its oil production and three-quarters of its extracted gas to the EU (BP, 2008), with oil and gas together having comprised nearly one-half of Russia's total 2006 exports by value and roughly 15 per cent of its overall GDP (World Bank, 2007). The United Nations (2002, pp. 850, 853; 2007, p. 5) has indicated a 19-per cent increase (from 42 per cent in 1999, at the depths of Russia's earlier economic crisis, to 61 per cent in 2007) in the mineral fuels-based proportion of Russia's overall export portfolio by value. This implies that Russia cannot facilely embargo energy supplies to European customers, as it has done with Former Soviet Union (FSU) importing countries, without harming itself.

Even if the focus is limited to the issue of how consumers can ensure *physical* supplies, individual countries rely on different total energy demands, various mixes of energy sources, disparate volumes of imports (overall and by fuel source) and varying ranges of external suppliers. Therefore, a single country or a distinct aggregation of countries can experience different permutations of dependency with divergent geopolitical implications. At one end of the continuum, economic growth might require no incremental input of energy. By contrast, consumer prosperity could be tightly shackled to specific volumes and portfolios of fuel supplies from one foreign producer. Most economies lie somewhere in between these extremes. For example, an economy may import a particular fuel from only one exporting country without relying much on large overall volumes of imports to satisfy its demand for that source of energy. Another economy may import sizable quantities of a fuel, but from a wide array of exporters. Whatever the case, a country's respective advantage or predicament in this regard has a significant bearing on the political stance it takes vis-à-vis its most salient energy suppliers. Simultaneously underscoring both a need for and an impediment to a common energy policy, disparate levels and types of energy dependency across EU member states have undeniably frustrated efforts to ensure that 'Europe speaks with one voice and acts accordingly' on matters of crucial urgency to its energy security (European Commission, 2008a, p. 10).

EU energy demand trends: is pro-environment also pro-Russia?

Chapter 3's brief survey suggests that long-term trends in both overall demand for energy and energy imports as well as in the consumption and importation of specific fuels can help situate Russia in the analysis of how and to what extent the EU's economy remains vulnerable from an energy standpoint. As Table 4.1 indicates, over a 15-year post-Cold War period ending in 2007, the EU27's gross inland energy consumption grew by 11 per cent, with this expansion concentrated in the EU15. While growth in EU27 oil demand just kept pace with its rising total energy demand, nuclear power use rose by 15 per cent, but use of solid fuels, centrally coal, fell by 18 per cent. The EU27's respective demands for gas and renewable energy rose by 46 and 81 per cent over the period 1992–2007, with EU15 gas demand increasing by 57 per cent and consumption of renewable energy sources in EU10-coterminous territory growing by 150 per cent from a smaller baseline. While some of this change has accompanied efforts to comply with environmental

Table 4.1   Gross inland energy consumption – EU and Turkey

	1992	2007	Change (%)
Austria	25873	33809	31
Belgium	51756	57377	11
Denmark	18973	20516	8
Finland	28102	37630	34
France	239055	270272	13
Germany	342601	339568	−1
Greece	23174	33488	45
Ireland	9914	15883	60
Italy	154789	183452	19
Luxembourg	3801	4655	22
Netherlands	70959	84542	19
Portugal	19065	25975	36
Spain	95476	146812	54
Sweden	46431	50564	9
United Kingdom	215738	221092	2
EU15	**1345707**	**1525634**	**13**
Cyprus	1792	2726	52
Czech Republic	44778	46241	3
Estonia	6944	6029	−13
Hungary	25203	27020	7
Latvia	6135	4764	−22
Lithuania	10845	9151	−16
Malta	619	946	53
Poland	97431	97982	1
Slovakia	17662	18074	2
Slovenia	5277	7346	39
EU10	**216687**	**220278**	**2**
Bulgaria	20731	20341	−2
Romania	46924	40083	−1
EU27	**1630049**	**1806336**	**11**
Turkey	54770	101510	85

Units: 1000 tonnes of oil equivalent (toe).
Source: Eurostat (2010a).

commitments mandated in the 1997 Kyoto Protocol to the 1992 UN Framework Convention on Climate Change, the EU10(12) slashed its aggregate coal use by one quarter, largely due to the downsizing of their antiquated Soviet-style heavy industrial sectors.

The International Energy Agency (2009f, pp. 632–3) has projected expansion in overall EU27 demand for energy to slow to less than 2 per cent during the period 2007–30, with coal, oil and nuclear power declining, both in absolute and in relative terms, at the expense of natural gas and a basket of various renewable energy sources. Accordingly, total CO_2 emissions from the EU area have entered a downward trajectory. They fell by 4 per cent between 1990 and 2007 and are expected to fall another 10 per cent by 2030. The respective 33 and 26 per cent fractions of total 2007 emissions generated by the burning of coal and natural gas are projected to reverse places by 2030, with oil retaining its relatively larger share of 41–2 per cent.[2]

Since the end of the Cold War, the fuel mix of the EU's energy basket has undeniably shifted. As Table 4.2 shows, natural gas, which supplied nearly 18 per cent of the EU27's fuel consumption requirements in 1992 and drove approximately three-quarters of its total energy demand

Table 4.2   Energy mix – EU and Turkey (% of gross inland energy consumption)

	Solid fuels		Oil		Gas		Nuclear		Renewables	
	1992	2007	1992	2007	1992	2007	1992	2007	1992	2007
Austria	13	11	44	41	21	21	0	0	21	24
Belgium	19	8	41	39	17	26	21	22	1	3
Denmark	36	23	44	41	11	20	0	0	7	17
Finland	17	19	34	29	9	10	18	16	19	23
France	8	5	38	34	12	14	37	42	8	7
Germany	30	26	40	33	17	23	11	11	2	8
Greece	35	32	59	51	1	10	0	0	5	5
Ireland	31	14	49	55	19	27	0	0	2	3
Italy	8	9	58	44	27	38	0	0	5	7
Luxembourg	27	2	51	63	12	26	0	0	1	3
Netherlands	12	10	37	44	47	40	1	1	1	4
Portugal	15	11	69	54	0	15	0	0	15	18
Spain	22	14	52	48	6	22	14	10	5	7
Sweden	5	5	31	28	1	2	36	34	27	31
United Kingdom	28	18	39	36	24	38	9	7	1	2
EU15	20	15	43	38	18	25	14	14	5	8
Cyprus	1	1	99	96	0	0	0	0	0	2
Czech Republic	61	46	18	22	13	15	7	15	1	5
Estonia	65	61	22	19	10	13	0	0	7	10
Hungary	20	12	31	28	31	40	14	14	2	5
Latvia	9	2	41	34	28	29	0	0	16	30
Lithuania	4	3	37	30	26	32	35	30	3	9
Malta	0	0	100	100	0	0	0	0	0	0
Poland	76	57	14	26	8	13	0	0	2	5
Slovakia	33	22	20	21	28	28	16	22	2	5
Slovenia	30	22	30	35	12	12	20	20	11	10

EU10	**55**	**41**	**21**	**26**	**15**	**19**	**7**	**8**	**2**	**6**
Bulgaria	36	39	27	25	20	15	14	19	2	5
Romania	23	25	26	26	45	33	0	5	5	12
EU27	**25**	**18**	**39**	**36**	**18**	**24**	**13**	**13**	**5**	**8**
Turkey	31	29	43	32	7	30	0	0	18	9

Source: Calculations based on Eurostat (2010a).

growth, came to meet nearly 24 per cent of overall EU27 energy needs by 2007. Gas is projected to fill nearly 29 per cent of the EU27's 2030 energy requirements. This fraction grew less dramatically for the EU10, rising from 15 to 19 per cent of their collective energy demand. Oil and nuclear power have accounted for relatively static shares – 37–8 per cent and 12–13 per cent, respectively – of the EU27's overall energy demand, although these respective proportions are projected to fall to 31 and 11 per cent of the 2030 demand mix. The EU10's aggregate oil consumption rose from 17 to nearly 21 per cent of its total energy demand.

During the same time period, coal's one-quarter share of the EU's 1992 energy consumption fell to nearly 18 per cent in 2007, with the EU10 easing its combined reliance on coal from a relatively higher 55-per cent baseline to 41 per cent. Accounting for nearly the same proportion of the EU27's total growth in gross inland energy consumption as oil, use of renewable energy sources (inclusive of hydropower) soared in absolute terms across the entire EU27, as this basket of myriad fuel sources expanded from a relatively negligible level. In short, the EU27 has essentially substituted cleaner-burning renewable sources and natural gas for coal, a process that has in turn confronted the EU with the pressing question of how to access more non-Russian sources of external gas supply.

Rising EU dependence on Russian oil joins an enduring reliance on its gas

Due to steady growth in its energy consumption requirements, nearly all of this increase having been motored by the EU15, the EU27 became dependent on imports to meet over half of its total energy needs between 2003 and 2004 (Eurostat, 2009a, pp. 456–7). Analysis of the three main hydrocarbon fuel categories – coal, oil and natural gas, in which importation is salient, helps to pinpoint where this dependency is most relevant in terms of identifying and strengthening the weakest links in EU energy security.

Coal

Trends relevant to the sub-categories of brown or soft coal (lignite) and black or hard coal serve as strong proxy measures for what is happening in terms of the overall consumption and importation of solid fuels in the EU. While imports met less than one per cent of the EU27 area's 2007 lignite consumption requirements, with Russian brown coal rising from 27 per cent of total imports in 1992 to 89 per cent in 2004 before dropping off to 17 per cent in 2007, thus showing no definitive trend, the proportion of EU27 black coal demand met by external suppliers rose from just under one-third in 1992 to nearly three-fifths in 2007. Moreover, Russia's share of these imports climbed from a comparatively minuscule 7 per cent in 1992 to roughly one-quarter 15 years later.

Import dependency has been even more pronounced and subject to a sharper rate of increase within the EU15 core. Reliance on foreign suppliers to meet EU15 collective black coal needs rose steeply from 46 per cent in 1992 to just over four-fifths in 2007, with Russia's share of these imports also growing from about 5 per cent to just over one-fifth. Even though Russia accounted for a relatively steady 24 per cent fraction of aggregate EU10 imports over the period 1992–2007, imports as a percentage of total lignite consumption dropped off sharply. Conversely, imports supplied an expanding fraction of EU10 hard coal demand, with Russia's share of that import basket climbing from 18 per cent to just over two-thirds. Nonetheless, for environmental and geological reasons, coal fills a declining portion of EU energy demand, thus mitigating the countervailing trend of rising dependency on general imports and Russian supply.

Crude oil

Both crude oil consumption in the EU and exports to this area grew slightly between 1992 and 2007. While combined EU10 oil demand rose by nearly 23 per cent, EU27 crude consumption grew by only 10 per cent over the period in question. Growth in EU27 importation approximated 4 per cent. However, as shown in Table 4.3, dependence on external suppliers to meet its oil demand remained high, making the EU27 most heavily import reliant in terms of oil, and imports of Russian crude into the EU experienced a phenomenal ascent, soaring from just over 1 per cent of extra-EU27 imports in 1992 to one-third in 2007, with the EU10 coming to depend on Russia to fill over nine-tenths of its collective oil import basket. Consequently, the presence of Russian supplies

Table 4.3 Crude oil-import dependency ratios – EU and Turkey

| | Non-EU crude imports | | | | Russian crude imports | | | | | |
| | % Crude consumption | | % Energy consumption | | % Non-EU crude imports | | % Crude consumption | | % Energy consumption | |
	1992	2007	1992	2007	1992	2007	1992	2007	1992	2007
Austria	84	87	37	36	0	3	0	3	0	1
Belgium	95	94	39	37	0	50	0	47	0	19
Denmark	47	26	21	11	20	0	9	0	4	0
Finland	57	83	19	24	23	89	13	74	5	22
France	90	91	34	31	0	14	0	13	0	4
Germany	83	82	33	27	0	38	0	31	0	10
Greece	104	106	61	55	2	32	18	34	1	17
Ireland	101	63	49	35	0	0	0	0	0	0
Italy	95	95	56	42	0	19	0	18	0	8
Luxembourg	0	0	0	0	0	0	0	0	0	0
Netherlands	89	78	33	34	0	36	0	28	0	12
Portugal	93	99	64	54	0	0	0	0	0	0
Spain	94	98	49	47	0	23	0	22	0	11
Sweden	76	68	24	19	7	49	5	33	2	9
UK	53	62	21	22	4	13	2	8	1	3

Table 4.3 (Continued)

| | Non-EU crude imports | | | | Russian crude imports | | | | | |
| | % Crude consumption | | % Energy consumption | | % Non-EU crude imports | | % Crude consumption | | % Energy consumption | |
	1992	2007	1992	2007	1992	2007	1992	2007	1992	2007
EU15	85	85	35	33	10	27	8	22	3	9
Cyprus	103	0	102	0	0	0	0	0	0	0
Czech	99	97	18	21	0	65	0	63	0	14
Estonia	0	0	0	0	0	0	0	0	0	0
Hungary	73	93	23	26	0	97	0	90	0	25
Latvia	100	0	41	0	0	0	0	0	0	0
Lithuania	99	100	37	30	0	96	0	97	0	29
Malta	0	0	0	0	0	0	0	0	0	0
Poland	99	103	14	26	0	97	0	100	0	26
Slovakia	98	102	19	22	0	100	0	102	0	22
Slovenia	99	0	30	0	0	0	0	0	0	0
EU10	94	100	16	21	0	93	0	92	0	19
Bulgaria	92	100	25	25	100	65	92	65	25	16
Romania	50	65	13	17	0	55	0	36	0	9
EU27	83	85	33	31	1	33	1	28	0	10
Turkey	83	90	35	23	2	39	2	35	1	9

Source: Calculations based on Eurostat (2010a).

grew from nearly 12 to 28 per cent of EU27 oil demand, as though the EU was still engaged in a process, dating back to the 1973–74 Arab oil embargo (Goldman, 2008, pp. 46–7), of moving *away from* Organization of Petroleum Exporting Countries (OPEC) in the direction of Russia.

Because the EU27's collective crude oil demand rose by nearly one-tenth from 1992 to 2007, increasing dependency on one particular exporter that has utilised pipelines extensively to ship not only gas but also oil counsels prudence against becoming complacent about the oft-touted capacity of oil's prevailing 'spot market' structure to adjust and compensate for shortfalls from any one particular supplier. In 2007, for example, five EU member states – the Czech Republic, Germany, Hungary, Poland and the Slovak Republic – together received 63 million metric tonnes per annum (mmta), just under one-third of all exports of Russian crude and Transneft-controlled crude, through the Druzhba ('Friendship') Pipeline (Energy Information Administration, 2008b, p. 5). After the main trunk of the pipeline forks into two at Mozyr, a Belarusian refining hub, the northern branch carrying most of Druzhba oil serves Germany and Poland and the southern branch, from which spurs connect to the Odessa–Brody and Adria pipelines, carries the minority share to the three other EU member states (International Energy Agency, 2010, pp. 23–4). While this volume made up 35 per cent of EU27 crude oil imports from Russia, but only 11 per cent of all EU27 crude imports and 10 per cent of EU27 crude oil demand, for the five member states served by it, this pipeline supplied approximately 87 per cent of their total crude oil imports from Russia, nearly half of their overall imports, and 43 per cent of their crude oil demand. Bulgaria, the Czech Republic, Finland, Hungary, Lithuania, Poland, Romania and the Slovak Republic, four of whom are also supplied by 'Friendship', looked to Russian oil to provide at least half of their respective oil imports and, with the exception of Romania, to supply at least three-fifths of their respective oil consumption requirements in 2007. This oil-import dependency profile bears at least a passing resemblance to that of natural gas.

Natural gas

Because of its predominantly pipeline-based and multi-jurisdictional transit along the Eurasian landmass, natural gas forms a salient focus of our geopolitical analysis. As indicated by Table 4.4, EU27-area gas imports nearly doubled over the period 1992–2007.

Table 4.4 EU and Turkish imports of non-EU gas (terajoules – gross calorific value)

	Extra-EU27 gas			Russian gas		
	1992	2007	Change (%)	1992	2007	Change (%)
Austria	193225	379607	96	193225	216419	12
Belgium	254898	381798	50	0	31528	+10000
Denmark	0	0	0	0	0	0
Finland	115204	173166	50	115204	173166	50
France	1076912	1438678	34	446260	238022	−47
Germany	1225841	2586105	111	838330	1436060	71
Greece	0	155138	+10000	0	118819	+10000
Ireland	0	0	0	0	0	0
Italy	1083613	2469718	128	503757	863613	71
Luxembourg	2	55948	+10000	0	0	0
Netherlands	98413	0	−100	0	0	0
Portugal	0	174947	+10000	0	0	0
Spain	225149	1465575	551	0	0	0
Sweden	0	0	0	0	0	0
United Kingdom	220519	866401	293	0	0	0
EU15	**4493776**	**10147081**	**129**	**2096776**	**3077627**	**47**
Cyprus	0	0	0	0	0	0
Czech Republic	254451	327343	29	254451	259008	2
Estonia	33381	37372	12	33381	37372	12
Hungary	191344	372938	95	191344	300491	57
Latvia	99298	61201	−38	99298	61201	−38
Lithuania	128699	138425	8	128699	138425	8
Malta	0	0	0	0	0	0
Poland	248080	352748	42	248080	260533	5
Slovakia	222888	238667	7	222888	236839	−6
Slovenia	27960	35364	26	20094	21657	8
EU10	**1206101**	**1636265**	**35**	**1198265**	**1315526**	**9**
Bulgaria	188931	128088	−32	188931	128088	−32
Romania	166688	179802	8	166688	164124	−2
EU27	**6055496**	**11152628**	**98**	**3650630**	**4685365**	**28**
Turkey	169937	1385956	716	169937	857649	405

Note: Gas imports into the EU27 area from *non-EU* supplier countries are calculated by subtracting *intra*-EU27 imports from *total* EU27 imports for each EU27 member state and by summing to obtain the various respective totals
Source: Calculations based on Eurostat (2010a).

As elaborated on further in subsequent chapters, much of the EU27's rising import dependency did not necessarily leave Gazprom with a tighter chokehold on European gas supplies. While EU15 imports of Russian gas grew by nearly half, EU10 imports rose only slightly, boosting EU27 gas shipments from Russia by 28 per cent over 1992–2007. Yet, as Table 4.5 illustrates, the Russian *share* of EU27 gas imports fell from its high of three-fifths in 1992 to nearly 39 per cent in 2007. Nonetheless, as demand and general importation rose, Russian gas dropped less dramatically as a percentage of EU gross inland gas consumption, from 27 to 23 per cent. According to data given by the International Energy Agency (2009d, pp. II. 30–3, II. 46–9), pipelines supply 85 per cent of the EU27 gas import basket, and Russian gas, all exports of which to the EU27 have been piped, accounted for 46 per cent of the EU27's piped imports.

Most EU member states, with the exception of Denmark, Ireland, the Netherlands, Romania, Sweden and the UK, depended on imports from *outside* the EU27 area to meet more than half of their respective natural gas needs in 2007. Of those relying on *extra*-EU27 imports to meet over half of their demand, only Belgium and Poland imported less than 70 per cent of their gas needs that same year. Moreover, of those EU27 member states who imported over seven tenths of their gas needs, nine smaller economies – Bulgaria, the Czech Republic, Estonia, Finland, Greece, Hungary, Latvia, Lithuania and the Slovak Republic – also relied on Russia to meet over seven tenths of their respective overall gas importation requirements, with six of these countries also highly dependent on Russian crude oil. Of those states, only Hungary depended on Russia to supply less than 70 per cent of its gas consumption needs in 2007.

On the whole, EU member states, especially within the EU15 core, display a wide variety of gas consumption and import-dependency profiles. In one anomalous case, Russia filled just over 90 per cent of Romania's import basket, but, because Romania imported only 30 per cent of its 2007 gas demand, Russia met only 27 per cent of this need, not far above the EU27 average. The import dependencies of EU15 giants Germany and Italy soared by 30 and 20 per cent, respectively, but, while both relied on Russia to fill just over two-thirds and 46 per cent of their respective import baskets in 1992, they cut these respective dependencies on Russian gas to 55 and 35 per cent by 2007. Conversely, France imported a constant 80 per cent of its gas demand between 1992 and 2007, but purchased only 17 per cent of these imports and 13 per cent of all its total gas needs from Russia.

Table 4.5 Gas-import dependency ratios – EU and Turkey

| | Non-EU gas imports | | | | Russian gas imports | | | | | |
| | % Gas consumption | | % Energy consumption | | % Non-EU gas imports | | % Gas consumption | | % Energy consumption | |
	1992	2007	1992	2007	1992	2007	1992	2007	1992	2007
Austria	77	117	18	27	100	57	77	67	18	15
Belgium	61	55	12	16	0	8	0	45	0	1
Denmark	0	0	0	0	0	0	0	0	0	0
Finland	100	100	10	11	100	100	100	100	10	11
France	81	80	11	13	41	17	34	13	4	2
Germany	46	73	9	18	68	56	32	40	6	10
Greece	0	100	0	11	0	77	0	76	0	8
Ireland	0	0	0	0	0	0	0	0	0	0
Italy	57	76	17	32	46	35	26	27	8	11
Luxembourg	0	100	0	29	0	0	0	0	0	0
Netherlands	6	0	3	0	0	0	0	0	0	0
Portugal	0	99	0	16	0	0	0	0	0	0
Spain	83	99	6	24	0	0	0	0	0	0
Sweden	0	0	0	0	0	0	0	0	0	0
United Kingdom	9	23	2	9	0	0	0	0	0	0

	40	58	8	16	47	30	19	18	4	5
EU15	**40**	**58**	**8**	**16**	**47**	**30**	**19**	**18**	**4**	**5**
Cyprus	0	0	0	0	0	0	0	0	0	0
Czech Republic	94	98	14	17	100	79	94	78	14	13
Estonia	100	100	11	15	100	100	100	100	11	15
Hungary	53	75	18	33	100	81	53	60	18	26
Latvia	124	97	39	31	100	100	124	97	39	31
Lithuania	100	103	28	36	100	100	100	103	28	36
Malta	0	0	0	0	0	0	0	0	0	0
Poland	69	61	6	9	100	74	69	45	6	6
Slovakia	96	100	30	31	100	99	96	100	30	31
Slovenia	98	83	13	11	72	61	70	51	9	7
EU10	**81**	**85**	**13**	**18**	**99**	**80**	**80**	**68**	**13**	**14**
Bulgaria	100	91	22	15	100	100	100	91	22	15
Romania	17	30	8	11	100	91	17	27	8	10
EU27	**44**	**60**	**9**	**16**	**60**	**39**	**27**	**23**	**5**	**6**
Turkey	96	98	7	33	100	62	96	61	7	20

Source: Calculations based on Eurostat (2010a).

'Thou shalt not pass'? The problematic movement of Russian hydrocarbons to Europe

As Map 4.1 illustrates, a central feature of EU energy security involves the physical transit of much of its importation of Russian and other FSU hydrocarbons across ex-Soviet territories Belarus and Ukraine.

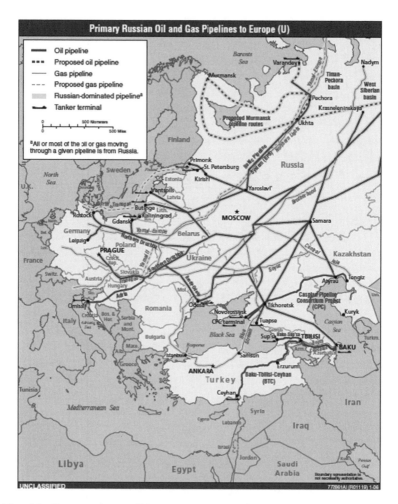

Map 4.1   Europe-orientated Eurasian energy pipelines.
Source: Energy Information Administration (2008b).

Both transit countries overwhelmingly depend on imports of Russian oil shipped by monopoly pipeline operator Transneft, even though they re-export fractions of the oil as crude or refined products. In fact, 2007 Ukrainian oil imports of 15–16 mmta covered 78 per cent of its total oil supply but only 11 per cent of its total energy needs, while Belarus imported approximately 20 mmta of crude in 2007, which supplied 90 per cent of its oil needs and 46 per cent of its total energy supply. Ukraine exported around 4 mmta, and Belarus 14 mmta, of refined products that year (International Energy Agency, 2009a, p. II. 73, II. 218). Gas met roughly two-fifths of each country's total energy supply (Ibid.), with exports by Gazprom exports covering two-thirds of Ukraine's 67-bcma requirement and nearly all of Belarus's 2007 gas demand of 21 bcma (International Energy Agency, 2009d, pp. II. 9, II. 17, II. 33).

These transit countries have exemplified the difficulty of balancing the potentially clashing roles of import-dependent consumer and reliable transit pipeline operator. As they were historically part of the Soviet Union, they consequently enjoyed gas and oil subsidies similar to those in the Russian Republic, a residual legacy of centralised control that continued into the post-Cold War period. Thus, a common element in Russia's bilateral disputes with most FSU countries has been the threat or use of sudden price hikes and energy cut-offs, which are albeit more potent weapons when markets favour sellers, to increase ownership and control over local assets and operations and to stop the economic and political gravitation of these countries and their energy-related assets into US and European orbits (Woehrel, 2009, pp. 7–14).

These disputes have been the main cause of periodic interruptions in Russia's pipeline-based energy deliveries. Belarus hosts both spurs of the aforementioned 'Friendship' Pipeline, the southern leg of which continues into Ukraine before forking again into the EU territories of Hungary and the Slovak Republic (and thenceforth into the Czech Republic). It can also transport oil through another pipeline that forks into both Latvia (Ventspils Port) and Lithuania (the ports of Butinge, in the Mazeikai oil complex, and Klaipeda). Belarus is the only non-Russian transit territory shipping Druzhba oil to Poland and Germany. This northern spur conveyed just under three quarters of this pipeline's oil flow in 2007, accounting for approximately 23 per cent of Germany's extra-EU27 crude oil imports and 18 per cent of its crude oil demand and nearly all of Poland's crude oil imports and demand (Energy Information Administration, 2008b, p. 5; Eurostat, 2010a). While its prevailing 'spot market' structure makes the oil trade literally and figuratively more 'fluid' than the natural gas trade, a large share of oil in international transit nonetheless moves by pipeline (Energy Information Administration, 2008c, p. 1), and it has been observed that disruptions in Druzhba's operation could inflict some economic damage on its terminus countries as well as raise global prices at the margin (Clover, 2010, p. 2; Kramer, 2010a, p. 9).

Indeed, in January 2007, Transneft halted oil deliveries to Belarus. This occurred in retaliation for a Belarusian failure to accede to Transneft's demand that it accept higher prices and pay an export tariff commensurable to what Belarus was earning from refining Russian oil and re-exporting it to Europe, thus imposing an opportunity cost on Transneft of relinquishing tax receipts that it might have garnered from the direct export of those oil products had they been processed and shipped by Russian exporters. The imbroglio, which resulted in a 3-day stoppage of westbound oil supplies, ended upon Belarus's consent to remit one-third of the normal export duty to Transneft in return for suppressing transit fees required of the latter monopoly Russian oil pipeline operator (International Energy Agency, 2010, p. 23). At the same time, and 1 year after the first of the more renowned halts in the flow of Gazprom gas to Ukraine (see below), Gazprom's threat to halt gas shipments to Belarus was staved off only by an agreement to double Belarusian gas prices over 2006 levels, raise them gradually to world levels by 2011 and give Gazprom a majority stake in local monopoly operator Beltransgaz (Woehrel, 2009, p. 13).

By 2009, Belarus's joining of the EU's Eastern Partnership programme signalled the possibility that a new threshold had been reached in the weakening of President Alexander Lukashenko's fealty to the Kremlin. With the expiration of the previous agreement, concluded for a 3-year period at the end of the previous dispute, the oil dispute reared its head again. Transneft issued a differentiated request, indicating that it wanted to obtain the full tariff rate (then approximately $267/metric tonnes (mt)) on all Russian crude processed in Belarus and re-exported westwards (about 71 per cent of Belarus's crude imports from Russia), but not on the 29-per cent remainder of Russian oil consumed there domestically (International Energy Agency, 2010, p. 23). On 2–3 January 2010, after reneging on the offer not to impose export taxes on Belarus's domestically consumed oil and thus provoking a Belarusian counter-threat to raise the price charged for the pure transit of Russian oil from $3.90/mt to $45/mt, Transneft cut shipments to Naftan and Mozyr refineries, although westbound transit supplies apparently continued without disruption, unlike during the 2007 dispute (International Energy Agency, 2010, p. 23; Kramer, 2010a, b). Even if another cut-off were to have occurred in early 2010, all five potentially affected EU27 and IEA member states would have been able to draw down on 90-day emergency oil stocks and resort to alternate routes (such as the Adria Pipeline that brings oil from Croatia's Omisalj Port to Slovakia and pipelines that convey oil from Italy's Trieste Port to the Czech Republic), although the dispute did raise the price of oil futures (International Energy Agency, 2010, p. 23).

However, the most salient issue tied to the tenuous balancing act between consumer and energy transit conductor concerns Ukraine's role in sending four-fifths (roughly 120 bcma) of Russia's gas exports to Europe, thus ensuring that the EU27 continues to obtain the Russian-controlled gas that supplies over one-fifth of its collective gas demand. The first major Gazprom gas cut-off to Ukraine, starting on the last day of 2005 and lasting less than a week, reverberated further 'downstream' into the EU after Ukrainian officials diverted supplies from the transit pipeline, but the next major stoppage, occurring exactly 3 years later, spanned 3 weeks after flows into the transit line were halted to prevent a repeat of Ukrainian diversions (Woehrel, 2009, pp. 7–10). This resulted in a cumulative loss of 7 bcm over the relevant time frame (International Energy Agency, 2009d, p. I. 5).

These disputes revolved around quarrels over Ukraine's accumulated debt for past gas imports from Gazprom, the price it would pay for future imports, and the amount that Ukraine would earn as transit host. However, the seminal dispute of January 2006 also took place in the politically charged context of the 'Orange Revolution' associated with the landmark 2005 election of pro-Western President Viktor Yushchenko (Goldman, 2008, pp. 144–5; Lucas, 2008, p. 168). It was at least partially resolved at the time by creation of joint venture UkrGazEnergo, which granted now defunct partner and intermediary firm RosUkrEnergo, itself half owned by Gazprom, 50 per cent of the Ukrainian market. A brief cut-off to Ukraine in March 2008, depriving it of half of its imports from Gazprom, ended before the burden was passed onto the EU because Ukraine eliminated UkrGazEnergo in favour of conceding to Gazprom direct access to the lucrative industrial market (White, 2008). While the EU had by then developed the storage capacity which would allow it to respond more effectively to the 2009 cut-off (International Energy Agency, 2009d, p. I. 5), economic recession, which reduced Ukrainian gas demand and bolstered stocks, and the concomitant price decrease from \$450 to \$271 per thousand cubic metres facilitated a new gas-payment arrangement (Woehrel, 2009, pp. 9–10). As of early 2010, having concluded a deal with newly elected Ukrainian President Viktor

Yanukovich to cut the price of natural gas by 30 per cent (at a cost to Gazprom of $30 billion) and waive another potential $2 billion fine for non-purchased gas in exchange for Ukraine's 25-year extension on Russia's naval basing rights in the Crimea, Moscow revealed its continued interest in consolidating control over Ukraine's gas-transit network via a proposed merger between Gazprom and Ukraine's Naftogaz (Barry, 2010).

'Externalising' EU energy policy 'upstream'

As detailed in Chapter 3, it has been understandable for the EU to bring material and institutional leverage to bear in trying in attain implementation of the *acquis communautaire*, the EU's growing panoply of directives and regulations, even in the territory of its 'upstream' energy suppliers. While 'upstream' aptly describes Russia and other source countries, it also encompasses non-EU *transit* countries, which could potentially include Turkey, since the energy sectors in both sets of territories have been distorted by the pervasive and perverse application of subsidies that have deprived them of clear market incentives to extract, consume and transport hydrocarbons more efficiently and switch to environmentally friendlier renewable energy sources. In lieu of having substantial military power-projection capabilities, the EU has had to fall back on 'soft power' tools of (dis)suasion and economic (dis)incentives. However, while its aforementioned market power serves as a basic deterrent to deliberate exporter-initiated cuts in the flow of energy to EU territory, preventing or mitigating abrupt stoppages arising out of disputes between source and transit countries, akin to *force majeure* incidents (so-called acts of God) from the perspective of the consuming economy, necessitates the use of more nuanced instrumentalities.

The EU's ability to leverage financial assistance is indirectly located in its collective or in its separate member states' presences in a number of multilateral bodies. These include the European Bank for Reconstruction and Development (EBRD), the 61 current members of which include all current EU member states, the European Community and the European Investment Bank (EIB); the International Monetary Fund (IMF), which can exert its clout in the energy sector through a number of facilities, notably its conditional stand-by loan arrangements; the World Bank; and vehicles of political summitry such as the Group of Eight (G8). The EU can also provide direct assistance via the EIB, which was created, along with the European Community, by the 1958 Treaty of Rome. In 2007, the EIB's Corporate Operational Plan set € 4 billion as a lending target for projects in five EU priority areas, including not only the improvement of trans-European energy networks (under the official aegis of the EU's Trans-European Networks-Energy (TEN-E programme)), but also the security of external energy supplies passing through countries in the EU's neighbourhood. The EIB's Board of Governors also approved a separate multi-annual € 3 billion facility to finance energy sustainability and supply security in external countries (European Investment Bank, 2007).

The EIB is heavily involved in the TEN-E programme, which is specifically focused on raising EU funds and targeting them on enhancing the efficacy and operability of the internal electricity and gas markets, a mandate that necessarily involves a number of external countries in the vicinity of EU territory. Part of the TEN-E budget is derived from third-party lending vehicles such as the European Neighbourhood and Partnership Instrument (ENPI), but it is supported mainly by the European Regional Development Fund (ERDF) and the EIB, which can fund up to half of a project's costs and use its 40-per cent contribution to the European Investment Fund (EIF) to underwrite additional loans (European Commission, 2009a). However, the TEN-E budget is primarily directed towards feasibility and engineering studies (European Parliament and European Council, 2006, p. 2), so it has been allocated only about € 20 billion for each of the last 5 years and € 155 million for the period 2007–13 (Checchi, 2009, p. 2; European Commission, 2009g, p. 1). Thus, even the Commission, in its Second Strategic Energy Review of November 2008, has conceded the inadequacy of the TEN-E budget as a tool for catalysing EU priority energy projects and proposed that it be replaced by an 'EU Energy Security and Infrastructure Instrument' (European Commission, 2008a, pp. 6–7). The aforementioned ENPI has been allocated about € 12 billion over the period 2007–13, 6 per cent of which is channelled into a Neighbourhood Investment Facility (NIF) that is to be pooled with individual member-state contributions entrusted to the EIB. The ENPI has emerged as another source of monies targeted at cross-border cooperation (CBC) initiatives, governance reform and 'twinning' projects that pair up EU member-state public agencies with their non-EU counterparts (European Commission, 2009e, 2010).

Russia and other countries at the EU's energy 'headwaters'

While the EU has a range of economic tools at its disposal, institutional colloquy has constituted its most visible vehicle of active engagement with its major external energy suppliers. Efforts to promote 'dialogue' and 'partnerships' have existed between individual European importing countries and oil-producing states since the 1973–74 Arab oil embargo, but the EU in its current incarnation has also been engaged in its own specific formal process of dialogue with OPEC, its major oil supplier, in an 'energy partnership' with the African Union, which includes states instrumental in an effort to construct a Trans-Sahara pipeline to take Nigerian gas to Europe (see Chapter 5), and in the International Energy Forum.

The EU's seminal post-Cold War concern with the energy sectors of its FSU 'upstream' suppliers, especially Ukraine, which experienced the Chernobyl meltdown in 1986, revolved around ensuring the safety of their NPPs. However, the novel EU that was created by the 1992 Maastricht Treaty gave strong support to the Energy Charter Treaty (ECT), which was signed in the same year that General Agreement on Tariff and Trade (GATT) was incorporated into the new World Trade Organization (WTO) and was intended to harmonise EU–FSU energy trade with GATT/WTO free trade principles. Given the extensive involvement of EU firms in energy investments and trade with Russia and other landlocked FSU countries, it is logical from the EU's standpoint that the treaty stipulates that the transit of hydrocarbons comply with Article V of General Agreement on Tariff and Trade (GATT). Thus, since 2000, ECT contracting parties have been discussing the addition of a Transit Protocol that would 'develop a regime of commonly-accepted principles covering transit flows of energy resources' (Energy Charter Secretariat, 2004, p. 15; van Aartsen, 2009, pp. 3–4). While Ukraine is a contracting party, Belarus and Russia are significant non-parties.

Nonetheless, the EU has persisted in its endeavour to bring its energy relations with 'upstream' territories into conformity with WTO market principles. It smuggled this objective into a raft of Partnership and Cooperation Agreements (PCAs) with FSU states, including Russia, which in 2003 agreed with the EU on a 'Road Map of Common Economic Space'. In 2000, the EU and Russia launched their ongoing Energy Dialogue, which has provided a forum for both parties to air their respective views of energy security to each other. In addition to advocating energy efficiency and savings, which could release more Russian hydrocarbons for export, the European Commission implicitly prefers that its strategic partnership lead to Russia's elusive ratification of the ECT (Europa, 1997, pp. 16–17; Europa, 2003). Nonetheless, the competing perspectives exhibited by Russia as a source country and the EU as a 'downstream' consuming party remain somewhat distant. The tenth Progress Report on the EU-Russian Energy Dialogue, issued in

November 2009, indicates Russian disagreement with the EU's assessment that its 'Third Energy Package' provides 'an attractive and stable regulatory framework also for Russian investments into the EU electricity and gas sector' and EU concern over Russia's 'Federal law on Foreign Investment in Industries of Strategic Importance for State Defense and Industry' (Piebalgs and Shmatko, 2009, p. 7).[3]

Transit countries: managing the flow of Russian energy 'midstream'

With observably limited capacity to exert direct influence over the policies and decisions of governments in the producer countries, especially during seller's markets, the EU has tried to align the economic, political and regulatory structures of extra-EU27 transit countries with the *acquis communautaire*. This 'convergence' objective strongly embodies the functionalist integration logic underlying the European Coal and Steel Community (ECSC), the EU's seminal predecessor. Efforts in this regard have been centrally focused on implementing market reform in Ukraine, largely in order to improve the efficiency and transparency of gas transmission operations there. As elaborated on below, however, some European companies have instead concentrated their investment capital on obviating the need for transit countries altogether via joint ventures in pipeline projects that will forge direct bilateral energy connections with Russia. Implicitly sanctioned by their governments, these actions may even reverse the trend of declining EU dependency on Russian gas.

In parallel with its 1997 agreement with Russia, the European Community signed a PCA with Ukraine that came into effect in 1998. This was essentially designed to focus 'Ukraine's approximation efforts on the legal framework of the EU's single market and of the WTO system' (European Commission, 2009c). The agreement's underlying purpose of integrating the Ukrainian energy sector into a larger market economy is indicated in its application of GATT Article V on 'freedom of transit in goods' and in PCA Article 53, which explicitly declares that energy-related cooperation 'shall take place within the principles of the market economy and the European Energy Charter, against a background of the progressive integration of the energy markets in Europe' (European Commission, 1994b, p. 28). In 2004, EU territorial boundaries extended to Belarus and Ukraine, prompting articulation of an ENP. The ENP underscored the importance of bilateral action plans, which, in the field of energy, included fostering 'further gradual convergence of energy policies and the legal and regulatory environment' and '[r]einforcing networks and interconnections', both deemed 'necessary for ensuring the security and safety of energy supplies and for extending the internal energy market to partner countries' (Ibid., p. 17).

This policy was concretised in the EU–Ukraine Cooperation Council's February 2005 endorsement of a new EU–Ukraine Action Plan. The introduction to this plan plainly announced that, 'Enlargement offers the opportunity for the EU and Ukraine to develop an increasingly close relationship, going beyond co-operation, to gradual economic integration and a deepening of political cooperation' (European Commission, 2005a, p. 1). In the area of energy, the plan called for '[g]radual convergence towards the principles of the EU internal electricity and gas markets' (Ibid., p. 33). Moreover, it explicitly referred to an EU directive on 'the financial and legal restructuring of the gas transit business ... and unbundling and transparency of accounts' (Ibid., p. 34). In December 2005, just before the first Gazprom cut-off, the institutional content of their energy relationship crystallised in the signing of a highly detailed memorandum of understanding (MoU) on EU-Ukraine energy cooperation. The MoU stated that 'the gradual adoption by Ukraine of the EU energy *acquis* would constitute a significant step towards Ukraine's objective of gradual economic integration and deepening of political co-operation with the EU' (European Commission, 2005c, p. 1). Ukraine was considered for observer status in the South-East Europe Energy Community Treaty (SEEECT), which specifies a graduated adoption timetable for a dozen measures contained in the energy *acquis* for the EU and non-EU countries of Southeast Europe (Ibid., p. 9).[4] Finally, both parties assented to set up a Joint Hydrocarbon Technical Support Group to carry out work on 'enhancing the hydrocarbons security and transit conditions and operations' (Ibid., p. 10).

Russian gas cut-offs and threats of stoppage have infused the EU–Ukrainian energy relationship with an immediate saliency. The EU attention is now more strongly focused on how to ensure, from Russia via Ukraine, ' "the continuous availability of energy in varied forms, in sufficient quantities and at affordable prices" ' (United Nations Development Programme, 2001 cited in Checchi et al., 2009, p. 2). The EU has kept pushing in its pre-crisis vein for greater convergence between EU and Ukrainian energy practices, policies and institutions, although it has been more willing to fund this effort. Ukraine obtained observer status in the Energy Community in November 2006, signed a 'road map' on 'energy efficiency, renewables and measures to tackle climate change' in March 2008, a month during which it narrowly averted another gas cut-off, and 1 year later, following the second major EU gas 'crisis', it hosted a conference designed to assemble multiple sources of invest-ment to modernise its gas transit system (European Commission et al., 2009). While the latter conference occurred soon after the January 2009 cut-off, it also represented the culmination of numerous Commission studies estimating the cost of rehabilitating Ukraine's pipeline system for 2009–15 at € 2.5 billion (Europa, 2009b). The conference's joint declaration acknowledged the strategic importance of Ukraine's gas tran-sit system, which the Ukrainian side suggested expanding from 120 to 180 bcma, before addressing Ukraine's intention to carry out a 'Gas Sector Reform Programme' in 2010–11 and spelling out the Commis-sion's willingness to use ENPI/NIF outlays to leverage funding from the World Bank, EBRD and EIB, co-signatories to that declaration (European Commission et al., 2009).

The economic crisis commencing in late 2008 complicated the issue of funding efforts to secure a stable flow of gas through Ukraine. On the one hand, by weakening the Ukrainian economy, it also lowered the lat-ter's demand for Gazprom-controlled flows of gas. Although this did not prevent the January 2009 crisis, it did, over the course of 2009, lead to more gas being routed from Ukrainian consumers, especially large indus-trial concerns, into storage (European Commission, 2009d).[5] By the end of August, the Ukrainian government reported that its gas reservoirs, with a capacity of 27 bcm, were full, leading experts to suggest that Ukraine's warnings in May and June that gas levels were too low to prevent another winter shortage crisis had been exaggerated (Valasek, 2009).

In 2009, the Russo-Ukrainian gas dispute seemed to move closer, albeit haltingly, to a final resolution. A confluence of factors, centrally the cuts in heating supplies to households in up to 20 European countries over a 2-week period when temperatures had plummeted to as low as –20°C (–4°F) as well as an estimated $1 billion revenue loss to Gazprom, made it vitally imperative to conclude the 21 January 2009 agreement that led to the official resumption of supplies (Traynor, 2009, p. 26). Under this new 10-year arrangement, Ukraine assented to pay double the pre-crisis price of nearly $180 per thousand cubic metres for Gazprom gas, with the resulting $360 figure still 20 per cent less than the market price of $450, as well as pay its previous month's gas bill by the end of the first week of the successive month. Russia, for its part, received a commensurate one-fifth discount on the fee it was to pay to send the gas to Europe. After 2009, market prices for all bilateral gas-related transactions were sup-posed to prevail, a deal that was aided by the recession-induced decline in gas prices and reaffirmed in a 19 November 2009 meeting between the

Ukrainian and Russian prime ministers (Dejevsky, 2009, p. 44; EurActiv Network, 2009b; Olearchyk, 2009a, p. 6; Kramer, 2009a).[6] Conversely, the same economic crisis that lowered GDP and local currency values and allowed Ukraine to obtain a $16.4 billion IMF stand-by loan also raised the risk that Ukraine would cease paying for and receiving Gazprom gas during the summer of 2009, when it needed to stockpile 19 bcm for winter release (Mortished, 2009, p. 42). While this enhanced the circumstances in which Ukraine could plausibly request an emergency loan package of $4 billion, apart from its stand-by loan, Ukraine's inability to make further progress on gas-sector reform and electorally related promises by then Prime Minister Tymoshenko to raise government spending lowered donors' willingness to spend additional monies (Ibid.; European Commission, 2009d, p. 4; Olearchyk, 2009b, p. 5).

Cutting out the 'middleman': direct pipelines to Russia

Given its – and possibly others' – perspectives on the aforementioned hydrocarbon transit 'crises', Russia has attempted to route more of its energy exports around its most 'problematic' transit partners. Given its salient petroleum-related disputes with Belarus, Estonia, Latvia, Lithuania and even Turkey (more indirectly in relation to questions of how much Russian and FSU oil can feasibly be channelled into the Bosporus Straits, through which cargo traffic cannot be assessed tolls by Turkey according to the provisions of the 1936 Montreux Convention), the Kremlin and its authorised oil-export monopoly Transneft have achieved large strides in routing oil exports around these territories. Transneft pipes about 75 mmta, some of which used to reach world markets via Lithuania's Ventspils Port or Belarus, to Russia's Primorsk via the Baltic Pipeline System (BPS) and is working to expand this route's throughput capacity (Energy Information Administration, 2008b, p. 5). The availability of the BPS has already enhanced Russian firms' ability to cut off oil supplies to Latvia and Lithuania, as was done in 2002 and 2006, respectively (Woehrel, 2009, pp. 12–13). To the south of Russia, Transneft has been pursuing the Burgas–Alexandroupolis oil pipeline project with Italian firm Eni to create a new route that bypasses Turkey's Bosporus Straits (Energy Information Administration, 2008c, pp. 7–8). In diametric contrast to their relations in the area of natural gas transit, Russo-Ukrainian oil trade has been relatively smoother, with both sides agreeing in early 2010 to increase transit fees to Ukraine and price these fees in euros, raise export volumes from Yuzhny and re-start shipments to major Ukrainian refineries (International Energy Agency, 2010, p. 26).

The same drives and imperatives have appeared in the case of natural gas. Joining Gazprom in its efforts to bypass transit countries altogether have been major European energy firms. As opposed to a genuine policy of diversifying not only transit routes but also suppliers, this policy of diverting Russian gas around 'problematic' transit territory seems strongly motivated by the desire for some reciprocal share of Russia's rich upstream sector. First elevated to the public agenda in April 2005 after having received EU endorsement much earlier, the Northern European Gas Pipeline (NEGP), or Nord Stream, project, which partners key Germany energy firms BASF-Wintershall and E.ON-Ruhrgas, Dutch company Gasunie and France's GDF-Suez, which collectively own 49 per cent, with Gazprom, in control of the remaining 51 per cent, will, if built by the end of 2011 at the earliest, consist of two parallel pipelines estimated to cost € 7.4 billion (in late 2009) and capable of transporting 55 bcma across a 1200-km stretch of the Baltic Sea from Vyborg in Russia to Greifswald in Germany (Larsson, 2007, pp. 21–5; Bryant, 2009, p. 11; EurActiv Network, 2009a; Kramer, 2009b). It has been criticised for enhancing Russian state leverage over and eliminating transit revenues to the Baltic states, Belarus, Ukraine and Poland, where the foreign minister likened it in 2006 to the 1939 Molotov–Ribbentrop Pact. Moreover, given the prominent position of former German Prime Minister Gerhard Schröeder on the Nord Stream board, it has come to symbolise the powerful tendency of bilateral member-state and firm interests to trump EU solidarity, even though it received TEN-E project status (but no funding) in 2006. Although candidate routes passing through territorial waters of EU10 Baltic states were precluded, fellow EU15 Baltic member state Finland withheld approval of the final version of the project until conceding in early 2010 (Larsson, 2007, pp. 6–7; Bryant, 2009, p. 11; EurActiv Network, 2010).

The analogous South Stream project has been exposed to similar criticisms. As part of a July 2007 memorandum between Italian firm Eni CEO Paolo Scaroni and then Gazprom Vice-President Alexander Medvedev, this project, cost estimates for which vary from Putin's lower-end estimate of € 8.6 billion ($12 billion in mid-2009) to larger estimate of € 12 billion, was originally intended to ship up to 31 bcma (matching its rival Nabucco's capacity), 900 km across the Black Sea to Bulgaria, where it would fork into a southwestern branch moving gas to Greece and then undersea to Italy and a northern line taking gas via Serbia, Hungary and either Austria or Slovenia to Italy (Baran, 2008, p. 1; Gorst and Hoyos, 2009, p. 3). Nearly 1 year later, Vladimir Putin and Silvio Berlusconi, prime ministers of Russia and Italy, respectively, agreed to double the pipeline's capacity to 63 bcma, 'enough to supply more than four-fifths of Italy's total gas consumption', leading Eni CEO Scaroni to explicate that, '1 bn cubic meters more here will be 1 bn cubic meters less gas crossing Ukraine'. Resembling the deals that German firms arranged with Gazprom on Nord Stream, Eni and subsidiary Enel agreed to sell Gazprom 51 per cent in three West Siberian gas fields (Gorst and Hoyos, 2009, p. 3). Towards the end of 2009, electricity firm EDF of France, of which GDF-Suez was blocked by Turkey from joining the Nabucco consortium, became the third partner in South Stream (EurActiv Network, 2009a). It has been reported, however, that its possible passage through Ukraine's EEZ may give the latter country a veto over South Stream (Kommersant, 2008).

Conclusion

While the crises sparked by the Russian gas cut-offs of January 2006 and 2009 and the averted stoppage of March 2008 possess an obvious saliency and immediacy that concentrated minds on finding the most readily available solutions, these stoppages could not easily be likened to the sort of blunt and deliberate exercises of power that Arab oil exporting countries wielded against Western oil consuming nations in 1973–74. Moreover, given the post-Cold War decline in dependency by the EU and many of its member states on Russian gas (but not oil), joint ventures by major EU15-headquartered energy firms and Russian state pipeline monopoly operators Transneft and Gazprom to build direct linkages between Russian and EU territory via the Burgas–Alexandroupolis oil pipeline (Eni and Transneft) and the Nord Stream and South Stream gas projects may actually allow Russia to demonstrate more clearly that it has no intention whatsoever – or conversely *every* intention – of wielding any energy 'weapon' against Europe.

However, the majority of EU states that acceded in 2004 or 2007 are more heavily reliant on Russian pipeline-transported energy, primarily gas but also oil. Given their history in the Soviet bloc, they tend to sympathise more closely with the Ukrainian view that Moscow directs or condones Gazprom gas cut-offs to keep them ensconced in the Russian economic and political orbits. Consequently, the EU needs to continue increasing energy efficiency and renewable energy production, which also mesh with its environmental treaty commitments, integrating its energy networks more tightly via greater gas storage capacity and interconnections (i.e., reversible pipelines), and applying regulatory apparatuses to ensure that these infrastructures work for member states' common good. Otherwise, the most vulnerable of the EU12 may follow, as they have already shown evidence of doing, some of their EU15 counterparts down the path of unilateral action, in the form of self-centred bilateral ties with Gazprom or re-activation of risky NPPs. In short, a common energy policy could facilitate stronger collective action on projects of 'European interest', including those designed to widen the diversity of export routes for non-Russian suppliers, the subject of our next chapter.

5
The EU Outreach to Non-Russian Energy

Introduction: no refrain from the 'great game'

In one sense, shifting the focus to European Union (EU) importation of non-Russian energy supplies simply inverts the previous chapter's analysis. However, more substantively important here is a discussion of the nature by which and the extent to which explicit policies articulated at the EU institutional level, mainly by the Commission, have sought to alter the EU's current portfolio of supplies and suppliers, one that evolved largely as a cumulative result of the pursuit of various policies and the unfolding of economic processes at the national level. In an acknowledgement of the limits to which the EU27 can ensure its energy security in the absence of new external fuel sources, the European Commission's (2007a) proposed common energy policy has enumerated measures intended to further diversification. These consist of a number of priority 'projects of European interest' that have received Trans-European Networks-Energy (TEN-E) financing for feasibility studies and been assigned project coordinators to ensure their progress. However, the EU energy budget, dominated by TEN-E financing, remains structurally underfunded (Andoura et al., 2010, p. 37), a deficiency that complements the diversification objective's lack of *acquis*-related regulatory force.

In addition to intra-EU27 divisions on the need and ways to fulfil this objective, diversification, as discussed in a subsequent section, also faces countervailing moves by Russian state interests, including those running Gazprom, to consolidate relationships with firms, often 'national oil companies' (NOCs), in those key producing countries that might provide larger alternative supply sources. Given the Russian energy sector's unlikely combination of onerous legal and practical restrictions on foreign direct investment (FDI), many imposed or re-imposed since 2003, and the perpetual failure of its leading state firms, exemplified by Gazprom, to plough enough sales revenues back into core operations to lessen the long-term need for new infusions of private investment (Goldman, 2008, pp. 126–35; Lucas, 2008, pp. 96–7, 182–5), it is not surprising that the Kremlin would display an acutely keen regard for how other producing regions could expand their European markets at Russia's expense. Russia's efforts to enter cooperative arrangements with other producing countries' state-influenced NOCs in order to gain a hand in shaping or steering the use of their respective upstream sectors could be construed as part of a larger drive to maximise obtainable rents from all links of the chain of energy value production.

As it supplies the plurality 39-per cent share of EU27 gas imports, Gazprom serves as central inspiration for our conceptualisation of gas 'w-a-r-s' ('wide-area rent-seeking'). As discussed below, our concept is not meant to connote that producing, transit and consuming states are poised to engage in military struggle over gas or the terms of its delivery – their interdependency, albeit highly asymmetrical according to the time frame and geographic area in question – minimises the likelihood of warfare. Rather, it implies that many energy-centric international tensions have arisen in large part from strong resistance to attempts to acquire ownership and operational control of different segments of the value chain that are located outside of the initiating firms' home jurisdictions. However, as it operates predominantly on the basis of long-term contracts mandating indexation of gas prices to those of oil, 'take-or-pay' requirements and prohibitions against importers' 'on-selling' to third parties, the natural gas trade reflects the comparative strength of exporters' rent-seeking imperatives. Indeed, the 'rentier state' has characteristically dominated commodity trade outflows in many if not most countries that depend heavily on commodity export revenues (Colombo and Lesser, 2010, p. 7). Gazprom's rent-seeking strategy has two prongs, what we term 'near encirclement' and 'far encirclement'. The former prong consists of actions to gain greater control over transit-pipeline operations and downstream assets and the latter entails efforts to influence the availability of supplies from their respective third-party 'upstream' sources, with both working in tandem to constrain the number of non-Russian gas supplies entering the EU27 area. In short, Moscow has been anything but a passive spectator, even in realms of the energy game outside Russia's traditional sphere of influence.

EU energy relations branch out beyond Russia

While this trend certainly does not apply to member states in any uniform manner, as examined in this section, growth in the EU's growing collective reliance on hydrocarbon imports has far outpaced the expansion in its source regions, which remain comparatively limited as a result. As Russia supplies nearly one-quarter of EU27 gas consumption and two-fifths of its total import requirements, while Middle Eastern Organization of the Petroleum Exporting Countries (OPEC) states account for a slightly larger fraction of EU oil imports, diversification retains the imperative quality imparted to it in a series of green papers that the European Commission (2001, p. 2) first launched in the new millennium. Nevertheless, this same agency (Ibid., pp. 22–3) has implicitly conceded that the present profile of EU hydrocarbon dependence on Russia, the Caspian, the Middle East and North Africa is unlikely to change markedly. For gas, the EU largely relies on Algeria, Norway and Russia. While imports from Norway occur within the regulatory compass of the energy *acquis*, contracts governing those from Russia and Algeria are less informed by EU legal strictures. The discussion below addresses the nature and extent of the ongoing proliferation of gas supplies and suppliers to the EU before turning to an examination of the strategy and policies by which EU institutions have been promoting further diversification of gas supplies.

EU27 Gas-import diversification through liquefaction

As suggested in the Chapter 4, most EU27 countries and thus the area in its economic entirety became considerably more dependent on natural gas imports from external (non-EU) sources between 1992 and 2007, but relatively less beholden to Russia to fill their rising gas demand. To reiterate, although imports rose from 44 per cent of consumption in 1992 to three-fifths of 2007 consumption, imports from Russia fell from three-fifths of all gas imports to slightly less than 40 per cent. As delineated in Table 5.1, nearly 11 countries in the present EU27 depended fully or almost fully on Russia to fill their import basket in 1992, but only six of them remained in this situation by 2007. Indeed, relative dependency on Russia escalated in only two member states, Belgium (from 0 to less than 10 per cent) and Greece (from zero to over three-quarters). In other member states, it generally dropped, sometimes drastically, as in the case of Austria, where Russian gas fell from 100 to 57 per cent of the total import basket. The collective proportion of the EU27 import basket occupied by the three largest suppliers also fell. In 1992, the present

Table 5.1 Gas-import diversity profiles – EU and Turkey

| | Non-EU supplier country (% of non-EU imports) | | | | | | | | | | | | | | | |
| | Russia | | Norway | | Algeria | | Nigeria | | Libya | | Qatar | | Egypt | | Trinidad & Tobago | |
	1992	2007	92	07	92	07	92	07	92	07	92	07	92	07	92	07
Austria (1 in 92, 2 in 07)	100	57–88*	0	12–15	0	0	0	0	0	0	0	0	0	0	0	0
Belgium (2,5)	0	8	28	60	72	4	0	0	0	0	0	23	0	0	0	1
Denmark (0,0)	0	0	0	0	0	0	0	0	0	0	0	0	0	0	0	0
Finland (1,1)	100	100	0	0	0	0	0	0	0	0	0	0	0	0	0	0
France (3,5)	41	17	23	38	35	22	0	9	0	0	0	0	0	3	0	0
Germany (2,2)	68	56	32	40	0	0	0	0	0	0	0	0	0	0	0	0
Greece (0,2)	0	77	0	0	0	23	0	0	0	0	0	0	0	0	0	0
Ireland (0,0)	0	0	0	0	0	0	0	0	0	0	0	0	0	0	0	0
Italy (2,4)	46	35	0	9	54	38	0	0	0	14	0	0	0	0	0	0
Luxembourg (0,0)	0	0	0	0	0	0	0	0	0	0	0	0	0	0	0	0
Netherlands (1,0)	0	0	100	0	0	0	0	0	0	0	0	0	0	0	0	0
Portugal (0,2)	0	0	0	0	0	34	0	66	0	0	0	0	0	0	0	0
Spain (2,7)	0	0	0	6	72	37	0	24	28	2	0	12	0	12	0	6
Sweden (0,0)	0	0	0	0	0	0	0	0	0	0	0	0	0	0	0	0
UK (1,0)	0	0	100	0	0	0	0	0	0	0	0	0	0	0	0	0
EU15																
Cyprus (0,0)	0	0	0	0	0	0	0	0	0	0	0	0	0	0	0	0
Czech (1,2)	100	79	0	21	0	0	0	0	0	0	0	0	0	0	0	0
Estonia (1,1)	100	100	0	0	0	0	0	0	0	0	0	0	0	0	0	0

Table 5.1 (Continued)

	Russia		Norway		Algeria		Nigeria		Libya		Qatar		Egypt		Trinidad & Tobago	
	Non-EU supplier country (% of non-EU imports)															
	1992	2007	92	07	92	07	92	07	92	07	92	07	92	07	92	07
Hungary (1,1)	100	100*	0	0	0	0	0	0	0	0	0	0	0	0	0	0
Latvia (1,1)	100	100	0	0	0	0	0	0	0	0	0	0	0	0	0	0
Lithuania (1,1)	100	100	0	0	0	0	0	0	0	0	0	0	0	0	0	0
Malta (0,0)	0	0	0	0	0	0	0	0	0	0	0	0	0	0	0	0
Poland (1,1)	100	100*	0	0	0	0	0	0	0	0	0	0	0	0	0	0
Slovakia (1,1)	100	99	0	0	0	0	0	0	0	0	0	0	0	0	0	0
Slovenia (2,2)	72	61	0	0	28	39	0	0	0	0	0	0	0	0	0	0
EU10																
Bulgaria (1,1)	100	100	0	0	0	0	0	0	0	0	0	0	0	0	0	0
Romania (1,1)	100	91–100*	0	0	0	0	0	0	0	0	0	0	0	0	0	0
EU27	60	39	17	25	22	16	0	5	0	3	0	2	0	2	0	1
Turkey**	100	62	0	0	0	13	0	4	0	0	0	0	0	<1	0	<1

Note on sources: The bulk of these calculations are based on Eurostat (2010a), but 2007 calculations of Russian supplies for Hungary, Poland and Romania include volumes from Uzbekistan and either Turkmenistan (for Hungary and Poland) or 'Other FSU' (for Romania), based on volumes specified as such by the International Energy Agency (2009d, pp. II. 30–II. 33) and implied as belonging under BP's (2008, p. 30) category 'Other Europe & Eurasia'. However, in the case of Austria, BP (2008) indicates no imports falling under the latter category for 2007, and the International Energy Agency (2009d) designates as 'Non Specified' a volume that amounts to 28 per cent of Austrian imports of extra-EU27 gas after Russian and Norwegian supplies are taken into account.

**17 per cent of Turkey's gas imports came from Iran.

EU27 depended on Algeria, Norway and Russia to meet nearly all of their collective need for gas imports from external sources. By 2007, however, EU27 reliance on this trio declined by nearly one-fifth, with Russia and Algeria losing respective market shares not only to Norway, but also to Libya and liquefied natural gas (LNG) exporters Egypt, Nigeria, Qatar and Trinidad and Tobago.

While this point has not yet received due emphasis, diversification is not genuine if dependence on Russia is simply replaced by dependence on another single country. In most cases, member states importing natural gas from outside the EU27 had typically managed by 2007 to widen their external supplier portfolio from a single entity to at least two entities, and in rarer cases, to three or more. Norway grabbed an additional 8 per cent of the EU27 market, increasing its overall share of it to one-quarter. Seven countries increased their demand for Norwegian gas, four of them (Austria, the Czech Republic, Italy and Spain) from a 1992 baseline of zero. Only two member states, the Netherlands and the UK, imported no Norwegian gas in 2007. Algeria's share dropped from 22 to 16 per cent of the EU27 gas-import basket. Belgium, France, Italy and Spain all cut their respective relative demands for Algerian gas, for which gains in the smaller markets of Greece, Portugal and Slovenia could not offset larger losses. Belgium slashed its heavier reliance on Algerian gas in 1992 by tapping a wider array of external suppliers, not only Norway, one of its previous extra-EU27 suppliers, but also Russia, Qatar and Trinidad and Tobago.

As analysed in the previous chapter, even large member states France, Germany and Italy, headquarter countries to large firms that have entered or are seeking to enter major joint undertakings with Gazprom, lowered their relative need for Russian gas. Thus, these joint ventures do not necessarily reflect any official policy of supplication to a major supplier country, even if the bypassing of ex-Soviet Bloc space inadvertently threatens to undermine the national interests of those new member states that posses only transit leverage to counter-balance their almost exclusive reliance on Russia gas. While Germany simply shifted the relative weight of its dependence from Russia to Norway, France widened its supplier base to include Egypt and Nigeria and Italy added gas from Libya and Norway.

In a few expected cases, Russian gas never factored into decisions to diversify relevant supplier portfolios. The Iberian Peninsula stands out for its noticeably broad diversification of suppliers as well as modes of supply, especially LNG. Spain, which never imported Russian gas, widened its base of external suppliers from two to seven or eight, five of which (Egypt, Nigeria, Oman, Qatar and Trinidad and Tobago) supply exclusively LNG and two of which (Algeria and Libya) added LNG to their export baskets. LNG exports meet nearly 70 per cent of Spain's gas imports, with the latter in turn accounting for over half of total EU27 LNG imports. In 1992, Portugal used no gas of any sort, but by 2007, was piping in gas from Algeria and receiving LNG shipments from Nigeria, with the latter African country's LNG exports filling nearly two-thirds of the Portuguese gas-importation and consumption baskets. The EU27 buys over three-fifths of Algerian LNG exports and nearly two-thirds of Nigerian gas exports (BP, 2008, p. 30; International Energy Agency, 2009d, pp. II. 30–3, II. 46–9, II. 55).

In fact, those EU states that have diversified their extra-EU27 gas supply base most broadly seem to have amassed the requisite capacity for major LNG tanker shipments. LNG, accounting for roughly one-fifth of natural gas imports into the EU area, with the latter market concentrated in seven member states (Belgium, France, Greece, Italy, Portugal, Spain and the UK), is poised to make even further inroads into expanding the EU27's supply portfolio as the whole. While the EU draws in 20 per cent of the world's LNG exports, two-fifths of the latter supply is shipped to Japan alone, which draws from 13 different suppliers (International Energy Agency, 2009d, p. II. 55). Between 1999 and 2008, € 4.4 million in TEN-E financing was allotted to LNG-related projects in Greece, Italy, Portugal and Spain (European Commission, 2009g), of which Revithoussa in Greece and Sines in Portugal have been completed (International Energy Agency, 2009d, p. II. 56).

The EU's official diversification strategy and policy priorities

The EU's efforts to diversify types and countries of origin and transit have been ongoing for nearly one decade. According to the European coordinator of the 'southern corridor' for natural gas, the EU's diversification of partners 'is in a way just another translation amongst many of the underlying free-market and competition-based pillars on which the European Union is based' (van Aartsen, 2009, p. 3) and has been motivated by the broader objectives of dampening prices and widening consumer choice (Andoura et al., 2010, p. 27). Nonetheless, diversification as an official EU energy policy strategy received fresh impetus from the 2006 Russian gas cut to Ukraine. Commission efforts to promote greater diversification, centrally for those EU12 states that remained, for historical reasons, predominantly dependent on Russian gas and its trans-Ukrainian and Belarusian passage, were inextricably coupled to appeals for greater solidarity between the EU15 and EU12 sub-groups. Greater gas storage and interconnectivity, essentially involving the capacity for inputting supplies from anywhere in the EU27 area into a network that could convey them to a larger number of intra-EU27 locations, have been deemed crucial not only to enhancing the liquidity component of a fully integrated internal gas market (Checchi, 2009, p. 1) but also to allowing member states to present a credibly united front in the face of external gas cuts (Gillman and Martin, 2009). In fact, the 2009 gas 'crisis' might have had been worse for EU12 populations had there been no earlier storage build-ups nor any flow reversibility to send gas from Greece to Bulgaria and from the Czech Republic to Slovakia (Chaffin, 2009, p. 8; Hope and Troev, 2009, p. 2).

However, the Commission has also stressed the importance of implementing physical and legal mechanisms for accessing new sources of gas and oil supplies. Right after the first Gazprom cut-off, the European Commission (2006b, p. 15) identified the necessity of 'independent gas pipeline supplies from the Caspian region, North Africa and the Middle East into the heart of the EU, new LNG terminals serving markets that are presently characterised by a lack of competition between gas suppliers, and Central European oil pipelines aiming at facilitating Caspian oil supplies to the EU through Ukraine, Romania and Bulgaria'. This green paper called for a strategic energy review that 'could acknowledge the concrete political, financial and regulatory measures needed to actively support the undertaking of such projects by business' (Ibid.).

In the following year, stronger synergistic linkage between greater network connectivity and wider diversity of suppliers and supply routes materialised in the Energy Policy for Europe. In its January 2007 communication to the Council and Parliament, the European Commission (2007a, p. 9) identified a 'Priority Interconnection Plan' that included four central projects, each with its own 'European co-ordinator': 'the Power-Link between Germany, Poland and Lithuania; connections to offshore wind power in Northern Europe; electricity connections between France and Spain; and the Nabucco pipeline, bringing gas from the Caspian to central Europe.' In fact, the latter, led by Austrian firm OMV, had already received approximately € 6.5 million for basic engineering studies by 2004 (European Commission, 2009g). Two other enumerated priorities under this Plan included establishing a 5-year deadline 'within which planning and approval procedures must be completed for projects that are defined as being "of European interest" under trans-European Energy Guidelines' and '[e]xamining the need to increase funding for the Energy Trans-European networks, particularly to facilitate the integration of renewable electricity into the grid' (European Commission, 2007a, p. 9).

At the end of 2008, just prior to the second major gas cut-off, the EU issued its 'Energy Security and Solidarity Action Plan'. While acknowledging that the EU27's import profile 'represents a reasonably well-diversified supply picture', the European Commission (2008a, p. 4), in its Second Strategic Energy Review of November 2008, lamented that, 'a number of Member states rely on a single supplier for 100% of their gas needs.' This report more sharply delineated the infrastructure that the Commission preferred the Community to prioritise. It underscored the necessity of a 'southern gas ring' to carry Caspian and Middle Eastern supplies as 'one of the EU's highest energy security priorities' and pointed out the interest in exploring the cost effectiveness of a 'block purchasing mechanism for Caspian gas ("Caspian Development Corporation")... in full respect of competition and other EU rules' (Ibid., pp. 4–5) – in other words, a block 'Gas Purchasing Group' supervised by a supranational 'Gas Supply Agency' (Andoura et al., 2010, pp. 115–6). This strategic energy review then proceeded to emphasise the utility of enhanced LNG facilities (proposed for a separate action plan) and the importance of a Mediterranean 'energy ring' that would link the region's large potential reserves of solar and wind power to the European continent (Ibid., p. 5). Even if production of renewable energies did not suffer from geographical confinement (Andoura et al., 2010, p. 66), the respective private and official initiatives Desertec and Med Solar Plan, which could diversify European energy suppliers and suppliers in an environmentally sustainable manner, have not been wholeheartedly embraced by potential non-European source countries (Colombo and Lesser, 2010, p. 10).

As later chapters elaborate in further detail, pipelines thus continue to assume a prominent role in Commission plans to diversify gas supplies. As indicated in the most recent Progress Report on 'natural gas route 3' (NG3), covering those 'projects of European interest' linking Caspian and Middle Eastern gas supplies to Europe, '... the European Union has designated (in the TEN-E programme) three... pipelines as of strategic importance', the Turkey–Greece–Italy Interconnector (TGII), Nabucco and White Stream (van Aartsen, 2009, p. 7). These three, in addition to the Trans Adriatic Pipeline (TAP), received nearly € 23.7 million in TEN-E funding for various feasibility and engineering studies between 1999 and 2008 (European Commission, 2009g). The smallest portion of this financing, roughly 3 per cent, was allocated in 2007 and 2008 to the most recently proposed White Stream Project, which is projected to bring Caspian gas to various new member-state EU markets via Ukraine, while nearly 13 per cent went to TAP, which is to transport gas from Italy to various Southeastern European countries. On the other hand, over half of the funding was dedicated to the sub-sea TGII, with the now operable Turkey–Greece leg receiving about € 4.5 million, or just over one-third of the total funds that had been allocated to TGII through 2008, and the Greece–Italy leg obtaining the remaining € 8.6 million. Turkey, ineligible for direct receipt of these monies, is crucial to the building of pipelines that attracted nearly two-thirds of TEN-E financing for NG3 projects.

Gas 'w-a-r-s'

Rising energy prices create a hospitable climate for rent-seeking. While the state's deliberate creation of tightly controlled spheres of economic activity can lead to the same debilitating competition to grab the associated monopoly rents (Krueger, 1974), higher prices, notably for geographically clustered resources, may raise the value of the existing prize enough to divert social effort from productive activity to re-distributive (rent-seeking) contestation (Wick and Bulte, 2006, p. 458). During the period 2003–08 real energy prices doubled (World Bank, 2009, p. 51). Consequently driven and enabled to act more assertively by these favourably changed circumstances, governments of states with hydrocarbon-rich territory moved to consolidate control over 'their' upstream assets and extraction activities. After more than a decade of comparative openness to FDI in the buyer's market of the 1990s, exporting states, including Russia, acting on behalf of their NOCs, reversed course to wrest not only larger royalties and tax revenues from multinational majors, who had been enjoying relatively advantageous terms of Production Sharing Agreements (PSAs), but also majority shares of ownership from these foreign investors and concomitant decision-making power over the disposition of field equipment and operations (Hulbert and Arian, 2009; World Bank, 2009, p. 104). Not surprisingly, control over upstream assets and operations gravitated to NOCs, with foreign investors relegated to minority equity-holders or service contractors, even in post-Saddam Iraq (Kanter, 2009).

Officials from exporting countries have long sought to deflect blame for the price of fuel at the petrol pump and elsewhere, criticising end-use taxes in importing countries as doing more to enrich governments of the latter than to curtail consumption. Whatever the veracity of this argument, different parties do compete to aggrandise the lion's share of the large value that comprises the differential between low production costs and high retail prices (Victor and Victor, 2006, pp. 138–9). Given that they may control at least 85 per cent of the world's viably productive 'upstream' territory (Hulbert and Arian, 2009), which in turn intensifies the focus on the geopolitical concerns that are saliently operative in the 'Regions and Empires' storyline (Correljé and van der Linde, 2006) reviewed in Chapter 2, NOCs are preeminent, but typically inefficient, generators of national income in major exporting countries (and in some major importing countries as well), so they seek out remunerative income-generating opportunities 'downstream'. Thus, the entire hydrocarbon value chain provides ample opportunity for governments and firms to obtain large financial returns by occupying one or preferably more of its potentially lucrative niches. Indeed, it is not surprising that firms headquartered within their respective territories would first try to obtain the greatest share of value that can be generated from activities and niches over which their states exercise sovereign control.[1] Afterwards, they may seek to expand their range of influence along the value chain beyond those nodes over which they posses direct territorial control. With resources scarce and 'a significant part of the world's supply and demand...controlled by authoritarian states', competition remains intense, but not 'in the "*Smithian*" sense' (Andoura et al., 2010, p. 76).

In a relatively reciprocal relationship, openness granted at one link of the chain to actors associated more strongly with another node of the supply chain can be conditioned on access to the latter links. Yet, symmetrical reciprocity rarely exists at any given moment. Specifically, seller's markets raise fears on the part of firms based in consuming states – typically multinational majors – that access to 'upstream' sectors will shrink, while buyer's markets instil in producing-state firms a corresponding fear of 'downstream' market loss. By logical corollary, buyer's markets may help open up upstream sectors in exporting countries to direct investment by preeminent importing-country firms, although extraneous factors, such as future expectations of renewed price upswings (Hulbert and Arian, 2009) and greater saving of revenues in such vehicles as stabilization or 'sovereign wealth' funds during the boom phase of the commodity cycle for counter-cyclical spending in the 'bust' phase (World Bank, 2009, pp. 106–7), may forestall (re-)liberalisation. In contrast, seller's markets may make infrastructure assets in large consuming markets available for purchase or other forms of cooptation, via bartering or asset swapping, for example, by dominant exporting-country firms.

Russia's state-dominated Gazprom has earned renown for crafting and implementing strategies to earn more from every phase of its pipeline-structured natural gas trade with Europe, from upstream production to transit operations to downstream storage and distribution. As Meister (2010, p. 24) asserts, Gazprom aims 'to be able to provide the entire value chain... on the European market'. In terms of what we call 'near encirclement', it has pursued assets primarily by negotiating to buy into an array of extant and future infrastructure assets dispersed across the widest swath of its most economically salient geography, especially in countries located in what was once the former Soviet bloc. It has also sought to dominate the construction and operation of new prestige projects like the earlier described Nord Stream and South Stream gas pipelines, just as Transneft has also sought to wield influence over oil projects, like the trans-Black Sea Burgas–Alexandroupolis pipeline. In its strategic prong of 'far encirclement', Gazprom has been looking to consolidate inroads into the upstream sectors of the Caspian, Middle East and Africa, which are poised to fill a greater portion of EU-orientated future gas pipelines and LNG cargoes. This has taken the form of official bilateral forays and exploratory work within the Gas Exporting Countries Forum (GECF), a so-called gas OPEC, to achieve greater coordination of world output and prices in a more globalised and LNG-based future gas market. Whatever the likely end result of these efforts, Russia has shown a clear regard for its present and future share of key energy markets.

'Near encirclement'

The EU energy market has been liberalising under Commission pressure on national authorities to 'unbundle' ownership of energy production from that of its distribution. Consequently, Gazprom has sets its sights on more than just expanding basic trunk-pipeline capacity and maintaining or acquiring a dominant share of the arms-length contractual purchases of extra-EU27 gas imports by EU member states' incumbent firms. It has also sought to buy into local storage nodes and distribution channels within the EU, in such critical gas storage and transmission points as Austria (Lucas, 2008, pp. 179–80), raising fears that it would simply apply a model of doing business throughout the Former Soviet Union (FSU) that has featured use of non-transparent intermediary trading companies, such as the three successive entities set up to market Russian and Turkmen gas in Ukraine – ITERA, EuralTransGas and RosUkrEnergo (Goldman, 2008, pp. 145–7; Woehrel, 2009, pp. 7–10).

Were it to enlarge its major EU markets via success of these endeavours, Gazprom could effectively use its acquisition of this infrastructure both to crowd itself 'in' and to crowd rival foreign supplies out of the European markets at critical intervals, thereby opposing the diversification process that the Commission has been promoting and individual member states have been pursuing.

Just as it may be able to aggrandise its shares of EU markets at the expense of rival foreign suppliers, Gazprom may be able to ensure the pliability of certain transit states, those most highly dependent on Russia. Thus, 'near encirclement' also connotes the possibility that new Gazprom-led pipeline projects, such as the Northern European gas pipeline (NEGP), or Nord Stream project, with Ruhrgas (Germany), and the South Stream project, with Eni (Italy), will not only bypass FSU transit territories of Belarus and Ukraine, which have long been regarded by Russia and many core EU15 member states as nettlesome partners, but also to leave new member states like Poland and those on the Baltic Sea more vulnerable to gas cut-offs if they choose to deviate from Moscow's expectations of how they should behave, especially if and when the added pipeline capacity exceeds the availability of Russian and other gas sources to fill it (Lucas, 2008, p. 182; Woehrel, 2009, p. 5). These behavioural expectations may encompass a spectrum ranging from questions of access by Gazprom and other Russian firms to the relevant sectors of their domestic economies to the overall foreign policy stances of EU12 member states.

Two distinctions are worth pointing out. One concerns the particular context in which the strategy is applied. Gazprom and other firms headquartered in preeminent exporting countries, typically state-backed NOCs, may simply announce rises in the price of near future gas exports to 'downstream' consumer markets according to contractual terms or forgo these price hikes in exchange for obtaining offsetting ownership of infrastructure of comparably appraised value, which can also help maintain or expand respective sales domains. The first mode of rent-seeking occurs most often vis-à-vis developed markets, while the second is more typically pursued in conjunction with threatened price hikes addressed to consumer markets that are subsidised by exporting companies, a situation apropos of Gazprom's myriad bilateral relationships with national entities of various FSU states that it inherited from the ex-Soviet Ministry of Energy (Woehrel, 2009, pp. 7–14). Both efforts are facilitated by the higher revenues earned under seller's market conditions, but they can also be motivated by an interest in defending relative positions in 'downstream' territories when the market shifts to the advantage of buyers.

Another related distinction concerns the process by which the strategy is pursued. Rent-seeking can be done transparently, according to the rules and regulations of a liberalised market that the EU27 area is becoming. For instance, the justificatory rationale of declarations of intent to raise contracted prices or to lift subsidies can be measured according to standard price-setting criteria. By contrast, unilateral price hikes can be presented as *fait accompli*, perhaps masking an ulterior motive to build a monopoly position that precisely contravenes the laws and spirit of liberal competition. Even if monopolisation attempts can later be identified as unfair market practices and subsequently neutralised by application of legal regulations in 'downstream' markets, it may prove more difficult by then to recoup the cumulative opportunity costs of lost or reversed diversification that resulted from the preceding market-cornering behaviour.

These distinctions often blur in practical terms. For example, Gazprom appears to have complemented its expressed interest in gaining 10 per cent of the UK's natural gas market with purchase of a 10-per cent share of the Bacton-Zeebrugge Interconnector that runs between Belgium and the UK, a 25-year agreement with Fluxys to build an underground storage site in northern Belgium, and an effort to acquire a share of the BBL pipeline between the Netherlands and the UK (Lucas, 2008, p. 175; Weaver, 2009, pp. 49–50). The latter effort fits into an early 2010 agreement to permit Gazprom to store gas shipped through Nord Stream, now 9 per cent owned by Dutch firm Gasunie, in Holland's Bergermeer storage facility, which could hold enough gas to supply 1 year of Dutch demand or be sold in the UK market (Steen, 2009, p. 16). Gazprom has met resistance from this northwestern corner of Europe that does not depend much on Russian gas anyway. In August 2007, Belgian authorities quashed Gazprom's bid for the Zeebrugge storage-pipeline complex (Lucas, 2008, p. 175), while UK political opposition to Gazprom's earlier attempt to acquire Centrica, reflecting antipathy towards Moscow's restrictions on FDI in the Russian energy sector and the opacity of Gazprom's business dealings elsewhere in Europe and the FSU, forced Gazprom to scuttle its purchase (Roberts, 2010, p. 27).

The influence of Gazprom and other Russian energy firms grows larger and arguably less transparent as countries approach the former Soviet bloc. This phenomenon is not confined to EU12 territory.

Gazprom enjoys a large presence in the gas storage, distribution and retail marketing sectors of those EU member states where Russia dominates the gas-importation basket, including the aforementioned Baltic countries, the Balkan states of Bulgaria and Romania and the Central European nations of the Czech Republic, Hungary, Poland and Slovakia (Weaver, 2009, pp. 51–2). It has also made certain inroads into the EU15 as well. Like several EU12 states, including fellow Baltic countries Estonia, Latvia and Lithuania, Finland remains fully gas-dependent on Gazprom, which also owns sizable shares of all their gas monopolies (Ibid., pp. 50–1). Thus, while it held out the longest of the EU member states involved (including Denmark, Germany and Sweden) against allowing the passage of Nord Stream through its territorial waters, ostensibly for environmental reasons, Finland eventually conceded its approval, partially because the project enlisted the support of former prime minister Paavo Lipponen (Kramer, 2010c). His German counterpart Gerhard Schröeder was appointed to head up Nord Stream's shareholder's committee, apparently in the wake of the latter's approval of German financial guarantees to Gazprom, a transaction that fomented enough suspicions for the Commission to launch an investigation into whether these amounted to illegal state subsidies (Larsson, 2007, pp. 28–33). In moves probably designed to undercut the 'downstream' viability of the Nabucco Project and foster competition with neighbouring Hungary, Russia has promised to transform Austria into a 'hub' for Gazprom-controlled gas exports, consistent with the building of a € 260 million facility capable of storing 2.4 bcm and Gazprom's gaining of rights to acquire shares of Austria's gas transit and distribution sectors (Lucas, 2008, pp. 179–80; Weaver, 2009, pp. 49–50).

'Far encirclement'

As suggested earlier, Russian energy interests capitalised on earlier seller's market conditions to do more than simply defend their extant portion of the European gas market. They have also acted to extend or strengthen their influence vis-à-vis other third-party regions, including not only the Caspian Sea basin, an integral component of ex-Soviet territory, but also the Middle East and Africa, where key producers are supplying European energy consumers either through pipelines extending under the Mediterranean to the European continent or via LNG shipments. Gazprom has developed a budding presence in some of the following producing regions and countries. While some of this presence, albeit inchoate and often tenuous, has grown out of direct bilateral arrangements between Gazprom and other Russian energy firms with the respectively dominant NOCs in those countries, another source of inroads into these alternative EU supplier countries has arisen via joint ventures and asset-swap transactions with major EU member-state firms that continue to nurse their hopes of maintaining or obtaining reciprocal footholds in the upstream Russian market.

As embodied in our label 'far encirclement', this apparent Russian strategy of expanding inroads into newer extra-regional and global (LNG) energy sectors suggests that EU member states should avoid becoming unduly complacent about premising their energy security strategies and plans on tapping more gas from outside Russia's traditional sphere of influence. In short, 'far encirclement' as a strategic vision suggests that Gazprom seeks cooperative, coordinative or cooptative relationships with a number of NOCs in other key gas producing areas of the world, whether through a formal 'gas-OPEC' type of mechanism or, most probably, through a series of ad hoc bilateral marketing arrangements, in order to curtail the nature and degree of competition it faces in 'downstream' markets. The capacious geographic compass of Gazprom's strategic vision may necessitate more active efforts to ensure that the various limbs of Europe's increasingly interconnected pipeline network are capable, not merely physically, but also politically, of advancing the collective EU interest in diversification of routes *and* suppliers.

The Caspian Region

As detailed to a greater extent in Chapter 6, since the end of the Cold War, EU institutions, member states and headquartered firms have been seeking to establish and consolidate a European presence not only in Russia, but also in the non-Russian territories of the FSU. However, even if they were to overcome the full array of barriers to realising more profitable returns on their FDI in the states of this region, firms seeking to augment their hydrocarbon exports from the disparately energy rich states of the Caspian Sea Basin still channel the bulk of those exports across the Russian land mass that lies between most of the non-Russian FSU Caspian states and potentially lucrative European markets. During the Cold War, the Caspian Basin was largely Soviet territory, so most pipelines of the formerly integrated political unit became de facto export routes crossing Russia. Subsequent control over the physical movement of natural gas from Kazakhstan, Turkmenistan and Uzbekistan, via the

Soviet-era Central Asia Centre (CAC) Pipeline, fell under Gazprom, giving this 50.01-per cent state-owned company dominant purchasing leverage over Caspian gas to complement its monopoly vis-à-vis many FSU and new EU member states. Only in recent years have non-Russian routes come online. Azerbaijan's oil can now go via the Baku–Supsa line to the Black Sea via Georgia and the Baku–Tbilisi–Ceyhan (BTC) pipeline to Turkey via Georgia and some gas travels through the Baku–Tbilisi–Erzurum (BTE) pipeline to Turkey via Georgia. Kazakstan's oil has found a direct outlet to China, while Turkmenistan's gas can now be shipped not only through the older Korpedzhe–Kurt–Kui line to Iran, which delivered about 6 bcm in 2007, but also through the newer Dauletabad–Sarakhs–Khangiran line, which is slated to deliver up to 12 bcma to Iran, and another one that may eventually deliver up to 30 bcma to China via Uzbekistan and Kazakhstan (International Energy Agency, 2008b, pp. 28–9, 62–3).

Nonetheless, the construction of these non-Russian pipelines from the Caspian Basin, principally those taking energy west, proceeded rather fitfully to surmount formidable economic and political obstacles. The latter arose largely out of a situation where pipelines that had already been commissioned in the Soviet era and currently lie under the respective controls of Gazprom (formerly the Ministry of Gas Industry) or Transneft generated benefits for those possessing an 'incumbent' position with respect to any proposed challengers, thus helping lock many FSU states into Russia's economic orbit (Wohlforth, 2004). Russia's cost advantage was reinforced by the evident doubts, especially in the buyer's market of the 1990s, about the financial wisdom of building the 'multiple pipelines' that lay at the core of the Clinton administration's seminal promotion of an East–West energy corridor (Jaffe and Manning, 1998–99, p. 118; Bahgat, 2002, p. 323). Finally, the period prefacing the US-led invasion of Iraq in March 2003 generated expectations that an underexploited source of oil would deluge world markets, thus forcing all energy prices further down and obviating any remaining need for new non-Russian Caspian pipelines (Andrianopoulos, 2003, p. 80).

Consequently, EU efforts to diversify its supplier portfolio by accessing more Caspian gas via the 'southern corridor' have been strongly hindered by the historical imposition and Gazprom's utilisation of Moscow's presence in this region. In fact, the more explicit determination by the Commission to support the creation of independent European-orientated export routes for Caspian gas largely seems to reflect greater awareness of the necessity of hedging against the increasing unlikelihood of obtaining Russian ratification of the 1994 ECT and its Transit Protocol, which would serve as the legal mechanisms for eliminating Gazprom's and Transneft's respective chokeholds over the CAC and the various oil pipelines that terminate at Russia's Black Sea and Baltic ports or cross directly into Europe (Olcott, 2006, pp. 222–6; Roberts, 2006, pp. 217–18; Belkin, 2007, pp. 3, 11).

The energy seller's market certainly did nothing to assuage Moscow's opposition to ratifying these measures. It even encouraged Russian officialdom, acting through Transneft, which has a one-quarter share in the Caspian Pipeline Consortium (CPC) pipeline carrying oil from Kazakhstan's Tengiz field to Novorossiysk, one of Russia's foremost ports and energy export centres, to ratchet up the stringency of its conditions, including higher transit tariffs and Kazakhstan's *quid pro quo* participation in the aforementioned Transneft-led Burgas–Alexandroupolis Pipeline, for agreeing to allow expansion and use of the CPC, the only physical route that traverses Russia but also enjoys legal independence from Moscow and is dominated by a consortium of foreign corporations (Socor, 2007b; Ritchie, 2008).

By 2008, talk of a new Gazprom-spearheaded project (the Prikaspiiski Pipeline) to carry additional Turkmen and Kazakh gas northwards along the Caspian littoral to and via Russia to Europe was threatening to make the existing Russian chokehold even more restrictive (Rodova, 2008a; Blank, 2010). The economic crisis that achieved near-epic proportions in the latter half of 2008, thereby eroding both energy prices and the concomitant value of Gazprom's capital stock, should logically have caused many of the latter firm's projects to be shelved or scaled back. Although Gazprom had long been re-exporting gas to Ukraine and Europe from Turkmenistan, which the successor government to Saparmurat Niyazov had forced Gazprom to buy at higher prices earlier in 2008, the negative effects of the market collapse reverberated back up the value chain, leading some European importers to renege on 'take-or-pay' contracts with Gazprom and the latter in turn to spurn further purchases of Turkmen gas on previously agreed terms. Turkmen authorities, who attributed an April 2009 explosion on the Dauletabad–Deryalyk leg of the CAC pipeline to a Russian decrease in flow intake, consequently halted gas exports, which later resumed on modified terms in January 2010, after the inauguration of new pipelines to China and Iran (Moscow Times, 2009, p. 3; ITAR-TASS, 2010). Notwithstanding the economic downturn and related Russo-Turkmen imbroglio, Gazprom has steadfastly pursued Russia's abiding interest in securing agreements with its three Central Asian partners to proceed with expansion of the CAC's capacity to take more of their gas to Russia (Xinhua, 2008; Gorst, 2009, p. 2).

The Middle East

The Middle East, long an arena of competition, first among Western powers for its energy reserves and later between the US and Soviet Union for overall regional influence, has become another area towards which Russian energy firms have shown growing interest that reflects a combination of business and geopolitical motivations. With the world's largest combined reserves of oil and gas, the Persian Gulf and North Africa, which, as described below, have not been immune to Soviet and later Russian influence, represent areas that have been among the least susceptible to the EU influence. For one, due to a longer period of colonial dominance and convenient access to seaborne transportation routes, this region has fully developed extraction and exportation infrastructure, adding another element of 'incumbency' that can make it costlier to bring new sources of supply and modes of delivery into global energy trade equations. In addition, regional countries have exerted output and pricing power through a series of actions involving the expropriation of multinational majors' assets, the implementation of embargoes and their participation as OPEC members in the cartelistic activity of setting overall output ceilings and dividing up production quotas among themselves. As they did after the 1973–74 Arab oil boycott (Skeet, 1988, p. 118), and as they are now doing with Russia, European countries have largely adopted non-confrontational strategies along the lines of 'dialogue' and other exertions of 'soft power' in seeking to lower or stabilise energy prices. Indeed, the European Commission (2001, p. 73) has for at least the past decade proclaimed that it is highly attuned to the 'expectations of several producer countries regarding political developments in the Middle East'.

Russian firms have still struggled to maintain their foothold in Iraq's energy sector, even though the latter has thrown up many obstacles in the way of both investors and customers. For the past 30 years, Iraq has been a major exporter of crude oil, with a smaller but significant fraction of these exports conveyed by the Kirkuk–Yumurtalık, or Iraq–Turkey (IT), pipeline (actually two parallel lines), which terminates in Ceyhan, Turkey's major Mediterranean oil export terminus. Post-occupation sabotage in Iraq disrupted pipeline operations (Williams, 2006) until late 2007, when the IT line's return to functionality played a major role in lifting Iraqi annual crude output by nearly one-fifth from its 2003–07 range to 115 mmta by the end of 2007 (International Energy Agency, 2007a, p. 21). Even though the IT route remains vulnerable to attack, its throughput later reached sustainable volumes equivalent to 20 mmta and aided Iraq in bringing annual oil output to 122 mmta (International

Energy Agency, 2010, pp. 16–17). Motivated perhaps by this favourable turn of events, a Russo-Iraqi agreement to cancel Iraq's Saddam-era debt in return for Baghdad's reconsideration of the validity of Russian firm Lukoil's earlier 1997 oil contract to develop the West Qurna 2 field (International Energy Agency, 2008a, p. 22) may have prepared the ground for Lukoil's successful 2009 bid, co-offered with Norway's Statoil, to develop this field (Kanter, 2009). Encouraging signs in the oil sector, especially in the Kirkuk region's production and export sectors, imparted fresh impetus to a 1996 bilateral proposal to develop the capacity to pipe 10 bcma of gas from northern Iraq to Turkey (Roberts, 2004, p. 7; Winrow, 2004, p. 34; O'Byrne, 2007). Iraq, holding slightly less than 2 per cent of global gas reserves, but more than Norway or the combined reserves of Azerbaijan and Kazakhstan (BP, 2009, p. 22), may provide another source of supply for the EU's Nabucco Pipeline Project.

Moscow has acted even more vigorously to establish inroads into Iran, Iraq's neighbour and perennial competitor. Iran holds the world's second largest gas deposits (Ibid., p. 22) and has been estimated as capable of covering more than one-tenth of the EU's medium-term needs (European Commission, 2005d, p. 15). Given that most Iranian gas to Europe will flow through Turkey, which actually imported less gas from Iran than the latter obtained from Turkmenistan in 2008, in respective volumes of 5.8 bcma versus 6.5 bcma (BP, 2009, p. 30), bilateral Turco-Iranian disputes have cast uncertainty on the prospects of assimilating this route into a 'southern corridor'. Related to the underlying issue of Turkey's periodic over-buying of imported gas supplies on a 'take-or-pay' basis, which also applies to Russia, Turkish authorities stopped importing Iranian gas in early 2003, just weeks after the 10 bcma-capacity Tabriz–Erzurum pipeline commenced operations, in order to force changes in price, volumes and destination restrictions (Winrow, 2004, pp. 29–30). Yet, the flow of gas into this conduit has also been cut from the Iranian end, ostensibly to cover domestic shortages in recent winters, and decreases in the flow from Turkmenistan, such as one that occurred in 2008, have in turn impinged on the now operational Turkey–Greece Interconnector (Platts, 2006; Reuters, 2008).

Just as European expectations of obtaining more gas from Iran have been diminished by application of sanctions on Tehran over the latter's uranium enrichment program and by specific difficulties that Turkey has experienced in its energy dealings Iran, Moscow has cultivated a range of mutual interests with Tehran, including those in the energy field. Moscow has refused to use the leverage afforded by its permanent seat on the United Nations Security Council (UNSC) to approve comprehensive multilateral sanctions extending to Iran's energy sector, not least because it has sought to have a role in developing civilian nuclear power at Iran's Bushehr site. In 2008, Gazprom also signed memoranda of understanding (MoUs), one on investing in Iran's oil and gas fields, notably the vast South Pars formation, thus filling the breach left by departing private-sector firms, such as Spain's Repsol, France's Total and Japan's Inpex (Eqbeli and Shiryaevskaya, 2008; Socor, 2008), and another on entering the Iran–Pakistan–India ('Peace') pipeline project, which India approved in return for promised participation in Russia's Sakhalin II (International Energy Agency, 2008b, pp. 29, 32). Thus, Russian plans for Iranian gas do not seem to help EU27 member states in getting more of it for themselves.

Africa

EU members cannot be complacent about the future potential nature and volume of African energy supplies to Europe, especially those from its bastions in North Africa, as Gazprom has attempted to leverage Soviet-era alliances with relevant regimes to enter various African energy sectors. Egypt, a new LNG exporter, which shipped nearly 45 per cent of its 14 bcma in exports to EU member states (BP, 2009, p. 30), may also wish to use Turkey (after Jordan and Syria in succession) to pipe its gas to Europe. Accordingly, Egypt, Jordan, Syria, where Gazprom's partially owned construction company Stroitransgaz built the Syrian leg, joined Turkey in agreeing to extend a proposed Arab Gas Pipeline (AGP) project to Turkish territory, where additional connections could link it up to Nabucco (Winrow, 2004, pp. 34–5; APS, 2008). In Libya, from where a trans-Mediterranean pipeline supplies 13 per cent of gas imports (BP, 2009, p. 30) into Italy, which is part of the proposed TGII, Gazprom acquired assets from a subsidiary German BASF firm, which is party to Nord Stream (Socor, 2006; RIA Novosti, 2008). In 2008, in returning for agreeing to coorganise the marketing of additional Libyan gas supplies to Europe, Gazprom, replicating its strategy vis-à-vis Caspian FSU states, offered to purchase the entire volume of Libya's export-bound oil, gas and LNG supplies (Socor, 2008).

Some of these moves have been abetted by EU-headquartered firms. Enticed by the prospect of securing greater access to the Russian upstream sector and ensuring the future profitability of their joint South Stream venture to pipe Gazprom's gas under the Black Sea into Southeastern Europe, Italy's Eni firm not only purchased one-fifth of Gazprom's oil business, which was assembled from Yukos's confiscated assets, but also offered Gazprom inroads into Libya's oil and gas sector.

Although Eni's own share of Libya's giant Elephant field had been reduced by Tripoli to less than one-third in 2008, Eni agreed to divide with Gazprom a share that had been shrunk to 32 per cent in 2008, although the exact terms of Gazprom's entry into Libya have still not been finalised (Crooks, 2007, p. 26; Hoyos, 2008, p. 17; BBC, 2009). Compared to Libya, which supplied less than 4 per cent of the European market, Algeria forms a much bigger fixture of the EU gas-importation portfolio. It provided 59 bcma (just under two-thirds of which came in the form of piped supplies to Italy and Spain), or 17 per cent, of the EU27's total 2008 gas imports and nearly twice as large a proportion of Italy's imports (BP, 2009, p. 30). In 2006, Gazprom agreed with Sonatrach, Algeria's state energy firm, to produce gas and jointly market it to Europe in return for permitting the latter entity to join an LNG development in Russia (Socor, 2007a), although this never progressed very far even during the height of the 2003–08 commodity boom (Gorst, 2008, p. 25). Gazprom also broached the idea of helping to produce Nigerian gas for domestic use, even as France's Total has taken the lead in proposing to build a 4128-km trans-Sahara pipeline at a cost of € 15 billion that could transport 20–30 bcma of this gas under the Sahara to Algeria and then to Europe (Gorst, 2008, p. 25; Green, 2009, p. 5; Weaver, 2009, p. 50). Although it does not directly supply the Iberian Peninsula, Gazprom has acquired 6–7 per cent of a Portuguese energy company with a share of the supply allotted to the planned Medgaz pipeline from Algeria to Spain (Weaver, 2009, p. 50).

All these instances or trends of 'far encirclement' may dovetail with Gazprom's efforts to shape the future LNG market. The latter interest has been evidenced by Russia's tentative support, together with major gas producers Algeria, Iran and Venezuela, for turning the GECF into a more active 'gas-OPEC' (Economist Intelligence Unit, 2008; Shchedrov, 2008; Shiryaevskaya, 2008). In December 2009, on the heels of a joint Russo-Iranian meeting where Russian Energy Minister Sergei Shmatko reputedly reaffirmed his country's support for Gazprom's involvement in the construction of a gas pipeline from Iran to India, GECF member states accepted Leonid Bokhanovsky, who had overseen pipeline building in Algeria, India and Syria as former head of Stroitransgaz, Gazprom's construction arm, as their head until the end of 2011 (Medetsky, 2009, p. 1). Nonetheless, effective market cartelisation is sure to be hobbled by supplier competition (Chazan, 2007), manifested in the egregious non-participation of non-Russian FSU Central Asian states in the organisation and exacerbated by soft prices. Thus, GECF 'activism' seems intended, at least for Gazprom, on gaining a stronger influence over a gradually globalising LNG market of which it recently became part.

Conclusion: will the EU end up energy diversified or upended by Russia?

The Commission articulated common energy policy in 2007 and promoted subsequent proposals, like the Second Strategic Energy Review in 2008, which advised in favour of prioritising further fuel supplier-diversification, *inter alia*, and TEN-E financing has been earmarked for identified 'priority' projects with their own specifically designated coordinators. Yet, vigorous top-down efforts have not been able to achieve greater cooperation and solidarity among EU27 member states, where headquartered energy corporations have succumbed to nation-centric *realpolitik* temptations to secure separate bilateral deals with Gazprom. The declared pledges contained in the 2007 Lisbon Treaty to let the Commission decide 'in a spirit of solidarity between Member States, upon the [appropriate] measures...if severe difficulties arise in the supply of...energy' (European Union, 2007, p. 72) do not impinge on a member's 'right to determine the conditions for exploiting its energy resources, its choice between different energy sources and the general structure of its energy supply' (ibid., p. 88). Thus, the treaty, which strikes a muddled balance between sovereignty concerns and supranational-action competency in the energy sector, retains 'pre-existing flaws and gaps' (Andoura et al., 2010, p. 76).

Part of the problem with characterising the default member-state-centric approach to EU energy security as *realpolitik* is that it seems a manifestly unrealistic way for the aggregate EU27 entity to try to guarantee uninterrupted physical deliveries of its collective present and future import needs from its external suppliers. As Andoura et al. (2010, p. v) remark, 'Member states are right to view energy as strategic, but wrong to believe that separate and/or diverging national approaches will enable them to achieve their strategic objectives.' Key features of the energy game make it amenable to rent-seeking *par excellence* and Russia's Gazprom remains one of the game's keenest participants (hence, the frequent references to the new 'great game' featuring Eurasian hydrocarbon resources). Thus, while this may reflect revenue-preservation motives more than purely expansionist imperatives and may not necessarily translate into the successful meeting of any larger Kremlin foreign policy objectives, Gazprom has trained a sharp eye on all developments that might affect Russia's main European customer base, including contrary

Commission campaigns to promote expansion of the EU27's import repertoire. Thus, it has worked throughout the entire gas delivery system to ensure that it controls, or at least continues to profit from, the widest swath of relevant upstream fields, transit routes and downstream networks, if necessary, at the expense of crowding out other extra-EU27 suppliers. As EU actors are engaged in gas 'wars' one way or another, whether or not they wish to be, they have not totally relinquished a vision of new routes of access to Middle Eastern and Caspian supplies that have become increasingly reliant on bridges crossing Turkey.

6
Roads to Europe for Caspian and Middle Eastern Energy Supplies

Introduction: opportunities and blindspots in the EU's quest for new foreign energy supplies

This chapter builds specifically on the previous examination of efforts to diversify the European Union's gas supplies and suppliers in line with the objective of ensuring that the European Union (EU) has more source countries from which to access energy as well as more evenly balanced dependency across them. The crafting of this objective, as articulated by the Commission, has been grounded in the plausible assumption that more strenuous market competition among suppliers should not only help to dampen or suppress price increases, but should also minimise the impact of future energy 'crises' arising out of disputes between specific producer and transit countries or precipitated by deliberate cut-offs. As examined previously, those member states, albeit limited in number, that have more fully equipped their domestic markets with the necessary intake infrastructure to re-gasify tanker shipments of liquefied natural gas (LNG) have also tended to achieve a wider broadening of their repertoire of suppliers that could be generalised to the rest of the EU area. In lieu of the EU27 becoming more widely capable of receiving and circulating LNG, individual EU member-state governments and firms have fallen back on maintaining their respective interests in tapping more gas (and more oil, in the case of the former) from a larger array of suppliers in the Caspian and Middle East regions via planned pipelines. This section includes a brief survey of changes in the relative availability of oil and gas reserves from regions that the EU has been accessing and those from which it could potentially import significantly greater volumes.

Our analysis then assesses the status of particular transportation infrastructure mechanisms by which various EU member states have sought to access additional Middle Eastern and Caspian region energy supplies. As embodied in the Pan-European and Odessa–Brody oil pipeline projects or the White Stream project for gas, all of which involve Ukraine, certain plans to transship hydrocarbons along an 'East-West corridor' have been conceptualised in such a way as to bypass both Russia and Turkey, with one environmental rationale for the afore-mentioned oil schemes being that they would decrease the flow of Russian-origin tanker traffic through the Bosporus Straits. However, as explained in Chapter 5, the extant bulk of Trans-European Networks-Energy (TEN-E) financing for the 'southern corridor' has gone to those projects crossing Turkey. Moreover, the current operation of smaller trans-Turkey pipeline flows of energy originating from the Middle East and the Caspian, the landlocked nature of which impose certain lim-itations on the feasibility of LNG exports, indicates that Turkey has become increasingly central to plans to diversify the EU's import bas-ket to a fuller geographical extent and thus more prominently located on the EU's energy security agenda. Thus, this chapter also previews Chapter 7's much fuller elaboration of how Turkey has already allowed the EU to attain a marginal widening of its pipeline-based hydrocarbon importation options.

On the other hand, the EU as a predominantly consumer-orientated economic area faces competition for supply from other importing-consuming countries. Consequently, efforts to obtain more energy supplies from the rich deposits located in the Persian Gulf and the Caspian Sea Basin regions are poised to encounter a considerable chal-lenge, not just from Russia on the supply side, as discussed in Chapters 5 and 7, but also from major Asian countries on the demand side.

A case in point, rapidly growing China has stepped more actively than the EU as an entity into the fray, with the former's state-influenced companies, prominent among them the China National Petroleum Cor-poration (CNPC) and its overseas subsidiary PetroChina, entering joint ventures in the exploration and production (E&P) sector and obtain-ing Beijing's underwriting of concessional loans and loan guarantees to shepherd the construction of the necessary complement of oil and gas pipelines to Kazakhstan, Turkmenistan and Uzbekistan on the Caspian's eastern rim. Thus, China has accomplished more than the EU to date in providing these landlocked states with an additional export outlet to an increasingly lucrative market that eases their dependence on Russia and, to a much lesser extent, Iran, fellow Caspian Basin states that have had many conflicts of interest with their various non-Russian Former Soviet Union (FSU) littoral partners. Accordingly, however, this diversification has favoured China, as well as the landlocked producing and exporting countries in question, without redounding to the benefit of Europe. Thus, this chapter devotes considerable space to examination of the extent to which Chinese projects pose a new threat to the viability of Europe-bound Caspian energy supplies and routes.

The EU'S access to world hydrocarbon reserves

Earlier chapters underscored that the area comprising the collective territory of the 27 EU member states has actually diversified *towards* Russia in meeting its oil import needs while actually diversifying *away* from Russia in terms of meeting its gas importation requirements. These cross-cutting trends do not represent the result of pursuit of an illogical or irrational collective-level policy. Rather, they mirror with some accuracy underlying trends in the distribution of world oil and gas reserves. However, they fall short of completely reflecting changes in the global distribution of the respective resources in question.

Surprisingly, non-Middle Eastern countries and regions have gained greater shares of world reserves at the expense of the Middle East, without displacing the latter in any meaningful way. According to figures derived from BP (2009, pp. 6, 8, 22–3), Europe and Eurasia (a BP-labelled category dominated by the FSU), Africa and Central and South America (a third category) came to account for a larger collective share, and respectively augmented regional shares, of the world's total oil reserves in 2008. In the two decades between 1988 and 2008, the first category's fraction of the world's oil reserves expanded from under 8 to 11.3 per cent, while Africa's grew from nearly six to ten per cent and the third category's portion of the world's oil reserves increased from nearly seven to ten per cent. Conversely, the Middle East's fraction of global oil reserves actually fell by over five per cent, from 65.4 per cent to just below three-fifths. While Russia supplied nearly one-third of EU oil imports and only a slightly smaller fraction of the EU's petroleum demand in 2007, it accounted for just over six per cent of 2008 global petroleum reserves. This mismatch indicates that the EU remains underserved by the collective oil riches contained in other regions of the world like Africa and the Persian Gulf, towards which the EU has also maintained an evident propensity for 'dialogue' and 'partnership'.

The scenario for natural gas differs markedly from that of petroleum supply. Because the gas trade remains dominated by pipeline movements, the EU area's importation profile may not become as widely diversified, relative to its oil basket, as would be suggested by the overall distribution of worldwide reserves. While Russia continues to supply just under two-fifths of the EU27 area's collective gas importation portfolio, it accounts for closer to 23 per cent of the latter's gas demand, a percentage that nearly matches Russia's share of world gas reserves. This suggests some basis for stability in the EU's present level of average dependency on Russia, albeit a mean that masks an uncomfortably wide range of variation across member states. However, as it imports another two-fifths of its gas from Algeria and Norway, two exporters that hold four per cent of global gas reserves between them, the EU may have to accelerate LNG capacity building to tap into regions holding the remaining 73 per cent of world's remaining gas reserves, the bulk of which are concentrated in the Persian Gulf.

Institutions of the EU recognise this necessity. Even the 'European Coordinator' responsible for monitoring and ensuring progress on those 'projects of European interest' involving the implementation of a 'southern corridor' for gas has recommended against the EU neglecting the utility of accessing more LNG from African and Middle Eastern sources and developing certain ports in Greece and Romania as new hubs for the trading of these supplies in Europe (van Aartsen, 2009, pp. 9–10). While the fraction of world gas reserves comprised by countries falling into the category of European and Eurasia declined from 40.6 to 34.0 per cent between 1988 and 2008, the Middle East's share climbed *pari passu* from 31.3 to 41 per cent (BP, 2009, pp. 6, 8, 22–3). African gas has also come to account for nearly eight per cent of global gas deposits. Thus, the slow but steady growth of LNG exports to European and other markets of Qatari gas reflects the fact that the latter constitutes nearly 14 per cent of the world's total, behind only Russia and Iran, which holds 16 per cent but has been hobbled in its ability to produce and export this gas by economic sanctions and mismanagement.

While the energy reserves of the Caspian Sea Basin have been subject to wildly vacillating estimates of their potential size and thus should not be unduly relied on to replace more mature producing regions like the North Sea, these hold an under-tapped potential to supply the EU27 economy, but most critically its newest member states, via export routes that do not traverse Russian territory. Russian and Iran also have Caspian littorals that extend out over energy beds, which have been the subject of lingering legal disputation (International Energy Agency, 2008b, p. 66), but posses more encompassing territories with direct marine outlets to world markets, in stark contrast to the four land-locked basin states of Azerbaijan, Kazakhstan, Turkmenistan and Uzbekistan. While oil from Azerbaijan and Kazakhstan, the main non-Russian FSU oil powerhouses in the Caspian Sea Basin, is already reaching markets without having to transit Russia, both territories taken together account for approximately four per cent of global oil reserves and therefore have room to grow to fill a slightly larger proportion of total European imports. Azerbaijan's oil can now reach Europe-orientated markets without having to traverse Russia out of geographical necessity, although China serves as the only non-Russian landborne exit route for Kazakhstan's oil at present. The four non-Russian FSU basin states, which collectively accounted for just under seven per cent of 2008 global natural gas reserves, represent the focus of considerable Euro- and Sino-centric efforts that have begun to achieve fruition. The former set of efforts have yielded a pipeline crossing Azerbaijan, Georgia and Turkey into Greece and the latter efforts have resulted in a pipeline extending from Turkmenistan across Uzbekistan and Kazakhstan to China, giving these landlocked states export outlets that bypass Russia while assisting the major consuming areas in question to broaden their respective supplier bases.

The EU and Caspian energy

Firms headquartered in European countries have provided the bulk of the material means and wherewithal to realise the energy-sector dimensions of the EU's Partnership and Cooperation Agreements (PCAs) with various non-Russian FSU states. By default, actors in Europe's corporate sectors have occupied the vanguard of EU-centric efforts to exploit gas supplies from the FSU Caspian littoral states, with notable albeit partial success in Azerbaijan and Kazakhstan that has not been replicated in Turkmenistan and Uzbekistan. As these multinational corporations have become more prominently involved in the Caspian energy sector, they have also shown a corollary interest in ensuring that the hydrocarbons they produce can be exported on the most competitive terms possible. While this interest reflects their preferences and those of their hosts for developing routes of hydrocarbon egress that are independent of Russia, given the capacity of state-led firms in the latter to buy captive energy supplies at lower-than-market prices and thus capture large rents from their passage, it is logical for EU institutions to back these projects, as they have done to a small extent via the TEN-E programme, for the sake of diversifying the EU27 area's portfolio of non-Russian-controlled imports.

By contrast, as amply underscored already, member governments have, until more recently, shown a more ambivalent attitude – one that reflects their disparate energy profiles – towards formalisation of EU efforts to access more Caspian energy, with an understandable degree of validity. As discussed in previous chapters, hesitancy on the part of some of them stems from many member states' desire not to jeopardise inflows of Russian gas and a variety of separate deals with Gazprom that have been pursued by a number of their major companies (Belkin, 2007, pp. 9–13). Indeed, to reiterate the common lament once more, the European Commission (2007a, pp. 18–19) admits that EU members have visibly struggled to 'speak with one voice' on common energy concerns, including how to build Europe-orientated connections to Caspian Basin energy supplies in the face of Russian efforts to prevent univocal EU forays in that endeavour.

In any case, the relative paucity of TEN-E financing for natural gas route 3 (NG3 or 'southern corridor') projects, which make up a specific section of a larger East–West energy corridor, as well as problems that individual companies have sometimes encountered in investing in and developing the various fields in the Caspian Basin region have made it costly and politically cumbersome for many of these firms to proceed as quickly as they and the governments of their host countries might prefer in readying their full panoply of upstream assets for production and export. In contrast, as discussed further below, contiguous People's Republic of China (PRC), opposite to the EU area in being relatively more dependent on foreign oil than gas, has made mammoth strides in developing and accessing its own secure landborne supplies of oil from Kazakhstan and gas from Turkmenistan, which are intended to balance its predominantly maritime importation of hydrocarbons from the rest of the world.

EU efforts to access Caspian Basin energy without Russia or Turkey

As companies headquartered in EU countries have been engaged in the partially fruitful development of Caspian Basin hydrocarbons for export, the EU has been correspondingly compelled to engage in prudent consideration of an array of candidate pipeline routes to ship these resources. Not all of these incorporate Turkey. In fact, although the volume of oil that they ship dropped by approximately one-quarter to 119 mmta in 2006, 5500 tankers exporting oil from around the rim of the Black Sea, but largely from Novorossiysk, already squeeze their way through the narrow Bosporus Straits between Turkey's Asian and European shores, occasionally colliding and spilling large quantities of petroleum in the environs of Istanbul (Energy Information Administration, 2008c, pp. 7–9). Consequently, one justification that some have cited in favour of these projects has been that they would help relieve this congestion. However, many of them have been hampered by some of the same key obstacles besetting major new expansions of Europe-orientated pipeline connection to Caspian energy that cross Turkey. Moreover, they have failed to obtain the necessary levels of financial and political backing that would put them on a competitive footing with those trans-Turkey pipelines that already exist. Indeed, the EU's institutional cooperation with non-Russian Caspian states has taken shape largely within the 'Baku initiative' and bilateral memoranda of understanding (MoUs) that were elaborated on in Chapter 3. Although the EU's approach has been based on '[t]he underlying idea that common energy interests can be advanced through a gradual process of regulatory approximation towards European norms', it 'has not captured the imagination of Caspian producers, who feel that the strategic and commercial value of the gas trade – rather than the details of the Gas Directive – should be the basis of their energy relationship with the EU' (International Energy Agency, 2008b, p. 45).

Oil: The Pan-European and Odessa–Brody pipelines

While interested in all conceivable non-Russian FSU sources of Caspian oil, the EU and major firms headquartered in its member states have focused primarily on developing the physical and legal means to bring additional supplies of petroleum from Kazakhstan. This oil is envisaged to cross, in succession, the Caspian Sea, Azerbaijan and Georgia, the two Caucasus region countries that already host the Baku–Tbilisi–Ceyhan (BTC) and Baku–Supsa pipelines as well as the railway terminating at Georgia's Batumi Port, and then the Black Sea.

The Pan-European Oil Pipeline (PEOP) has been designed to bring oil from Constanta, on Romania's Black Sea coast to Serbian and Croatian refineries and deliver the refined product onwards via Slovenia or the Istria peninsula to Trieste in Italy. Estimated to cost upwards of € 2 billion and expected to have throughput capacity of 60 mmta, this project, the subject of an April 2007 inter-governmental accord endorsed by the EU Commission at Zagreb and a development company founded 1 year later, appears to have garnered some interest from Kazakhstan. Five months after conclusion of the inter-governmental accord, state firm KazMunaiGas, which already owned Georgia's Batumi oil terminal, consented to acquire the vast majority share of a Romanian oil enterprise that included two refineries and over 600 petrol stations spread across seven countries. The project, however, has not advanced very far for several reasons. These include Italian and Slovenian absence from the project development company, Russian pressure on potential upstream supplier Kazakhstan to route most of its oil exports through the Transneft-controlled Burgas–Alexandroupolis Pipeline, and Gazprom's oil arm Gazpromneft's interest in gaining majority control over Serbia's NIS oil company (Ibid., pp. 55–7).

Progress on the Odessa–Brody Pipeline Project, another project that has received feasibility financing from the European Commission, has long been stymied by some of the same problems afflicting the aforementioned project. In 2001, Ukraine built a 674-km pipeline with a throughput capacity of 9 mmta that is now theoretically available to convey Caspian oil from the Pivdenny terminal at Ukraine's Odessa Port on the Black Sea northwards to Brody in western Ukraine, where the oil would enter that leg of the Druzhba trunk line that reaches the Czech Republic, Germany and Slovakia. However, without Kazakhstan oil yet accessible in sufficient quantities, Ukraine, then under the leadership of Leonid Kuchma, agreed in 2004 to accept the Anglo-Russian TNK-BP's proposal to reverse the direction of Odessa-Brody so that more Russian crude could reach the Black Sea (Ibid., p. 58; Kupchinsky, 2007). As the International Energy Agency (2008b, p. 58) has remarked, 'in this way, the project initially viewed as a means of relieving congestion in the Bosporus ended up increasing volumes seeking transit through the Straits'.

This project experienced a later upturn in fortune, albeit insufficient to bring about its full realisation. In August 2005, during the 2003–08 commodity price boom, the Commission became more highly motivated to award a contract to a European consortium to finalise studies on the feasibility of extending this pipeline to Poland (Kupchinsky, 2007). The following year, the northern spur of the Druzhba export pipeline, part of which supplies Russian oil to Lithuania, was shut off, persuading that EU member state to join fellow member state Poland, as well as Azerbaijan, Georgia and Ukraine, in setting up a consortium to extend Odessa–Brody another 500 km to Poland's Plock Refinery, making the project's cost equivalent to one euro per kilometre (International Energy Agency, 2008b, p. 58; Crooks and Olearchyk, 2007, p. 8). Nonetheless, with Kazakhstan declining to join this consortium, the project, while acquiring stronger EU-level support, continues to face uncertainty in terms of how it will be filled (Crooks and Olearchyk, 2007, p. 8).

Gas: White Stream Project

At its inception, the White Stream Project was known as the Georgia–Ukraine–European Union (GUEU) Pipeline. Like its counterpart oil projects, this project envisages the construction of a new sub-sea pipeline, up to 1355 km long – at an estimated cost of € 3.8 billion – to ship amounts of Caspian gas, rising from 8 bcma in its initial phase to 32 bcma, through Azerbaijan and Georgia to Romania directly via the Black Sea or indirectly via Ukrainian Crimea (International Energy Agency, 2008b, p. 65). White Stream has gained the strong support of Ukraine and received € 650 million in TEN-E funding (over the 2007–08 period), as a component of the EU's NG3 ('southern corridor') 'project of European interest' (European Commission, 2009g, pp. 1–2; van Aartsen, 2009, pp. 2–3).

This project confronts problems that also face others encompassed within the NG3 gas-corridor framework. As an initiative intended to provide a new route for gas supplies that skirts Russian and Turkish territory, it faces the ever-present possibility of being preempted by Gazprom. That firm has heretofore maintained control of most non-Azeri sources of FSU Caspian gas and, as further discussed in the next chapter, even agreed in 2009 to commence buying 0.5 bcma from Azerbaijan starting in January 2010 (Energy Information Administration, 2009a, p. 5). The latter has even agreed to send 56 million cubic metres per annum (mcma) of gas to traditional nemesis Iran (Blagov, 2010), with which it has had a lingering dispute over ownership of the Caspian seabed's Alov/Alorz energy deposits (International Energy Agency, 2008b, p. 66). Based on its central passage through Georgia, a characteristic of most other projects to transport more Caspian hydrocarbons to European markets, the International Energy Agency (Ibid., p. 65) has added that, 'More than other projects in the region, the viability of the White Stream project was called into question by the Russia-Georgia conflict [of August 2008].'[1] While concern over the viability of White Stream from a security standpoint focuses more on the effects of regional conflicts on the calculations of Caspian producers about where to send their exports in the long run, others have implied that potential revenue gains from the existence of direct Caspian-centric energy corridors to Europe should permit the cooptation of even the most aggrieved parties of local opposition within the transit states (Grgic, 2009, p. 9).

Turkey's growing involvement in Europe-orientated Caspian Basin energy projects

Another hurdle that the aforementioned projects face is the existing operation of oil and gas projects that now cross Turkey. This is not an insurmountable hurdle, as Iranian, Turkish and now Chinese projects themselves succeeded in eroding Russia's once formidable monopoly on Caspian-origin pipeline routes. As discussed more extensively in Chapter 7, since 2006–07, the BTC and Baku–Tbilisi–Erzurum (BTE) pipelines have been transporting the respective bulk of Azerbaijan's oil and gas exports to the Turkish land mass, from where some fraction of them are shipped or piped onwards to the EU area. Officials in Ankara, the Commission and in some member states have touted Turkey as a route for conveying significantly larger supplies of hydrocarbons originating not only from the Caspian Basin states of Azerbaijan, Kazakhstan and Turkmenistan but also from the Middle Eastern countries of Egypt, Iraq and Iran. These plans have moved forward sporadically, slowed down not only by expected opposition from Russian interests, but also by inherent difficulties with each of these candidate suppliers.

West Shore: Azerbaijan

UK firm BP, successor to British Petroleum, both descendants of their seminal predecessor Anglo-Persian, has continued to occupy the forefront of efforts to produce and export oil and gas from fields located in Azerbaijan's territory along the western shore of the Caspian Sea. With nearly one-third plurality shares in both related projects, BP led the Azerbaijan International Oil Consortium (AIOC), which developed the Azeri–Chirag–Guneshli (ACG) oilfield cluster. An overlapping group of licensees, including leader BP, Norway's Statoil, with a nearly nine per cent share, and EU-headquartered firms Agip and Total, uninvolved in the ACG project but each with a five-per cent share in this pipeline (International Energy Agency, 2008b, p. 9), built the BTC pipeline, discussed more fully in the following chapter. As ACG oil started becoming available first from Chirag in late 1997 and later from the Azeri fields in late 2005 to early 2006, prior to completion of the BTC line, shipments of this earlier oil had to be exported by rail to Georgia's Black Sea port of Batumi or by pipeline, either from Azerbaijan's Sangachal Port at Baku to Russia's Black Sea port of Novorossiysk or via the AIOC's Western pipeline extension from Baku to Georgia's Supsa Port. In precise contrast to Agip and Total, US firm ExxonMobil, the one ACG licensee without any corollary share in the BTC, continued to pipe its quota of ACG oil to Supsa, although the pipeline in question underwent repairs between October 2006 and November 2008 (Energy Information Administration, 2009a, p. 3).

Prior to the BTC pipeline's construction, Azerbaijan's production had clearly been restrained by lack of adequate exportation capacity. As apparent from annual data issued by BP (2009, pp. 9–10), Azerbaijan achieved a 45-per cent jump in output and a three-fifths spike in export volumes between 2005 and 2006, the year that the BTC line was ushered into operation. Between 1998 and 2008, Azerbaijan nearly quadrupled its output from 11.4 to 44.7 mmta (Ibid., p. 9), becoming the 'largest contributor to Non-OPEC supply growth during 2006 and 2007' (Energy Information Administration, 2007, p. 2). In 2006 and 2007, respectively, approximately 44–51 per cent and 43–49 per cent of Azerbaijan's crude oil exports were shipped to the EU area.[2] Italy reportedly purchased approximately two-fifths of Azerbaijan's 2008 oil exports (Energy Information Administration, 2009a, p. 2), although Eurostat (2010a) data indicate that Italy bought 40–50 per cent of the EU27 area's imports of Azerbaijan's oil in 2006 and 2007.

Several members of these consortia, with a few key exceptions, also participated in bolstering Azerbaijan's natural gas production and exportation capabilities. Most of Azerbaijan's gas has been extracted from the offshore Shah Deniz field. Development of this field originated in a 1996 Production Sharing Agreement (PSA) involving a seven-member consortium that comprises leaders Statoil and BP, each with 25.5-per cent shares and joint leadership responsibilities, separate ten-per cent shareholders Eni-affiliated LukAgip, France's Total, Iran's Naftiran and Azerbaijan's State Oil Company (SOCAR) and Turkish Petroleum (TPAO), which holds a nine-per cent share. This group of licensees built the Shah Deniz gasfield as well as its complementary project the South Caucasus Pipeline (SCP) – also known as the BTE pipeline (see Chapter 7) – in 2007.

East Shore: Kazakhstan, Uzbekistan and Turkmenistan

Across the Caspian Sea, other European firms have been more prominent than BP in the upstream sector. Similar to Azerbaijan in facing a more dire need for foreign investment and assistance, not only to extract hydrocarbons but also to build new export routes, Kazakhstan, under the longstanding rule of Nursultan Nazarbayev, assented to PSAs in the buyer's market of the 1990s that collectively granted majority shares in field and pipeline projects to multinational corporations. Made up of EU-headquartered firms Eni (lead operator), Total and Shell and American ExxonMobil, each with identical shares of 18.52 per cent, as well as smaller stakeholders ConocoPhilips, Inpex and KazMunaiGaz, the Agip Kazakhstan North Caspian Operating Company (Agip KCO) has been undertaking to develop the challenging Kashagan giant offshore oilfield, estimated to contain recoverable oil reserves of 1730 mmt and total reserves-in-places of 5070 mmt (Energy Information Administration, 2008a, p. 3). The Karachaganak Petroleum (KPO) consortium, which includes Eni and lead operator British Gas (BG), each with 32.5-per cent shares in early 2008, one-fifth shareholder Chevron and ten-per cent shareholder Lukoil, has been tasked with operating the Karachaganak field, estimated to hold 1100–1200 mmt of oil and gas condensate and over 1000 bcm of natural gas (Ibid., p. 4).

This field's crude had little choice but to go to Russia for processing until a new pipeline spur came online in 2003. This allowed the oil, approximately 12.5 mmta in 2007, to be rerouted into the Caspian Pipeline Consortium (CPC)'s pipeline at Atyrau. This conduit, respectively 19 and 24 per cent owned by Kazakhstan and Transneft, transported nearly 35 mmta in 2007 (from the Kenkiyak, Karachaganak and Tengiz fields), over half of Kazakhstan's total oil exports, nearly 1600 km to Novorossiysk (Ibid., p. 5). Kashagan oil could eventually feed the BTC pipeline (of which Total and Eni each own five per cent) either by sub-sea pipeline or barge, already a means of carrying approximately 10 mmta of Kazakhstan oil (Ibid.). Although less than one-fifth of this volume went to Baku in 2007 for onwards rail delivery to Georgia's Batumi Port, the Kazakhstan Caspian Transportation System will encompass a new port at Kuryk south of Aktau, an upgraded tanker fleet, a new uploading terminal at Baku, and an interconnection to the BTC (International Energy Agency, 2008b, p. 54).

However, even in landlocked Kazakhstan, changes in the balance of power driven by the 2003–08 commodity boom were bound to have a deleterious business impact on European and American investments prospects. The government introduced price-indexed 'rent' and 'windfall profit' export-taxation mechanisms, ended tax-stabilisation guarantees, and capped foreign shares in offshore projects at 50 per cent in early 2004, imposed legal preemptions on interfirm transfers of oil assets in 2005, paving the way for it to buy out BG's share of the Kashagan project, and even legalised the unilateral abrogation of contracts in late 2007 (Energy Information Administration, 2008a, p. 7). Despite the field's hydrogen sulphide content and burial under highly pressurised natural gas, factors playing a significant role in lead operator Eni's decision to push its start up from 2005 back to 2011, Kazakhstan, suggesting that this delay had helped to inflate project costs from $57 to $136 billion, brought operations to a cessation and demanded $10 billion in compensation from Agip KCO in late 2007 (Ibid., p. 3). Eni was also accused of various tax violations (Dinmore and Gorst, 2007, p. 5). This paved the way for a forced renegotiation that resulted in the doubling of KazMunaiGaz's stake to 16.81 per cent, a corresponding reduction in each of the four main foreign shareholders' individual shares to 16.66 per cent and additional recompense via price-indexed payments to the government (Crooks, 2007, p. 26; Stern, 2007; Energy Information Administration, 2008a, p. 3).

In Kazakhstan, as in Russia, contract revisions and operational changes have sometimes followed charges of environmental violations and accompanying fines. Given the manner of contract renegotiation related to Russia's Sakhalin II offshore project, observers have imputed novel pretexts for engaging in 'resource nationalism' to these types of charges (Belton and Crooks, 2007, p. 7). In mid-2005, the government mandated that companies lower Kazakhstan's oil output enough to eliminate any concomitant flaring of gas, estimated at 8 bcm in 2006. This restriction, coupled with a sudden shutdown of its generators in 2005 that released sour gas into the atmosphere, suppressed output from the Tengizchevroil (TCO) consortium's Tengiz oilfield in 2005–06 and compelled implementation of a new $1 billion Sour Gas Injection (SGI) innovation that started to reverse Tengiz production declines in late 2007. Nonetheless, the consortium incurred a $609 million fine in 2007 for storing over 9 mmt of waste sulphur (Energy Information Administration, 2008a, pp. 3, 8). Other companies have faced similar problems on different projects. Stoppage that same year on Kashagan work was at least partially supported by official claims that the project induced the deaths of coastal seals (Gorst, 2007, p. 11). Sufficiently alarmed by this train of events, EU Energy Commissioner Andris Piebalgs admonished that the EU ' "would take adequate measures if the legal rights of European companies were put at risk" ' (quoted in Gorst, 2007, p. 11). Nonetheless, EU-headquartered firms continued to absorb the costs of doing business. In 2009, UK firm BG, which had been levied tax fines by Kazakhstan earlier in 2004 (Hoyos, 2004, p. 26), invoked international arbitration to try to recover £ 616 million in extra duties that had been assessed by Kazakhstan on the export of Karachaganak hydrocarbons (Tobin, 2009).

Uzbekistan and Turkmenistan, the other energy endowed eastern Caspian littoral countries, have been among the least permeable to the influence of EU institutions or EU member state-headquartered firms.

Although both produce and export relatively miniscule amounts of crude oil compared to their FSU counterparts Azerbaijan, Kazakhstan and Russia, they occupy more salient positions in the natural gas sector. In 2008, according to data provided by the Energy Information Administration (2010) database, Uzbekistan exported as much as gas as Azerbaijan and Kazakhstan combined, with Uzbekistan and Turkmenistan collectively exporting 63 bcma, approximately one-quarter of Russian volumes. Yet, as each country has been governed by highly dictatorial regimes that have not offered clear and consistent ground rules, neither has been able to attract significant inflows of foreign direct investment (FDI) from the EU27 economy, nor have they built any independent capacity to transport their hydrocarbons directly to Europe. Indeed, any gas from these two countries that reaches the EU area has already been bundled into export streams that are controlled by Gazprom and mostly sold via opaquely intermediary trading arrangements.

Both countries' attitudes towards EU-centric investment and exports have ranged from indifferent to ambiguous. Uzbekistan President Islam Karimov, who has faced EU sanctions over his government's role in the 2005 Andijan massacre, has dismissed outright almost any prospects of shipping gas into a trans-Caspian pipeline (AFP, 2008). On the other hand, Turkmenistan's government, which changed hands from now deceased Saparmurad Niyazov, the self-styled 'Head of the Turkmen', to Gurbanguly Berdymukhamedov, has stoked new hopes on the part of foreign investors looking to enter Turkmenistan's upstream gas sector. In mid-2009, during the Russo-Turkmen imbroglio over Russia's sudden halt to the passage of Turkmen gas flows into the Central Asia-Centre (CAC) pipeline, which caused an explosion in the latter, the Berdymukhamedov government granted German firm RWE, the newest partner in the Nabucco Pipeline Project consortium, exploration rights in its Caspian Sea territory (Globe and Mail, 2009, p. B6). However, while other Western firms, including Chevron, BP and Shell, have expressed interest in gaining similar E&P rights to Turkmenistan's onshore deposits, Turkmenistan has thus far confined its enticements to less alluring service contracts (Shiryaevskaya, 2010).

Chinese resource demand and EU energy security

In contrast to the EU, the PRC, which stands out as one of the fastest growing economies, energy consumers and energy importers, has also sought to diversify its importation portfolio. In many ways, the nature of the growth in the Chinese economy and energy consumption has replicated the industrial revolution itself. While the sustained high rates of expansion in the Chinese economy have largely been powered by access to relatively abundant domestic coal reserves, the increasing intrusion of concerns over carbon emissions and mine safety have helped to accelerate efforts to develop nuclear power and find new sources of oil and gas, in which China had been relatively self-sufficient until sometime in the past two decades. Since the early 1990s, when it became a net importer of petroleum, China has largely become dependant on Persian Gulf energy sources, which it has had to import through an easterly succession of maritime channels (in turn, the Hormuz and Malacca straits) that pose an array of interdiction risks to this trade from armed conflict, piracy and terrorism. Thus, while its state-led corporations have notably expanded China's supplier repertoire by acquiring oil assets in Africa, especially the Sudan, they have also supported building new pipelines to Russia and establishing a larger scope of overseas routes to source countries in the Western Hemisphere, primarily Brazil, Canada, Ecuador and Venezuela.

While they will contribute to keeping some floor under prices, the ways in which China is attempting to fulfil its oil demand, may have a more direct impact on the US than on Europe. However, since 2006, China has been importing oil from Kazakhstan via pipeline, and this development, coupled with endeavours to build new Sino-Russian pipelines that officials in Moscow have implied will afford Russia greater diversity of export channels, could negate European-centric plans to augment Kazakhstan supplies for the BTC or Odessa–Brody routes. Moreover, China has looked in a similar direction, towards Russia and Turkmenistan, with which it inaugurated a new pipeline in late 2009 that also crosses Uzbekistan and Kazakhstan before reaching Urumqi in PRC's restive province of Xinjiang, in its efforts to augment its natural gas imports, most of which arrived heretofore in the form of LNG from Australia. As Turkmenistan's gas serves as one of the largest potential non-Russian sources of new European supply (via the aforementioned trans-Caspian options or less directly, through Iran), this Sino-Turkmen pipeline potentially removes these volumes from consideration.

China's energy demand

Although its economy was placed on a proto-capitalist footing as early as 1978, over a decade before the collapse of the Soviet Union, China has experienced prodigious growth in both its economy and its energy use over the past two decades.[3] This expansion has occurred in both absolute and relative terms. In absolute terms, China's total primary energy demand of 758.4 million tonnes of oil equivalent (mtoe), which accounted for 9 per cent of the world total in 1993, rose 164 per cent by 2008 to reach nearly 2003 mtoe, or 18 per cent of the world total. While it consumed approximately 57 per cent of what the EU15 consumed in 1993, by 2008, it was using 270 mtoe more than the EU. China's domestic coal reserves, which account for seven per cent of the global total, have continued to provide the lion's share of China's overall energy needs. While coal met three-quarters of China's energy demand in 1993, by 2008, this fraction had dropped only fractionally, to seven-tenths. In fact, over the 15-year period in question, while coal's share of world total primary energy demand increased from 26 to 29 per cent, China's coal use, which made up 26 per cent of world coal consumption in 1993, climbed by an even larger multiple (150 per cent) to account for 43 per cent of world coal consumption.

Because of the absolute and relative increase in its energy demand, which remains dominated by the burning of coal, China also became the top-ranking emitter of carbon dioxide by 2007.[4] In 1990, China's CO_2 emissions of 2.244 billion mt represented only 11 per cent of the global total, a fraction that paled in comparison to the EU's 19-per cent share and the 23-per cent US share. However, in line with its overall percentage increase in energy demand, China's CO_2 output rose 171 per cent to 6.071 billion mt, or 21 per cent of 2007 global CO_2 emissions, edging out the US and putting the PRC leagues ahead of the EU, where carbon emissions actually declined between 1990 and 2007. During this time frame, the rise in Chinese coal-related carbon emissions made up 80 per cent of global increase in coal-generated emissions and nearly two-fifths of the increase in total world CO_2 emissions.

China's consumption of other energy sources has risen in tandem with its high economic growth rates, although more in absolute terms than in relation to its coal usage. In the decade and a half between 1993 and 2008, China endeavoured to augment its use of energy sources that limit carbon emissions and dependency on imports. The country managed to quadruple its generation of hydroelectric power and treble its share of the world's total from 6 to 18 per cent, and its reliance on nuclear power climbed exponentially, from a modest base of 0.4 mtoe to nearly 15.5 mtoe. In an area where Chinese activity has drawn the most attention from the rest of the international community because of the significant amount of new importation entailed, China increased its oil consumption from 140.5 to 375.7 mmt, 53 per cent as much as in the

EU. Although oil continued to provide 19 per cent of total PRC primary energy demand, this increase doubled China's share to ten per cent of global oil demand. By 2008, natural gas demand by China had nearly quintupled to 72.6 mtoe, or nearly 81 bcma (three per cent of world natural gas demand), 17 per cent of EU demand.

The PRC's hydrocarbon import profile

Oil

Rapid expansion in China's economy and energy demand transformed it into a large net importer of fossil fuels.[5] While it was a net exporter of 35 mtoe of energy in 1990, it lost this capacity in mid-decade, turning into a net importer of 167 mtoe by 2007. While it covered its needs for hydroelectric power, nuclear energy and other renewables from domestic production, which provided just under 15 per cent of its total energy production in 2007, it imported over half of the oil component of its total primary energy supply (47 per cent of its crude oil needs) that same year. In 2007, crude oil filled over 95 per cent of China's total net energy import basket, and PRC net crude oil imports were third in size after those of the US and Japan. In 2008, China imported nearly 179 mmta of crude oil, nearly half of which came from the Middle East, three-tenths from Africa, three per cent from the Asia-Pacific region, and 17 per cent from an assortment of other source areas, and Saudi Arabia and Angola accounted for one-third of China's crude oil imports (Energy Information Administration, 2009b, p. 6). Chinese crude oil imports, which originated from a diverse array of suppliers comprising 40 countries, grew nearly 14 per cent between 2008 and 2009. Saudi Arabia gained another 15 per cent of the Chinese market to acquire the single largest share (24 per cent) and Angola obtained another seven to eight per cent to increase its portion to 16 per cent of PRC crude oil imports, thus bringing their combined share to two-fifths of the Chinese market (Chinaoilweb.com, 2010).

China has accelerated its acquisition of new assets and supplies from outside its traditional Middle Eastern and Asian-Pacific wellsprings. China slowly but gradually filled its import basket with more FSU and Latin American oil. While the Middle East and Africa continued to dominate the Chinese import basket, the FSU supplied nearly 11 per cent, with roughly one-third of this coming from Azerbaijan and Kazakhstan (see below) and two-thirds from Russia. Five South American countries – Argentina, Brazil, Colombia, Ecuador and Venezuela – covered slightly more than six per cent of PRC crude oil importation requirements

(Ibid.). As part of China's overall strategy of leveraging its deep official reserves to secure energy supplies from a range of developing producer countries, the return of an energy buyer's market in late 2008 found the China Development Bank in the enviable financial position of being able to underwrite new 'oil-for-loan' deals to Brazil (€ 7.4 billion, at the mid-2009 exchange rate, for up to 10 mmta of oil over 10 years to China Petrochemical Corporation, or Sinopec), Kazakhstan (€ 7.4 billion) and Russia (€ 18.5 billion) (Oster, 2009, p. B8). Between 2008 and 2009, Chinese consumption of Brazilian and Russian oil increased by nearly one-third (Chinaoilweb.com, 2010). Chinese loans to Rosneft and Transneft of $40 billion in 2009 were directed to building a 69-km spur to bring Russian oil via the Eastern Siberia–Pacific Ocean (ESPO) Pipeline to the Chinese border and then into a 961-km pipeline to China's longtime workhorse Daqing oilfield (Energy Information Administration, 2009b, pp. 7–8).

While much of the focus on the new 'scramble for Africa' or other drives to acquire new assets features China pitted against the US, the EU27 area, which is significantly more dependant on foreign oil suppliers than the US, might be proportionally more vulnerable to the effects of China's growing petroleum importation requirements. As implied by the increasing EU reliance on FSU energy, this involves Russia more than Africa, Latin America and the Middle East, from where EU27 imports decreased by approximately one-quarter, from 322 mmta in 1992 to 243 mmta in 2007 (Eurostat, 2010a). While EU27 energy security is analytically framed in the aggregate, vulnerability to expanding demand by external actors for the pool of the area's available energy supplies varies by member state and supplier country. For example, significant increases in demand for Angolan, Brazilian, Iraqi, Libyan and Russian oil could put China on a potential collision course with France, the single largest EU importer of Angolan oil, Portugal (Brazil), Italy (Iraq and Libya) and Germany (Russia) (Ibid.; Chinaoilweb.com, 2010). As discussed below, China's pipeline projects may also clash with EU aspirations vis-à-vis the FSU as well.

Gas

The gradual increase in China's natural gas demand has also driven a more energetic search for foreign suppliers. China became a net importer of this energy source in 2007, the year after it first resorted to foreign suppliers.[6] Until 2010, it had been receiving all of its natural gas imports as LNG, which it started shipping from Australia in 2006, in an annual amount of 950 mcm, which came to less than one per cent of global LNG trade, below two per cent of the EU's LNG imports, and just under five per cent of Australia's LNG exports (International Energy Agency, 2009d, p. II. 54). This gas is brought to Dapeng re-gasification terminal in Guangdong, a joint venture between China National Offshore Oil Corporation (CNOOC) and BP, under a 25-year contract to buy up to 4.395 bcma from Australia's North West Shelf liquefaction terminal (Energy Information Administration, 2009b, pp. 12–13). By 2007 and 2008, Chinese had raised its LNG import volumes to 4.020 bcma and 4.335 bcma, respectively, with over four-fifths of these coming from Australia (which in turn sent 16 per cent of its LNG exports to the PRC), and the rest from Algeria and Nigeria (both years), Oman (in 2007) and Egypt and Equatorial Guinea (in 2008) (International Energy Agency, 2009d, p. II. 55).

It appears on the surface that China is gearing up to place itself on a more competitive importation footing vis-à-vis LNG importers in the EU area. According to data found in the Energy Information Administration (2009b, p. 13), China has two re-gasification terminals, Dapeng and Fujian, and is planning to add seven more, lifting its initial LNG re-gasification capacity from 10 bcma to nearly 37 bcm per year, which, if expanded, could even reach 50 bcma within this decade. Two projects, Dalian and Rudong, slated to bring up to 8.7 bcma of Qatari gas after 2011, are being undertaken by the PetroChina subsidiary of CNPC. However, CNPC has reportedly entered into agreements with European firms Shell and Total and CNOOC has arranged to buy 4.8 bcma of Australian gas from UK firm BG over two decades (Ibid.). Thus, Chinese and EU interests have been more co-operative than rivalrous in terms of developing global LNG supplies. This is not necessarily the case in terms of laying pipelines to divert the coveted natural gas deposits of the FSU.

Chinese pipeline inroads to Central Asia

Pipelines may represent a type of Faustian bargain in the realm of energy security. This path was taken by then members of the European Economic Community (EEC), especially West Germany, when, in the wake of the 1973–74 Arab oil embargo, which compounded existing European concerns over coal-based pollution, they moved to supplant some fraction of their dependence on this oil with natural gas (and oil) from the Soviet Union. This, however, laid the foundation for European consumers' sometimes irksome dependence on Russian gas (Goldman, 2008, pp. 136–9). While Chinese plans in this respect were conceived in the 1990s, pipelines accessing oil from Kazakhstan and gas from

Turkmenistan (via Uzbekistan and Kazakhstan) have now been built and brought into operation. These projects were constructed with material assistance from Chinese state-influenced corporations, not so much to allay PRC fears of another oil embargo, but in order to reduce China's vulnerability to a myriad of other potential threats to their Middle Eastern petroleum supply bases (Williams, 2006, p. 1081).

Kazakhstan oil

As if Europe did not already have enough hindrances to overcome in attempting to develop and route a larger supply of Kazakhstan oil westward around Russian territory, now they must also factor in a potentially more serious source of demand-based competition from China to the east, which has a much larger and more dynamic economy than Russia. In relation to oil from the Persian Gulf, upon which China's import basket is most reliant, FSU oil shipments to China earlier in the twenty-first century were miniscule and based primarily on rail shipments, in volumes of 6–9 mmta from the erstwhile firm Yukos (Zweig and Jianhai, 2005, p. 28), which has been disbanded and its assets largely absorbed into by Gazprom's oil division. While China imported approximately 11.6 mmta of oil in 2008 and 15.3 mmta in 2009 from Russia, its imports of oil from Kazakhstan grew to over 5.5 mmta in 2008 and 6 mmta in 2009 (Chinaoilweb.com, 2010).

This represents the culmination of earlier Chinese efforts to build pipeline connections to access hydrocarbons from its Central Asian neighbours. Based on seminal Sino-Kazakhstan agreements, the first in 1997 to buy – some have claimed overpaid for – three-fifths of Kazakhstan firm Aktobemunaigaz and the latter's Aktobe oilfields and a second one in 1999 placing CNPC in charge of building and financing the pipeline (Williams, 2006, p. 1081; International Energy Agency, 2008b, p. 53), CNPC undertook to build a 2163-km pipeline in three phases to deliver oil from Kazakhstan to China. The shortest 449-km section, which actually routes oil in a westerly direction from Aktobe to Atyrau, was ironically the first to be completed, in 2004, so, while CNPC's accounting ledger may have been bolstered, China did not see any physical flows from Kazakhstan until the 2006 completion of the second phase of the project, a 962-km section that pumps oil from KazMunaiGaz's Kumkol field to Alashankou in China (International Energy Agency, 2008b, p. 53). Although the recent economic crisis pushed back completion of the pipeline's final 762-km leg between Kenkiyak and Kumkol, which could double the pipeline's present capacity to 20 mmta and is partially contingent on the Kashagan field's development, it also presented CNPC with an opportune moment, one not fully seized, to acquire a larger share of KazMunaiGaz assets with new loans (Energy Information Administration, 2009b, p. 7; Dyer and Lau, 2009, p. 1; International Energy Agency, 2008b, p. 54). The pipeline could provide about five per cent of China's current oil demand (International Energy Agency, 2008b, p. 54) and one-tenth of its import needs (Chinaoilweb.com, 2010).

Turkmenistan gas

China acted with even greater alacrity in securing contracts to import gas from Turkmenistan, which possesses the largest exportable supply among all Caspian littoral states except Russia but had, until late 2009, lacked direct export access to markets that were more lucrative than Iran. Following a seminal 2006 Sino-Turkmenistan agreement, CNPC in 2007 signed a coveted PSA to develop Turkmenistan's South Yolotan gas fields and another accord with state firm Turkmengaz to invest over $2 billion in building a 2000-km Central Asian Gas Pipeline (CAGP), extending from about 188 km south of the Turkmen–Uzbekistan boundary to the Sino-Kazakhstan border, to import gas over a 30-year period, in volumes starting from 10 bcma at the 2010 inception of the pipeline and reaching 30–40 bcma by 2012 (Energy Information Administration, 2008a, p. 9; 2009b, p. 12; International Energy Agency, 2008b, pp. 22, 62–3). Potential maximum post-2012 supplies from Turkmenistan could fill most of China's natural gas importation gap by 2020, which is projected to reach at least 40 bcma (International Energy Agency, 2008b, p. 22). In 2008, work accelerated on the Uzbekistan and Kazakhstan sections, the latter of which could be linked up to the internal Beynau–Bozoi–Akbulak Gas Pipeline to take smaller amounts of gas from Kazakhstan to China (Energy Information Administration, 2009b, p. 12; International Energy Agency, 2008b, pp. 22, 63).

The CAGP was inaugurated in December 2009, available to ship gas from Turkmenistan to the Chinese province of Xinjiang. In fact, the aforementioned April 2009 explosion on the CAC pipeline that Turkmenistan attributed to Gazprom's stoppage, which itself seems to have been related to its preference for lowering the price paid for Turkmenistan gas, helped to speed construction not only of the PRC-bound pipeline but also of a second pipeline to Iran, starting at 6 bcma (like the first one), but eventually rising to 12 bcma (Socor, 2009). While these pipelines certainly strengthened both Turkmenistan's exportation and China's importation options, they have potential negative ramifications for the prospects of broadening the EU's gas supply base.

Admittedly, given the lack of consistent and transparent information on the size of Turkmenistan's reserves, these projects may be less of a blow to Europe (less vis-à-vis the Iran-bound lines than the China-bound one) than to Russia, which eventually agreed to resume Gazprom's gas purchases on terms more favourable to Turkmenistan and to build the Prikaspiiski Pipeline to supplement the CAC's capacity (Blank, 2010). The most obviously relevant concern is that China, as a unitary actor that has weathered the latest economic crisis better than most European countries, has reduced Europe's pool of potentially available Turkmenistan gas and thus rendered the construction of any trans-Caspian sub-sea pipeline less viable. Conversely, others have pointed out that the most likely source of Turkmenistan natural gas for Europe, other than those volumes that might reach Europe via Iran and Turkey, would be western littoral deposits originating offshore or as gas associated with offshore oil output, not the eastern reserve base of Chinese supplies (Petersen, 2009; Socor, 2009).

Conclusion: Asian bumps or craters in the way of EU energy security?

Officials in EU institutions and member states have frequently implied and expressed their apprehensions not only about their reliance on their existing portfolio of non-EU energy supplies but also about proportionally increased reliance on the existing mix of suppliers located in this portfolio. As discussed in Chapter 5, only a subset of EU member states, including the UK and those on the southwestern coastlines of the European continent, have succeeded in achieving a wider range of gas-supplier diversity by developing the requisite infrastructure to receive and re-gasify tanker shipments of LNG, the bedrock of any future gas 'spot market' that would mimic the oil trade. For the most part, however, Europe and the EU have kept their dominant focus trained on the physical expansion and improved operation of the pipeline network – that is, by enhancing storage capacity and interconnectivity levels.

Though the state-backed corporate undertaking of projects with Transneft and Gazprom suggests an opposite tack, EU institutions, member-governments and headquartered companies have prudently refrained from putting so many of the Union's eggs in the Russian energy basket that they preclude the building of any other economic or physical links to foreign energy suppliers that require these connections to bypass Russia. In fact, the EU and its member states have shown clear recognition, as manifest in the Energy Commission-backed 'southern corridor' project, that the energy resources of the Caspian Sea Basin, especially those belonging to the non-Russian FSU littoral states of Azerbaijan, Kazakhstan and Turkmenistan, could serve as a valuable supplement to diversifying the EU27's energy supply repertoire if those producers had truly independent outlets for their exports. Some EU-based actors have expressed preferences for building such projects as the Odessa–Brody and PEOP and the White Stream gas route, which would transport non-Russian FSU Caspian energy reserves across Azerbaijan, Georgia and the Black Sea.

Those trans-Caucasian projects on the EU's planner avoid not only Russian but also Turkish territory. In fact, they have even been justified on the basis that they would relieve tanker-traffic congestion and reduce the risk of accident and environmental damage in the narrow Bosporus Straits, which separates Istanbul's and Turkey's European and Asian shores. However, these projects involve relatively miniscule volumes of energy, have attained negligible levels of financing and have also invited Russian efforts to thwart or subvert them. By contrast, the BTC oil pipeline and the BTE or South Caucasus (gas) Pipeline (SCP), the first projects brought into operation to access Caspian energy supplies without passing through Russia, do cross Turkey's terrain and have thus acquired a position of incumbency with respect to any future trans-Caucasian schemes. Conversely, the landlocked non-Russian FSU states on the Caspian's eastern rim have been busy crystallising their 'multi-vector' foreign policy orientation in the form of exports pipelines branching south to Iran and east to China. While not necessarily confining Europe-orientated trans-Caspian projects to oblivion, these pipelines heighten the immediacy of the EU27's need to act more concertedly in advancing its interests.

Part III

Turkey as a Transit and Candidate Country

7
Turkey's Role as a 'Trans-European' Energy Corridor

Introduction

Pronounced European Union (EU) reliance on oil and gas imports is exacerbated by the nature and limited number of its source regions. As Russia supplies one-quarter of EU gas consumption and 40 per cent of its total import requirements, while Middle Eastern Organization of Petroleum Exporting Countries (OPEC) states account for a slightly larger fraction of the EU's imported oil, it makes political–economic sense for the EU to diversify its supply sources (European Commission, 2001, p. 2). Nonetheless, despite advocating greater diversification of energy sources and suppliers, the European Commission (Ibid., pp. 22–3) understands that the present profile of EU hydrocarbon dependence on Russia, the Caspian, the Middle East and North Africa is unlikely to change markedly. Especially in the context of EU–Russian energy relations, the EU has recognised Turkey's potential value as a relatively secure *and* independent route for importing non-Russian energy supplies (Tekin and Walterova, 2007). This chapter analyses the role of Turkey as an independent (of Russia) conduit for third-party (notably Caspian and Middle Eastern) energy supplies to Europe, while remaining cognisant of the distinct possibility that Turkey, which is also highly dependent on Russian energy (especially gas) supplies, could also emerge as a new conduit for routing these supplies to the EU area.

Turkey's candidacy as a major energy corridor to Europe lies in its geographical propinquity to the energy-rich regions of Russia, the Caspian Basin and the Persian Gulf, thus complementing Europe's relatively favourable terms of access to North African sources. In fact, Turkey lies near regions possessing over 70 per cent of the world's proven oil and gas reserves (Roberts, 2004, p. 1). The United Nations Economic

Commission for Europe (2006, p. 9) has estimated that Turkey may host 6–7 per cent of global oil transport by 2012. Nonetheless, although Turkey's role as an oil-transit country is important for regional exporters, it is less vital for global importers because of oil's greater fungibility (Roberts, 2004, p. 19). By contrast, states in producing regions holding over one-third of gas reserves have expressed varying degrees of interest in using Turkey as a transit country to the EU (Roberts, 2004, p. 1; Tekin and Williams, 2009a, 2009b).

Most of this chapter is dedicated to the analysis of Turkey as an energy corridor between the producers in its neighbourhood and the consumers in Europe. It focuses on the question of how Turkey could fulfil such a role. It discusses Turkey's existing, but limited, role in transporting non-Russian gas to Greece (and in the near future to Italy) as well as the prospects for completion of the EU-backed Nabucco pipeline, which is slated to convey even larger volumes of non-Russian gas from the Caspian and Middle East. Here the chapter also considers the counter-scenario of a Pyrrhic victory for Nabucco, wherein the project is built but becomes used as a secure – but *non-independent* – conduit for Russian gas. However, before going into the subject of Turkey as an energy transit country, a short evaluation of Turkey's own energy needs is necessary for a fuller grasp of its energy policy motives.

Turkey's energy profile in brief

Turkish energy sector traditionally depended on natural gas, coal and hydropower. However, in the recent decade, it has attempted to expand into two new areas: renewable resources and nuclear energy. It ratified the Kyoto Protocol on 5 February 2009. As an overall energy strategy, Turkey aims to achieve the following targets by 2023 (Turkish Ministry of Energy and Natural Resources, 2010b, p. 1):

1. To be able to make complete use of its potential of indigenous coal and hydraulic resources;
2. To make maximum use of renewable resources;
3. To incorporate nuclear energy into electricity generation in the period until 2020;
4. To secure rapid and continuous improvement in energy efficiency in a way that parallels EU countries.

Turkey is highly dependent on external energy resources. Its limited indigenous energy resources are solid fuels and hydropower, which

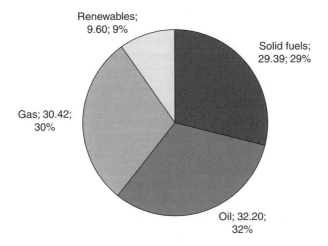

Figure 7.1   Turkey's gross inland consumption (energy mix in mtoe, %) (2007).
Source: Market Observatory for Energy (2009b, p. 7).

together made up 89 per cent of total domestic production of 27.3 mtoe in 2007. As Figure 7.1 shows, in the same year, Turkey consumed a total of 101.5 mtoe, with oil, gas and solid fuels each with approximately 30 per cent shares and renewables with the remaining 10 per cent. Recent forecasts indicate that the energy demand growth in Turkey will be 6–8 per cent per year for the foreseeable future.

Therefore, Turkey is highly dependent on energy imports, especially in terms of oil and gas. For example, in 2008, Turkey's oil and gas import dependencies were respectively 93 per cent and 97.3 per cent (Enerji ve Tabii Kaynaklar Bakanligi (Turkish Ministry of Energy and Natural Resources), 2010a, pp. 25–6). In 2007, Turkey imported its oil needs, albeit in declining volumes, from Russia, Iran and Saudi Arabia, with additional lesser volumes coming from Libya, Iraq and Syria (Energy Information Administration, 2009d). Furthermore, as Table 7.1 indicates, over the period 2000–06 Turkey imported its growing gas needs from four main suppliers. Important source countries include Russia, Iran, Azerbaijan, Algeria and Nigeria, with Russia alone supplying the most.

Turkey is poor in energy resources but neighbours the world's richest energy producing regions. Therefore, it is strategically positioned to act as a type of 'bridge' between Caspian and Middle Eastern oil and gas producers and European (and other) consumers. Indeed, 'Turkey's development as a European energy hub looks natural' and Turkey aims

Table 7.1   Turkey's natural gas imports based on source countries (million cubic metres) (2000–09)

Years	Russian Federation (WEST)	Blue Stream	Iran	Azerbaijan	Algeria LNG	Nigeria LNG	Spot LNG	TPAO	Total
2000	10,082				3,594	704		151	14,531
2001	10,928		114		3,626	1,198			15,866
2002	11,574		660		3,722	1,139			17,095
2003	11,229	1,231	3,461		3,794	1,107			20,822
2004	10,919	3,183	3,498		3,182	1,016			21,798
2005	12,639	4,885	4,248		3,815	1,013		136	26,736
2006	12,038	7,278	5,594		4,211	1,099		87	30,307
2007	13,565	9,188	6,054	1258	3,255	1,396	1117	40	35,873
2008	13,156	9,806	4,113	4580	4,220	1,017	333	895	38,120
2009	7,680	9,527	5,253	4960	4,486	903	259		33,068

Source: Enerji ve Tabii Kaynaklar Bakanligi (Turkish Ministry of Energy and Natural Resources) (2010b, p. 26).

to 'become a major European energy hub' (Barysch, 2007a, pp. 1–2). This has impelled a certain deepening of energy relations between Turkey and the EU, which views Turkey as a potential energy corridor that may ease the complications associated with its energy heavy dependence on Russia and extant transit countries Belarus and Ukraine. Currently, no specific energy agreements exist between the EU and Turkey to regulate its transit role. Turkey is an observer in the South-East Europe Energy Community Treaty (SEEECT), but negotiations on Turkey's full participation in the Community have been underway since September 2009 (Market Observatory for Energy, 2009b, p. 2).

In preview of the fuller discussion in Chapter 8, it is worth noting a distinction between the competing roles of 'energy hub' and 'energy corridor' – one with potentially critical political implications for Turkey's EU accession bid. While Turkey has strongly supported bringing more Caspian energy to Europe, its backing has been muddled by competing imperatives. As implied by one EU official (van Aartsen, 2009, pp. 6, 9), one vexing issue revolves around whether Turkey, itself highly dependent on Russian gas and showing little propensity to risk jeopardising that energy trade, will serve as an *acquis*-regulated train pulling new energy supplies along their tracks to Europe or an energy 'broker' capitalising on its transit position to obtain parochial rent-seeking advantages. The former posture would both assure EU member states of the long-term payoffs of underwriting trans-Turkey pipelines and place EU consumers in a less-mediated commercial relationship with the relevant group of suppliers, such that, unlike the cases of Belarus and Ukraine, Turkish 'transit' would become less politically freighted. By contrast, 'brokerage' behaviour could easily dissuade the EU from staking too much of its energy security objectives on Turkey.

Turkey's existing and planned pipeline systems

Geographical advantages have afforded Turkey the opportunity to play the role of an 'energy bridge' or 'energy supermarket' (Bahgat, 2002, p. 317). As Roberts (2004, p. 19) states, '[w]ith the EU already in receipt of large volumes of gas from the three main sources – Russia, the North Sea and North Africa – Turkey's goal is to become Europe's fourth main artery.' Thus, Turkey actively seeks to become a pipeline-based transit country.

Existing pipeline system

The Turkish system has two main corridors of energy transport: the East–West corridor and the North–South corridor. The East–West corridor extends from the Caspian, Iranian and Iraqi energy-producing areas via Turkey to locations in Europe. Currently, the central component of this corridor is the *BTC oil pipeline*, which runs for approximately 1768 km, connecting the Azeri–Chirag–Guneshli (ACG) field through Georgia to the Mediterranean port of Ceyhan in Turkey. Its construction began in 2002 and became operational in 2006. While taking nearly 40 mmta of ACG oil over the course of 2009 (Botas, 2010), this pipeline can actually carry up to 60 mmta, an amount that may rise to 80–90 mmta based on post-2012 availability of Kazakhstan's oil (International Energy Agency, 2008b, p. 55). The Baku–Tbilisi–Ceyhan (BTC) was the first pipeline specifically designed to export Caspian oil without going through Russia (Barysch, 2007b, p.3). Naturally, Russia as well as those who argued that the project was not profitable and politically motivated opposed the project (Pravda, 2005). On the other hand, it was politically supported both by the US and EU. As the world energy prices skyrocketed in the wake of the US-led occupation of Iraq in 2003, the concerns about the commercial viability of the BTC pipeline disappeared (Williams and Tekin, 2008). Needless to say, the project served as a strategic step to connect landlocked Azerbaijan to western energy markets though Georgia, boosting the economic and political confidence of these countries and showing the determination of Turkey to become an East–West energy corridor (Tekin and Walterova, 2007).

Another route in the East–West energy corridor is the *Kirkuk–Ceyhan* or *Iraq–Turkey (IT) oil pipeline*. Its first phase built in 1976, the pipeline extends 986 km and is Iraq's largest crude oil export pipeline. With the addition of a second parallel line in 1987, its total capacity reached 70.9 mmta (Botas, 2010). After the 1990 Gulf War, the pipeline was mostly shut down. Since the Iraq war in 2003, the pipeline has been used only sporadically (Fink, 2006, p. 2; Williams and Tekin, 2008). As Iraq becomes more stable and peaceful, the facilities will need to undergo repairs to reach their full operational capacity (Orekli, 2007, p. 8).

In addition to these oil pipelines, there are three gas pipelines in the East–West energy corridor. One of them is the *SCP* or *BTE pipeline*, built by the South Caucasus Pipeline (SCP) Company, which is itself owned by a consortium of BP, Statoil and other companies. Transmitting gas from the Shah Deniz gas field in Azerbaijan's sector of the Caspian Sea into Turkey's national gas grid, the SCP runs parallel to the BTC pipeline until it reaches the town of Erzurum in eastern Turkey. The initial capacity of the pipeline is 8.8 bcma. The capacity of Shah Deniz I was expected to top out at just under 10 bcma in 2010, but Shah Deniz Phase II, the commencement of which may nonetheless be pushed back until 2016 in the absence of a Turco-Azerbaijan transit agreement, is expected to bring 20 bcma onstream, making the SCP one of the most significant export routes from the gas-rich Caspian region (Alekperov, 2004, p. 120; Energy Information Administration, 2009a, p. 4). Gas delivery began at the end of 2006. As indicated in the US Energy Information Administration's database, Azerbaijan exported 1.15 bcma of gas in 2007 and 5.50 bcma in 2008. Most of this gas supplies the domestic needs of Georgia and Turkey, but a longer-term aim is to connect this gas up to the planned Nabucco Pipeline project (see below).

A second gas pipeline, the *Iran–Turkey natural gas pipeline*, has been in operation since 2001. It transfers gas from Iran's South Pars gas field to Turkey's gas grid near Erzurum. Iran currently provides 11 per cent of Turkey's total gas needs and is scheduled to fill about 20 per cent of Turkish consumption by 2020. This ranks Iran as the second largest gas exporter to Turkey after Russia. The Iranian pipeline is envisaged to become a supply route for the planned Nabucco pipeline. Nonetheless, Iran–West relations will need to improve for such a possibility to occur.

A third gas pipeline in the East-West corridor is the *TGII pipeline*. The first phase of the project, connecting Turkey and Greece, was built between 2005 and 2007 and inaugurated in 2007. The pipeline is 300 km long with current capacity of 7 bcma. Turkey–Greece–Italy

Interconnector (TGII) piped nearly 443 mcm in 2007 and 721 mcm in 2008 (Botas, 2010). When the second phase connects Greece and Italy as anticipated by 2012, capacity will rise to 11 bcma (Ibid.). In addition, there are plans to provide gas via this pipeline for a proposed Western Balkan pipeline as well as a 160-km branch pipeline connecting Komotini in Greece and Stara Zagora in Bulgaria (Tshkov, 2009). This pipeline has been viewed as an important component of South Eastern Gas Ring, which is supported by the EU as a Trans-European Networks-Energy (TEN-E) project. Given the level of European participation involved in the Shah Deniz Project and the volumes of gas that the latter is scheduled to produce for export into the SCP, much of this gas seems intended for sale in Europe. For instance, an accord between Turkey's state-run Botas pipeline operator and Greece–Italy Interconnector partners DEPA of Greece and Edison of Italy as well as a parallel 2006 tripartite inter-governmental agreement are premised on the projection that, after the trans-Adriatic (Greek–Italian) section of the TGII becomes operational, 16.6 bcma of gas will be available for division between Greece and Italy, with the latter obtaining over three-quarters of the total volume (Botas, 2010).

Azerbaijan's fields could conceivably supply this additional gas to Greece and Italy. However, given that the capacity of this 'southern corridor' interconnector pales in comparison to that of the Nabucco Pipeline (see below), which is also vying to take Caspian gas, and the Gazprom-backed South Stream Pipeline (see Chapter 4), rival projects to which Turkey has given its assent, Shah Deniz II gas will enjoy a more diverse choice of candidate transit routes to Europe. This may even include Russia, as suggested by a 2009 agreement to pipe more Azerbaijan gas to Russia contingent on modernisation of Soviet-era links (Energy Information Administration, 2009a, pp. 4–5). Whether it is eventually channelled into the TGII or into Nabucco, the SCP may serve as the intake point for Turkmenistan gas via a several proposed transportation options (see below).

Though these pipelines are important for energy transport in an East–West direction, Turkey already has an important gas route in the North–South corridor. The 1213-km *Blue Stream gas pipeline* cost $3.2 billion to build and was undertaken by Gazprom, Italian Eni and Turkish Botas. Officially inaugurated in November 2005, it is designed to deliver Russian gas directly to Turkey under the Black Sea. It consists of three parts: the Russian section extending from Izobilnoye to Dzhugba in Russia, a submarine leg across the Black Sea and the Turkish section connecting Samsun to Ankara (Gazprom, 2010). Blue Stream was due to reach a capacity of 16 bcma in 2010 (Barysch, 2007a, p. 3). This pipeline originally aimed to serve Turkish domestic needs as existing contracts do not allow for re-exportation of Russian gas to third countries. However, Turkish state company, Botas, and Gazprom have occasionally discussed the issue of using Blue Stream (or building and utilising a parallel Blue Stream 2) as a gas transmission corridor to serve other countries as well. Indeed, it is possible to use Blue Stream to ship gas from Russia to Europe as an alternative route to the Ukrainian one. Another alternative involves utilising expanded Blue Stream to deliver gas to Israel and a few other countries in the Middle East (Alexander's Gas and Oil Connections, 2007).

The North–South corridor includes another oil pipeline project in the construction phase: the *Unye–Ceyhan pipeline* (also called the Trans-Anatolian pipeline). The aim of this project is to pipe Russian and Kazakh oil from Turkey's Black Sea town of Unye to the Mediterranean oil terminal in Ceyhan, thus providing the potential capacity to reduce tanker traffic on the Turkish straits by up to 50 per cent. The project has been jointly undertaken by Italian Eni and Turkish Calik Enerji. This 550-km pipeline is estimated to cost $2 billion and come into operation by 2012 with a throughput capacity of 1.5 million barrels per day. This project is highly important as another means of bypassing the Turkish straits (Bosporus and Dardanelles), which have been under recurring environmental threat from heavy oil-tanker traffic (International Energy Agency, 2006).

Two oil and three gas pipelines in the East-West corridor and one pipeline each for gas and oil transportation (to become operational in 2012) in the North-South corridor comprise the current energy pipeline system in Turkey. Though Turkey has succeeded in building this relatively elaborate system, there are a number of new projects that, if realised, are likely to turn Turkey into an important energy hub within its surrounding region, especially one that can cater to Europe's current and future energy needs.

Projects in the planning stages

Relevant project plans include the Trans-Caspian gas pipeline, Arab gas pipeline (AGP) and Nabucco. The first two would connect gas-exporting countries with the Turkish grid whereas the latter would connect Turkey to the consuming countries of Europe. Therefore, one can consider the Nabucco pipeline and the existing and planned gas transmission routes as elements of a larger interconnected pipeline system.

The *Trans-Caspian gas pipeline* aims to transit gas from Turkmenistan (and possibly Kazakhstan) via the Caspian Sea to Azerbaijan. It would then link to the SCP delivering gas to Erzurum in Turkey, thus bypassing both Russia and Iran. This project was initially proposed by the US in the late 1990s and signed onto by Turkey, Georgia, Azerbaijan and Turkmenistan. In October 1998, Turkey and Turkmenistan signed a framework agreement to realise the Turkmenistan–Turkey–Europe natural gas pipeline, which was proposed to supply 30 bcma of gas, 16 bcma of which would be used by Turkey (Baran, 2005, pp. 115–6; Botas, 2010). However, due to strong Russian and Iranian opposition to a trans-Caspian pipeline on the basis of environmental concerns as well as the unresolved status of the Caspian Sea (see Chapter 3), the project never gained critical momentum. In the wake of the 2006 Russia–Ukraine gas dispute, however, EU support for the project firmed up while the Turkmen and Kazakh governments seemed to favour reviving the project. Yet, a year later in 2007, as elaborated on in Chapter 5, Russia signed a counter-agreement with Kazakhstan and Turkmenistan to deliver Central Asian gas to Europe through the Russia-bound pipeline system (Hagelund, 2009). A 2007 EU programme study identified two intriguing alternatives to what has shaped up to be an increasingly costly (both economically and politically) full-length subsea trans-Caspian Pipeline. One consists of relaying compressed natural gas (CNG) via an array of complementary apparatuses, including a compressor station, CNG shuttle carriers and a decompressor station. The other involves a shorter mid-Caspian bridge that would essentially join the extant Azerbaijan and Turkmenistan offshore pipeline infrastructures (International Energy Agency, 2008b, p. 64; Socor, 2009).

Another suggested new pipeline is the *Arab gas pipeline*, which connects Arish in Egypt to Kilis in Turkey. This pipeline has several parts. The first part is already operational, delivering Egyptian gas to Aqaba in Jordan since 2003. Including a 16-km subsea segment through the Red Sea, this part extends 248 km with a total capacity of 10 bcma. The second part travels 390 km through Jordan's Aqaba port to El Rehab near the Syrian border (Gulf Oil and Gas, 2003). The third section goes from the Jordanian–Syrian border to the Turco-Syrian border, traversing 600 km through Syria. In 2008, the 319-km first segment was completed and began operations (Forward Magazine, 2008). The second segment will extend from Aleppo in Syria to Kilis in Turkey. That same year, Syria and Turkey signed another agreement to build a 63-km connection from Aleppo in Syria to Kilis in Turkey within the framework of the AGP, the construction of which is expected to be completed in 2011.

Moreover, in 2006, Egypt, Jordan, Syria, Turkey and Romania signed an agreement to extend the AGP into the Turkish grid near Kilis to deliver gas to Europe via the planned Nabucco project in the future. Interestingly, the AGP could be also used for the delivery of Iraqi gas to European consumers via the planned Nabucco project. Though this agreement did not came to fruition, Iraq, Egypt, Jordan, Lebanon and Syria signed an agreement in 2004 to link the Iraqi gas grid to the AGP in order to facilitate gas exports from Iraq to Europe. The inclusion of Iraq in the AGP was welcomed by the EU Commission as a development potentially contributing to Europe's supply security (ABHaber, 2008).

Nabucco: piping gas through Turkey

Among projects in the planning stages, the most dramatic one is the Nabucco project, which aims to transmit gas from Turkey to Baumgarten in Austria. Nabucco differs from other planned projects in that, while the previous ones aim to transport gas from the producing regions of the Caspian Sea and Middle East (including Egypt) to the Turkish grid, it aims to deliver gas from Turkey to consumers in European countries. Map 7.1 below depicts the Nabucco pipeline system *inter alia*.

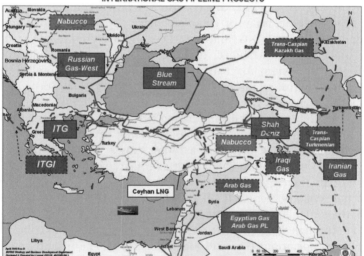

Map 7.1   Energy pipelines through Turkey and its neighbourhood
Source: Botas (2010).

The length of Nabucco is 3300 km if Turkey's eastern border with Georgia and Iran is taken as the departure point. It travels 2000 km in Turkey, 400 km in Bulgaria, 460 km in Romania, 390 km in Hungary and 46 km in Austria, where it will terminate at Baumgarten. But it can also be expanded into Central and Western European countries at a later stage. On the basis of the current market studies, the pipeline is designed to have a total capacity of 31 bcma. The total cost of the project is estimated at approximately €7.9 billion. The construction is due to start in 2011, with the first gas expected to flow in 2014 (Nabucco, 2010). The Nabucco is to supply between 5 and 10 per cent of the EU's projected total gas consumption in 2020 (Aras & Iseri, 2009, p. 6).

The project is led by the Nabucco Gas Pipeline International GmbH, of which the current shareholders include OMV (Austria), MOL (Hungary), Transgaz (Romania), Bulgargaz (Bulgaria), BOTAŞ (Turkey) and RWE (Germany). Each holds a 16.6-per cent stake in the project. State Oil Company of Azerbaijan Republic (SOCAR) is also expected to join the consortium in the near future and the Kazakh and Polish gas monopolies have expressed an interest in joining the project as well. Gaz de France's bid to join the project was vetoed by Turkey in retaliation for vocal French opposition to the Turkish EU accession bid. An Inter-governmental Agreement (IGA) on Nabucco was signed in Ankara by the governments of the Nabucco transit countries – Turkey, Bulgaria, Romania, Hungary and Austria – in July 2009. EU Commission President Jose Manuel Barroso and EU Commissioner for Energy Andris Piebalgs attended the ceremony along with US Special Envoy for Eurasian Energy Richard Morningstar and influential US Senator Richard Lugar, who represented American political support for the historical project.

It is not surprising that Nabucco has garnered such wide attention in EU circles and that discussions of it have reflected so many underlying issues and controversies at the heart of making common EU energy policy. The EU has inserted the project into the framework of the TEN-E programme, with Jozias van Aartsen appointed by the Commission to serve as the project coordinator for Nabucco in 2007. European Commission President Joe Manuel Barroso has praised the project, stating that Nabucco is 'a truly European project [that] will provide energy security to Turkey, to Southeast Europe, and to Central Europe' (Lobjakas, 2009). As the main motive of Nabucco has been to diversify sources and transit routes for energy supplies to Europe, with the underlying goal of reducing heavy EU dependence on Russia, the project has taken on considerable geostrategic importance. Nabucco International GmbH consortium has enumerated the project's main strategic goals as follows (Nabucco, 2010):

- to open a new *gas supply corridor* for Europe and for the countries involved in the project, deliver very cost-effective gas sources
- to raise the *transit role* of the participating countries along the route
- to contribute to the *security of supply* for all partner countries, and also for Europe as a whole
- to strengthen the role of the *gas pipeline grids* of all Nabucco partners in connection with the European gas network (emphases added)

The company has also stated that it does not intend to exclude any supply source for Nabucco. However, it considers Russian supply at best as an 'add on' to other sources. Yet, it is commonly argued that Nabucco is an alternative project to the South Stream pipeline project led by Gazprom. Since Nabucco is a project that lies at the analytical core of the subject matter of this book, a detailed analysis of its geopolitical aspects is amply warranted.

Nabucco: supply-side hurdles

Nabucco project is moving ahead, but has many hurdles to overcome before it comes to completion. Most of the hurdles stem from its strategic nature and profile, which have drawn in a larger range of proponents and detractors than might be the case for a less ambitious enterprise. These hurdles stem both from producer and transit countries as well as consumer countries, namely China (as discussed extensively in the previous chapter). In regards to the producer states in the Caspian region and the Middle East, an array of problems has arisen around and along the very fields and routes that will produce and carry the gas supplies in question.

Russian and Iranian obstructions on the status of the Caspian Sea

Through its energy supply networks dating back to Soviet times, Russia has played a fundamental role in the transportation of energy from the Caspian region. As Chapter 5 detailed, Russia has adopted policies aimed at capturing the lion's share of the Caspian area's potential resource rents (International Energy Agency, 2008b, pp. 14–20). Russian leverage was first undermined by the BTC project, which accordingly attracted strong opposition from Russia. Now Russian opposition to Nabucco is rooted in the same geostrategic concern for losing control over the pricing and routing of energy resources out of the region (Bacik, 2006; Winrow, 2005, 2007). Potential export routes for Caspian energy to Europe and China have empowered the Caspian states to negotiate more advantageous or at least equitable deals with Russia (International Energy Agency, 2008b, p. 4).

As suggested in Chapter 3, one way that Russia has obstructed projects to build alternative routes for Caspian energy is by invoking the contested legal status of the Caspian Sea. This issue has been on the table since the littoral Former Soviet Union (FSU) states gained independence following the collapse of the Union of Soviet Socialist Republics (USSR). Since no resolution of the issue has been achieved, energy rich Azerbaijan, Turkmenistan and Kazakhstan have been effectively blocked from laying trans-Caspian energy pipelines. In addition, Iran, another littoral Caspian state, shares Russia's legal position that the Caspian Sea is a lake rather than a sea, thus permitting only joint control by the littoral states. While Russia has demanded that each littoral state should control only a certain section of the basin and that the remaining centre of the body of water remain common property or a condominium, its ally Iran, with a relative paucity of energy reserves in its section, has argued for a collective approach and equal distribution of the offshore reserves (Rabinowitz et al., 2004, p. 32; Bahgat, 2005, pp. 6–8). The Russo-Iranian position has been challenged by the joint Azeri, Turkmen and Kazakh position that the Caspian Sea is indeed a 'sea', permitting implementation of the United Nations Convention on the Law of Sea that allows for each littoral state to have an exclusive economic zone up to 200 miles offshore (Rabinowitz et al., 2004, p. 31). The likelihood of resolving this problem seems low, as lack of resolution constitutes the very outcome that ensures that Russia and Iran can continue to obstruct trans-Caspian energy projects.

Another strategy of Russia designed to make Nabucco less appealing to the other FSU Caspian producers has been to offer higher prices for the region's gas resources (a strategy that was more viable at least until the economic downturn that commenced in later 2008). For example, in March 2008, Russia, Turkmenistan, Kazakhstan and Uzbekistan agreed that the gas trade among them would take place on the basis of the 'European-level prices', which is construed to be what Europe pays for Russian gas minus costs and a Gazprom fee (International Energy Agency, 2008b, p. 44). This Russian policy has been accompanied by a perception of increased geostrategic risk in the Caspian region in the aftermath of the Russian–Georgian conflict in August 2008. The projects now require stronger investment and credit assurances as well as stronger commitments from relevant governments (Ibid., p. 43).

Ethnic conflicts in the Caucasus

There are many frozen and not-so-frozen conflicts in the area that have stalled movement on building further energy transportation projects via Turkey. Conflicts of the region include, but are not limited to, the Chechen bid for independence from Russia, multiple inter-ethnic struggles within Georgia, the Nagorno-Karabakh conflict between Azerbaijan and Armenia, wrangles between Russia and Georgia and poor relations (or non-relations) between Turkey and Armenia. These conflicts have invited interference from outside powers such as Russia, US, Turkey and Iran, which complicates the stability and security in the region. As stated earlier, the 2008 Russian military interference in Georgia's internal restiveness visibly demonstrated the region's highly volatile security environment. Though the conflict did not stop energy flows in any significant long-term manner, it did affect strategic calculations on the part of the Caspian states regarding production and export of their resources. Therefore, energy companies have hesitated to invest significant sums of money in the area and have sought to get strong official multilateral political and financial backing before undertaking any projects in the region (Ibid., pp. 46–51).

Iran–Western relations

Iran holds the world's second largest gas reserves (after Russia), fourth in gas production, and only twenty-seventh in gas export (Central Intelligence Agency, 2009). It does have ambitious plans to rapidly expand gas production and export. Iranian gas constitutes another major alternative source for Nabucco (Nabucco, 2010). This potential source has been estimated as capable of meeting more than 10 per cent of the Union's medium-term needs (European Commission, 2005d, p. 15). Yet, it is unlikely in the medium term for Iran to have any gas surplus for export beyond the relatively small amount that it already pipes to Turkey.

Increasing Turco-Iranian ties in recent years has worked in favour of Iran's inclusion in the Nabucco supplier network. The Erdogan government in Turkey has accelerated a thawing in Ankara's relations with Tehran, to a degree to which some Western critics have objected. Turkey has tried to help broker a deal on Iran's nuclear program between Iran and the West, but with no concrete results at the time of this writing. Even into the US Presidency of Barack Obama, the impatience of Western countries (in particular the US) with Iran's ongoing uranium enrichment efforts has not ebbed noticeably in recent years, with the potential for a military showdown with Iran ever present. In any case, even if the conflict does not escalate further, Iran's energy development plans will be constrained by Western embargos and domestic political upheaval.

On the other hand, as a country with huge gas reserves, Iran plans, perhaps not very realistically, to produce 500 bcma of gas by 2017. Such a goal requires nearly doubling the existing average growth rate in the gas sector, which requires investment levels that domestic and foreign investors are not able or likely to provide (International Energy Agency, 2008b, p. 26). Iran presents a risky bet for investors. First of all, it has been under American sanctions since the inception of the Iran–Libya Sanctions Act in 1996 (ended in 2004 for Libya), which mandates the US President to impose sanctions against any foreign or domestic companies that invest more than $20 million in developing the Iranian energy sector. Secondly, the nuclear debacle also led to UN sanctions on financial transactions with Iran. As a result of the worsening of the conflict in recent years, a number of EU-based companies have withdrawn from Iran. For instance, due to increasing risk of conflict and the application of sanctions, Total, Statoil Hydro, Shell and Repsol have decided against investing further in Iran (International Energy Agency, 2008b, p. 27).

Due to the persistent conflict between Iran and the West, Iran has had to turn to other energy developing and importing countries in Asia, notably Russia, China and India. Gazprom and China's Sinopec have already signed agreements with Iran (National Iranian Oil Company) to develop oil and gas fields (mainly various phases of South Pars) and to pump oil from the Caspian to the Persian Gulf (Ibid.).

The future of Iraqi energy

Another potential source of gas for Nabucco is Iraq, which holds the world's third largest proven oil reserves after Saudi Arabia and Canada. Moreover, Iraq has the 11th largest proven natural gas reserves in the world, an amount equal to 3170 bcm. Only 20 per cent of Iraqi gas is, however, non-associated (with oil), mostly concentrated in several fields in the North. Iraq's gas reserves outrank those of Kazakhstan (14th), Norway (16th), Egypt (18th), Azerbaijan (19th), Uzbekistan (20th), Kuwait (21st) and Canada (22nd). Yet, despite this potential, Iraq produces only 3.5 bcm per year; it ranked, by 2009, 58th in production, and 168th in export (Central Intelligence Agency, 2009). Iraqi production of gas increased in the post-2003 period, but has only reached the meagre levels of the mid-1990s, when the country was under comprehensive UN sanctions imposed in the wake of the first Gulf War.

As mentioned before, there are proposals to pipe Iraqi gas via the AGP. Another option is to renew a 1996 bilateral proposal to develop the capacity to transit 10 bcma of gas from Northern Iraq to Turkey (Tekin and Williams, 2009a, pp. 346–7), gas that could be connected to Nabucco. Yet, the central government and the Kurdish entity in the North have had a major dispute over the issue of the control of oil and gas reserves in the North and the revenue they are expected to generate. Baghdad wants to participate in supplying Nabucco, but it wants to utilise gas fields other than those in Iraqi Kurdistan. Interestingly, though the Oil Ministry later declared this endeavour illegal, the United Arab Emirate's Crescent firm and its affiliate Dana Gas joined forces with Hungary's MOL and Austria's OMV, both Nabucco shareholders, at the end of 2009, in an \$8 billion project to develop gas fields in Northern Iraq with a view of supplying gas for Nabucco (Reuters, 2009).

The Russian question

Although the Nabucco Project's official website clearly – perhaps wishfully – identifies the Caspian Region, the Middle East as well as Egypt as potential gas suppliers, it also specifies that it does not rule out Russia as a potential supply source. The Nabucco Pipeline Company claims to be 'open for Russian gas as "add on" to other sources' and that it 'will treat all sources equally' (Nabucco, 2010). Indeed, it is highly feasible, from a technical standpoint, to divert Russian gas from the extant Blue Stream pipeline into Nabucco, even though this would contravene the Russian policy of constructing the South Stream as an *alternative* to Nabucco. If, however, Nabucco gets built before – or at the expense of – South Stream, for example, due to the latter's lack of financial wherewithal, Russia might indeed show a keener defensive interest in feeding gas into the Nabucco system via Blue Stream.

Turkey's general relations with its gas producing neighbours

Nabucco's fate will also depend on Turkey's relations with the natural gas producing and transiting countries to its east, north and south. In this respect, the evolution of Turkey's bilateral problems with its neighbours – countries in the South Caucasus (Armenia, Azerbaijan, and Georgia) as well as with Iraq and the Kurdish Regional Government (KRG) in Northern Iraq – are crucially significant. Considering that the main competition in the Caspian region between Nabucco and South Stream is over gas supplies from Shah Deniz, Turkey–South Caucasus relations are quite relevant. The territorial conflict between Azerbaijan and Armenia is well-known. Armenia occupied Nagorno-Karabakh and surrounding seven Azeri districts in 1992. While Russia upheld Armenia's claim to the occupied territory, Turkey has been the most ardent supporter of the Azeri position in the international arena. Turkey's close ethnic, cultural and historical ties with Azerbaijan were important factors in garnering Azeri support for Western-backed energy projects connecting the two countries in the face of strong Russian protests. The BTC and SCP were the fruition of such a rebalancing of power in the region.

However, Turco-Azerbaijan ties were shaken in 2009. In October of that year, under American and European pressure, Turkey signed protocols with Armenia to normalise relations in the form of opening of the Turco-Armenian border – which Turkey had closed in retaliation for the Armenian occupation of Azeri territories – in exchange for the Armenian state not pushing for recognition of 'genocide' claims against Turkey. Azerbaijan has perceived the Turkish opening of the border with Armenia as a sign of Turkish dismissal of Azeri concerns. It is commonly claimed that Azerbaijan retorted by signing a natural gas agreement with Russia only 4 days after conclusion of the Armenian–Turkish protocols. By January 2010, Azerbaijan had begun pumping the equivalent of 1 bcma of gas from the Shah-Deniz region to Russia as part of the agreement. Gazprom Chief Executive Officer (CEO) Alexey Miller declared that 'Russia will buy from Azerbaijan as much as Azerbaijan [would] supply' (Tuna, 2010). Baku also signed a short-term agreement in January 2010 to supply gas to Iran. These Azeri moves indicate that the country has refused to lend unequivocal support to Turkish-centred energy projects. Growing Azeri irritation with Turkey was also visible in President Aliyev's following statement at the World Economic Forum on 29 January 2010 in Davos: 'Azerbaijan has three energy routes apart from Turkey; Iran, Russia, and Georgia' (Ibid.). However, Ankara has been hesitant to bring these protocols to the Turkish Parliament for ratification. The protocols were signed largely to deter the Obama Administration and the US Congress from voicing the dreaded acceptance of the 'genocide' claim that has been levelled by some Armenian groups against Turkey. In lieu of US relaxation of pressure on Turkey over the Armenian issue, Ankara may never bring the protocols to Parliament, which could help Turkey repair its ties with Azerbaijan.

Though it seems to be a less significant problem for Nabucco, Turkish-Iraqi (and -Kurdish) relations are also important in the future. Turkey's struggle with the separatist Kurdish PKK, ongoing since the mid-1980s, has complicated the country's relations with Iraq. In post-Saddam Iraq, the Kurdish leadership in Northern Iraq has developed an autonomous Kurdish entity – the self-styled KRG – with strong backing from the

US. However, Northern Iraq also emerged as a haven for PKK operations, straining relations between Turkey, the KRG, Iraq and the US. Nonetheless, in recent years, under heavy pressure from the US on both sides, official relations between Turkey and the KRG have been gradually established, at least in a de facto sense. Tensions have eased within a broader framework that the Turkish government initiated with the goal of dissolving the PKK through partial amnesty and a so-called democratic opening package that offers more cultural rights to the Kurds in the country. In parallel, Turkey's relations with the Iraqi central government have also improved in recent years. The Turkish attitude towards receiving energy supplies from Iraq and the Kurdish region will be heavily influenced by how its own Kurdish question evolves and resolves itself and how much support Turkey receives from Baghdad and the KRG to neutralise the PKK. There have been certain positive signs in recent years, but it is difficult to gauge the future unfolding of this situation. Nonetheless, as mentioned before, Turkey has been interested in implementing a 1996 bilateral proposal to develop a gas pipeline capacity to pipe 10 bcma of gas from Northern Iraq to Turkey (Roberts, 2004, p. 7; Winrow, 2004, p. 34, Turkish Daily News, 2007).

Turkish–American Relations

For the success of the BTC, American support was vital. The question remains as to whether the US government will furnish the same level of backing for Nabucco, especially in a buyer's market for natural gas, one softened up on both ends of the economic equation by recession and discoveries of huge new quantities of American shale gas. Though the resolution of this question also hinges on the quality of trans-Atlantic relations, it suffices here to discuss what the evolving nature of Turkish American relations in recent years implies for US policy towards Nabucco (and related) projects. For one, the US has been supportive of the project as evidenced by the presence of the US Special Representative Richard Morningstar and Senator Dick Lugar at the Nabucco IGA signing ceremony in Ankara in July 2009. Conversely, Turkish–American relations have deteriorated over a few issues that bear on the viability of the Nabucco project. The main issue is the growing American suspicion regarding Turkish policies towards Iran, Syria, Israel and Sudan. A more specific problem concerns the Turkish support offered to the Iranian regime on the nuclear issue. Under these circumstances, the US may liken Tehran's involvement in the Nabucco project to the extension of a future lifeline for the Iranian regime. Another specific problem is the growing American pressure on Turkey to resolve its differences with Armenia, including the opening of the borders between these two countries as well as settlement of the Armenian 'genocide' claim in relation to the atrocities of 1915. These issues have strained bilateral relations in recent years, even as a succession of US Presidents have continued to eschew using the term 'genocide' to describe these events. Negotiations over these issues between Turkey and Armenia have also angered Azerbaijan, which vehemently opposes any deals between the former countries without a settlement of its own separate Nagorno–Karabakh dispute with Armenia. Thus, Azerbaijan has refrained from completely neglecting its own energy ties with Russia.

The lack of American support could hurt Nabucco's prospects by reducing the level of support for such a project within the EU itself. It seems that firm American support for the project, as with the earlier BTC and BTE projects, depends on how it continues to regard energy sources coming from Iran and Russia. On the other hand, if these American considerations are taken into account, energy importation from American allies in the Caspian and Middle East will find its strongest support from the US, although this may continue to leave the question of how to provide sufficient throughput into Nabucco less than fully resolved.

Nabucco and Russia: a pyrrhic victory for the EU?

Nabucco, once completed, will be a major undertaking that transports gas from the borders of Turkey to the heart of Europe, bypassing Russia. The project has broad support in Europe as an alternative conduit to Russia. The US government also supports the project. Yet the issue of who will supply gas to Nabucco is still an open question and continues to incite controversy. The Nabucco Gas Pipeline International consortium has argued that the pipeline will be open to any source, without discrimination, for example, to gas supplies from Russia or Iran. The company's director, Reinhard Mitschek, stated that a multisourcing approach is one of Nabucco's key selling points. Mitschek indicated that Nabucco will be open to Iranian gas if the current diplomatic problems subside, while EU Energy Commissioner Andris Piebalgs stated that 'Iranian gas in the long-run is an issue for Europe' (Pannier, 2008). On the other hand, US support is predicated on the condition that Nabucco does not pipe Iranian gas.

Nabucco exec Mitschek, who has considered the possibility of Russian gas supply for Nabucco, has pointed out that the Blue Stream pipeline already brings Russian gas into Turkey for domestic use and could thus contribute supplies to Nabucco in the future. While this logic may seem to be at odds with the European objective of diversifying European energy sources away from high(er) dependence on Russia as well as out-competing the Russian-backed South Stream pipeline project, Mitschek has advanced the argument that 'Europe's gas needs are big enough to accommodate both pipelines' (Ibid.). He has indicated that EU gas consumption in 2007 was 500 bcma, of which 200 bcma was produced in Europe, and that within the next 10–15 years, European production will drop to 100 bcma while gas demand will climb to 700 bcma. These projections show that the EU will double its current import of 300–600 bcma towards the end of this decade, underscoring a huge need for pipeline capacity. Mitschek has thus emphasised that 'Southeast Europe and all Europe will need a lot of these pipeline projects' (Ibid.).

Conclusion

This chapter analysed Turkey's role as an energy corridor for Europe in terms of its existing energy pipeline system as well as the projects in their planning or early construction phases. A particular focus on Nabucco, as Europe's fourth main energy artery, allowed for a more concrete exploration of the strategic and technical aspects of Turkey's role as a transit corridor role for Europe's present and future energy needs.

Turkey has indeed become an increasingly vital partner of Europe in energy transport from producers in Turkey's vicinity. Underlying this claim is the assumption that Turkish territory is a relatively cost effective means of conveying energy resources from East to West (Tekin and Walterova, 2007). While Turkey is not a globally essential oil corridor for the EU, its hosting of the BTC crude oil pipeline may help not only on prices, but also on getting Caspian crude into a position to compete with Russian and OPEC oil in European markets. Additional factors favouring landward Turkish oil transit is the fact that transporting Caspian oil by trans-Iranian pipelines to the Gulf may be less economically viable than exporting it via Turkey to the Mediterranean. Moreover, Azerbaijan and Kazakhstan crude blends are better adapted than many of the typically heavier and sourer grades of the Persian Gulf to European refineries regulated by stricter environmental directives (Adams, 2004).[1]

In terms of gas, Central Asia, the Caspian, Iran, Iraq and Egypt are believed to hold enough gas to supply Europe through Turkey at reasonable costs. Consequently, developing conduits to ship this gas to Europe via Turkey could restrain the overall price that Gazprom can demand for its supplies (Roberts, 2004, pp. 17–18; Gow, 2008).[2] Obviating the necessity of having to pin all hopes on Nabucco, the existing SCP, the Iran–Turkey pipeline as well as the TGII infrastructure can already be utilised to send gas to Europe. The planned Nabucco and Arab Gas Ring projects would, however, change the EU's gas supply picture even more favourably.

Though the strategic nature of Turkey's energy transit role seems rather clear, there are multiple challenges emanating both from suppliers and, to a lesser extent, consumers in Europe. This chapter dealt extensively with those hurdles arising from the supply side. However, we conclude that Nabucco's hurdles can be overcome and that the latter is highly likely to provide an ample supply of gas to pipe to Europe.

The Turkish energy corridor seems to offer one of the most obviously feasible modes of connecting a greater diversity of suppliers to Europe via secure and independent routes. However, treating Turkey's capacity and willingness to serve as a transit country, primarily in terms of gas, as a matter to be addressed within existing frameworks of cooperation may not be enough to ensure Europe's energy security. Proposed energy networks associated with such mammoth infrastructural undertakings as the TGII or the Nabucco Pipeline involve the higher standardisation and integration of regulatory environments characteristic of political union. Thus, more serious efforts by the EU to diversify supply and secure those diverse supplies may come to require exhibiting less ambiguity and ambivalence on the question of Turkey's accession.

8
Turkey's Energy Role and Its Accession Process

Introduction

This chapter focuses on the larger implications of Turkey's role as alternative pipeline-based energy corridor for bundled gas supplies to Europe. These implications may be viewed from the European Union (EU) and member-state perspectives, ranging from the choice of eventually allowing Turkey into the Union – as the ultimate destiny of its ongoing accession process – to considering energy cooperation as only one element of the myriad bilateral relationships that Turkey has with the EU or each of its member states. Indeed, we see evidence of both linkage and delinking strategies regarding Turkey's energy role and its accession process in the current political discourse in Europe. Conversely, a prevalent Turkish reading of the implications of Turkey's increasing energy role is based on the growing assumption of a strong association between these two matters. Thus, overall energy policy discussions have been occurring against a background based on the untested view of 'Turkey entering Europe through pipelines.'

Obviously, the official Turkish position sides with that faction of European interests that subscribes to the linkage between Turkey's energy role and its accession to the EU. On the other hand, Ankara suspects that proponents of bilateral energy cooperation wish to dampen Turkey's expectations on accession in favour of a 'privileged partnership' and has shown commensurable resistance on energy policy cooperation with these proponents. All in all, the EU seems ambivalent on the issue, with none of the factions seemingly dominant among member states, thus creating uncertainty on EU policy per se. This also makes the official Turkish positions rather difficult to gauge or at times rather unpredictable. These two contending readings are rooted in two different interpretations of Turkey's energy role. One assumes Turkey's energy role to be simply an alternative transit route for supplies not controlled by Russia, while the other one interprets it as an important contribution to European energy security through the country's accession to the EU.

In trying to decipher how the EU and Turkey view the implications of Turkey's energy role, we look at the evolution of the EU–Turkey cooperation on energy. We observe that the EU has attempted to extend its energy regulatory influence over its neighbourhood, which has been depicted as including Turkey. While this has been implemented mostly via the European Neighbourhood Policy (ENP) and bilateral mechanisms, the Turkish case has taken place mostly within the framework of the country's accession talks since 2005. However, EU policies are not limited to regulatory influence on energy matters. Rather, the Union is also active in the promotion of projects – such as the Nabucco project – that will strengthen its (external) energy position vis-à-vis its prominent dependence on Russian energy and Russian-controlled supply routes. The EU has utilised both market and geopolitical approaches in its energy policies, with implications for the energy role of Turkey and its accession to the EU.

This chapter examines these clashing perspectives through a study of energy policy developments in recent decades and their broader implications for Turkey–EU relations. In doing so, it first evaluates the existing status quo in EU–Turkey energy cooperation. It then turns to the issue of how the EU and its member states have treated their (energy) relations with Turkey and what their current and future expectations are in this matter. This precedes an assessment of the Turkish view of cooperation on energy security and how this is linked to the broader question of Turkish membership in the EU. As is clarified herein, energy-related issues have become tightly intertwined in the broader contours of EU–Turkey relations.

Turkey–EU relations and cooperation in energy issues

Turkey and the EU have a long-lasting relationship dating back to the 1950s when the European Communities were set up. The Turkish application for associate membership in 1959 resulted in the Ankara Agreement in September 1963. The Agreement foresaw a Customs Union between the European Economic Community (EEC) and Turkey by the end of 1995, with a stipulation that the parties would discuss the possibility of Turkey's full membership as the next step. Towards the end of the Cold War period, in 1987, Turkey applied for full membership. Since then, however, Turkey has been waging a protracted struggle to become a member of the EU. The first half of the 1990s saw the EU offer Turkey accession to the Customs Union, which was achieved by the end of 1995.[1] However, Turkish ambitions were not satisfied simply by joining the Customs Union, a sentiment manifested in the strong reaction of the Turkish government to the EU Luxembourg Summit decision in December 1997, which declared the start of the negotiations with the Central and Eastern European countries, Malta and Cyprus, while seeming to ignore the Turkish application (European Council, 1997). Turkey froze its relations with the EU until the latter changed its policy towards Turkey. That breakthrough came at the EU Helsinki Summit in December 1999, when EU leaders finally endorsed Turkey as 'a candidate State destined to join the Union on the basis of the same criteria as applied to the other candidate States' (European Council, 1999).

After years of wrangling, the EU opened accession talks with Turkey in October 2005. As historic as this might have been, the EU left Turkey's full membership issue shrouded in uncertainty, as the Negotiation Framework Document provided ample evidence of ongoing European ambivalence on the question of Turkey's accession (European Council, 2005). The document stresses that although 'the shared objective of the negotiations is accession, the negotiations are an "open-ended" process, the outcome of which cannot be guaranteed beforehand'. In addition, the document states that 'long transitional periods, derogations, specific arrangements, or permanent safeguard clauses', particularly in the areas of freedom of movement of persons, structural policies or agriculture, 'may be considered'.

Although these phrases may not be sufficient to preclude full Turkish membership in the EU, the overtly negative opinions that have been expressed by French President Nicolas Sarkozy, German Chancellor Angela Merkel and various Cypriot governments on the Turkish accession have bolstered the impression that negotiations with Turkey may not yield full EU membership after all.[2] Furthermore, the negotiating procedures now include the maximum number of national veto opportunities; for example, each *acquis* chapter's opening and closing requires unanimity in the Intergovernmental Conference among all 27 of the member states and Turkey. This affords any member state leverage by which to stall the accession process. Not surprisingly, a few member states have taken the option. As a matter of fact, Turkey and the EU have completed only one chapter and have opened

11 chapters, while 18 chapters have been frozen due to the exercise of national vetoes (Bagis, 2010, p. 6). Cyprus has vetoed the opening of eight chapters, including the crucial one on energy, in response to Turkey's rejection of the stipulation that it extend its obligations under the Customs Union to the Republic of Cyprus. In addition, France has vetoed the opening of five important chapters, arguing that these chapters lead to a deeper integration of Turkey that would presage full membership, instead of simply anchoring Turkey in European security structures as a 'privileged partner'. Overall, the accession process has become currently highly protracted and its outcome correspondingly uncertain.

Obviously each candidate state has to meet certain EU obligations contained in the *acquis communautaire*, but the criteria on which Turkey has been judged thus far seem to be more complex than the ones applied to other candidate states. Indeed, there have been strong currents in the EU against the Turkish membership, based on Turkey being, in the words of former EU Commissioner Frits Bolkestein, 'too big, too poor, too different'.[3] Yet, Turkey's energy role has added a new dimension to its perceived importance by the EU. Turkey's generally acknowledged potential contribution to the EU as an important military power has been joined in recent years by its advantageous geostrategic position on the energy security front. As the EU increased its efforts to bolster its energy security, it also began to view Turkey as a cooperative partner on the diversification of its energy routes. The Union's policy of augmenting its existing energy supply network with a 'fourth artery' through Turkey to reach the Caspian and the Middle Eastern resources has highlighted the country's role as a logical and cost-effective energy transit route (Tekin and Walterova, 2007).

The previous chapter described the operational and planned pipeline projects involving Turkey. It is clear that when the pipeline network is completed, Turkey will emerge as an important route linking energy suppliers and consumers. Various EU documents, such as the green paper of 2006, have pointed to Turkey as an important strategic element in the Union's external energy policy. The European Commission (2006a) has urged the EU to support Turkey's efforts to become an energy hub. Even the European Parliament has also recognised the possible linkage between Turkey's geopolitical roles in EU energy security and has invited others to take energy-related considerations into account when Turkey's EU membership is being discussed (European Parliament-Directorate

General External Policies, 2006). Many individual member states have also endorsed this view.

Contrary to the positions of EU institutions, however, several important member states, including heavyweights Germany and France, do not see or wish to see a strong link between Turkey's emerging energy role and its process of accession to the Union. The current governments of both countries have rightfully argued that becoming an energy hub for Europe does not absolve Turkey from its obligations to tackle other diplomatic, cultural and economic matters pertinent to the Turkish accession. Yet, they have gone a step further to argue against including Turkey as a member in the Union simply for the sake of energy security, which they imply can be satisfied by closer bilateral cooperation with Turkey. The following section details these divergent attitudes within the EU and among its member states on the proper implications of Turkey's energy role in its EU accession process.

European views of Turkey's energy role

While many have underscored the decisiveness of the moral and ethical logic behind the recent EU enlargement to Eastern Europe, others have emphasised the dominant role of geostrategic reasons (Sjursen, 2002; Moravcsik and Vachudova, 2003). For the latter, forward movement of the Turkish process over the period of 1999–2005 finds its strongest explanation in the rational calculations of the EU (Onis, 2000; Tekin, 2005). Indeed, the supporters of the Turkish membership have explicitly cited Turkey's advantages on energy security issue in EU Council internal debates. Some initially Turkey-sceptic leaders were seemingly convinced by this line of argument. Carl Bildt and Massimo D'Alema, foreign ministers of Sweden and Italy, respectively, wrote in a joint article that ' . . . Turkey is a key actor in the realm of energy security. Given the uncertain state of energy markets, and the stakes involved, it is our shared interest to incorporate Turkey in a functioning integrated system' (Bildt and D'Alema, 2007).

Official EU positions

As Chapters 2 and 3 indicated, the EU is seeking to establish a coherent external energy policy based on several goals and measures that include the construction of new infrastructure, bilateral and regional partnerships and dialogues with energy producing and transit countries and development of a pan-European Energy Community including 'certain essential strategic partners' like Turkey and the Caspian countries

(European Commission, 2006b, pp. 15–16). Given its growing role in the global energy market, Turkey seems to be one of the most suitable means by which the EU could realise its specified energy strategy.

As Chapter 7 delineated, Turkey is already plugged into the EU energy grid. The Turkey–Greece Interconnector has been in operation since 2007, with plans to extend it further to Bulgaria and, through the undersea Greece–Italy Interconnector, to Italy, creating the larger Turkey–Greece–Italy Interconnector (TGII) backbone of the 'southern corridor'. As a relevant document from the European Parliament has stressed, 'the potential of Turkey to become an important country for oil and gas transit from Russia, the Caspian Sea region and the Persian Gulf adds to the strategic importance of Turkey to the EU' (European Parliament-Directorate General External Policies, 2006, p. 3). The EP document continued to assert that *'political-strategic considerations play often an important role in discussions about Turkey's future EU membership or closer relations with the EU'* (p. 3).[4] As this statement indicates, the energy role of Turkey does not automatically translate into the country's eventual membership, as it could also lead simply to 'closer relations with the EU'.

The EU endorsement of the role of Turkey as a major transit country has become increasingly pronounced, especially in the gas sector. The Trans-European Networks-Energy (TEN-E) programme underpins the creation of an integrated internal energy market and aims at the development, interconnection and interoperability of cross-border networks for gas transportation. In this programme, Turkey plays an important role, as it is located at the intersection of two priority axes of natural gas: natural gas route 3 (NG3) and natural gas route 6 (NG6). The NG3 includes gas pipelines from Caspian and Middle East to Europe, such as the TGII, with its planned extension to the Balkans, and Nabucco. The NG6, on the other hand, involves connections between the Mediterranean member states and East Mediterranean gas ring. It therefore involves phases one and two of the South Europe Gas Ring project (the already operational Turkey–Greece Interconnector and the proposed Greece–Italy Interconnector) as well as the Arab natural gas pipeline project (European Parliament and European Council, 2006). Turkey has also received financial and technical assistance within the accession negotiations framework in order to increase energy efficiency, achieve legislative alignment and foster institution building (Europa, 2007a).

Besides TEN-E, Turkey has also played a significant role in Interstate Oil and Gas Transport to Europe (INOGATE) since its inception in 1995.

As explained in Chapter 3, the latter was introduced as a programme to foster energy cooperation among the EU and the Caspian and Black Sea littoral countries plus the Central Asian republics. The programme aims to provide greater assurance on energy security, promote foreign investment in infrastructure development and consolidate the progressive alignment of producer and transit countries' legislations with the EU *acquis* (Interstate Oil and Gas Transport to Europe, 2010).

Yet, Turkey does not participate in all possible EU-led energy frameworks. In this sense, it is significant that Turkey is still not a member of the South-East Europe Energy Community Treaty (SEEECT), but has chosen rather to limit itself to holding an observer position. This Treaty, initiated in 2006, aims to set up a regulatory and market framework in order to bring Western Balkan countries into line with the EU *acquis communautaire* on energy (Energy Community Treaty, 2010). While the EU invited Turkey to become a party to the SEEECT, the latter did not show interest in joining even after negotiations started in September 2009. While Turkey has been trying to adopt the EU *acquis* as a general component of the accession process, its hesitance to sign this treaty may have to do with its uncertainty on the eventual fate of its membership bid. While not necessarily viewing the treaty as a Trojan horse intended to sabotage its full-membership aspirations, Ankara nonetheless feels that the SEEECT is better suited to countries that are not eligible for EU membership anyway and that it could denigrate its own accession chances (EurActiv Network, 2005).

In summary, EU official positions remain disparate on the issue. On the one hand, Olli Rehn, then Commissioner for Enlargement, stated that 'the EU and Turkey share essential strategic interests e.g. in security, economy and dialogue of civilizations. That is one of the reasons why the EU decided to open negotiations for membership with Turkey.... [Energy strategy] is an area where both the EU and Turkey can gain from deeper cooperation' (Joint Press Release, 2007). On the other hand, the EU seems to have hedged in line with the uncertainties surrounding the eventual fate of the accession talks, as manifested in the statements of then Energy Commissioner Andris Piebalgs. While depicting the EU–Turkish energy cooperation as offering 'mutual benefits for both sides' and expressing determination 'to work together with Turkey to realize these mutual benefits', Piebalgs (2007) went even further to state that 'this is a process that...has nothing to do with the EU accession – the one does not prejudice the other or vice versa...they both stem from the understanding that further cooperation is needed between EU and Turkey in a number of fields.'

Even while emphasising the importance of Turkey in meeting EU energy policy objectives, EU official documents have used carefully guarded language in linking energy security issues to the Turkish accession process. The last Accession Partnership Document (APD) for Turkey suggests completing the alignment of national legislation with the *acquis* with a view to possible membership of the Energy Community Treaty and ensuring 'the implementation of fair and non-discriminatory rules for the transmission of gas' (European Council, 2008, p. 12). The APD also asks Turkey to give priority to 'projects of common interest listed in the European Community TEN-Energy Guidelines' (Ibid., p. 16).

The 2004 Progress Report on Turkey was the first one to discuss the details of energy security issues. It concluded that 'Turkey will play a pivotal role in diversifying resources and routes for oil and gas transit from neighbouring countries to the EU' (European Commission, 2004b, p. 116). The Progress Reports of 2006 and 2007 (2006c and 2007b) focus on the Tran-European Networks (TENs). The 2006 Report stated that 'The Nabucco natural gas pipeline project from the Caspian and Central Asian region to Europe via Turkey is among the priority projects of the EU, and Turkey should pursue efforts to support this project' (European Commission, 2006c, p. 55), while the 2007 Report mentioned the Nabucco project as one of 'the TEN-Energy projects of European interest' (European Commission, 2007b, p. 56). The 2008 report went further to label the Nabucco project as 'among the *highest* priority project of the EU' (European Commission, 2008b, p. 64).[5] The latest Progress Report (2009h) deals with energy issues more extensively. It stresses the relevance of Turkey's accession to SEEECT, on which the negotiations started in September 2009. On TENs, the report discusses the signing of the intergovernmental agreement (IGA) on the Nabucco pipeline by Turkey in July 2009, the objective of which was 'to set a common regulatory framework and facilitate the necessary investment decisions' (European Commission, 2009h, p. 67). The report evaluates the Nabucco project as follows:

> This project is an important strategic step towards closer energy cooperation between the EU, Turkey and other States in the region as well as towards the diversification of energy sources. The timely completion of the Southern Gas corridor, though notably the swift implementation of the Nabucco Intergovernmental Agreement, remains one of the EU's highest energy security priorities.
>
> (Ibid.)

The Screening Reports on the TENs and energy *acquis* chapters provide details of the developments within, and future expectations from, Turkey on energy security. The trans-European energy guidelines of 2006 identify priority projects and projects of common interest (European Council, 2006). Building upon these guidelines, the screening report on TENs points out that 'TEN-[Energy] respond to the growing importance for securing and diversifying the Community's energy supplies, incorporating the energy networks of the Member States and candidate countries, and ensuring the coordinated operation of the energy networks in the Community and in neighbouring countries' (Europa, 2007c, p. 2). Security of energy supply and the functioning of the internal energy market are key policy goals. Axes for priority projects and projects of common interest have been identified in this regard (Ibid.). The Screening Report on energy, among other issues, considers the Energy Charter Treaty (ECT) and related instruments. This report states that, 'as regards international agreements relevant for energy trade, market access and cross-border transit, Turkey ratified the ECT in 1998 and is actively contributing to its functioning, but has not yet ratified the ECT Trade Amendment (as of April 2010). Turkey has incorporated ECT dispute settlement mechanisms into relevant intergovernmental agreements' (Europa, 2007b, p. 6). The report also suggests that 'Turkey should now also ratify the ECT Trade Amendment. Turkey should adopt and implement an appropriate legal framework to facilitate the transit of energy materials and products' (Ibid., p. 11).[6]

According to both screening reports, the Turkish side has expressed its willingness accept the *acquis* regarding both TENs and energy chapters by the time of accession. The report on the energy chapter asserts that Turkey, 'located in the vicinity of world's greatest energy reserves', is a 'natural connector' between the producer countries and the European energy markets (Europa, 2007c, p. 4). Ongoing gas pipeline projects, connecting Turkey, Greece and Italy and Turkey to Austria (Nabucco), have both been designated 'TEN-E priority projects'. Turkey has also suggested that other projects, such as an Arab Gas Pipeline–Turkey interconnector, as well as the Baku–Tbilisi–Erzurum (BTE), Iraq–Turkey and Trans-Caspian pipelines, should be considered as EU priority projects as they can link up to Mediterranean networks (Ibid., p. 5). The report concludes that 'overall, Turkey has reached a satisfactory level of preparedness regarding the strategic development of the... energy networks in accordance with the design and objectives of the... TEN-E' (Ibid.).

In contrast to the reserved language contained in official EU documents, less formal language has been slightly more forthcoming in terms of linking Turkey's role in European energy security with its accession process. For instance, in June 2007, a conference in Istanbul was convened to address the common challenges and opportunities for the EU and Turkey in the energy field. The joint statement issued by Turkish and Commission leaders emphasised the importance of strategic cooperation and the exploitation of Turkey's geographic location in providing energy security for Europe. More precisely, these leaders indicated that 'as Turkey is moving forward in the accession process, coherent policies will need to be implemented with a view to ensuring secure access to the energy resources of the region and their safe arrival to the markets' (Joint Press Release, 2007). In sum, the EU as an institution recognises Turkey's potential value as a secure and independent (of Russia) route for EU energy supplies, which may in turn assist Turkey's accession process.

Member-state positions

It is not unreasonable to propose that Turkey's energy role has had at least some shaping influence on the attitudes of some EU member states on Turkish accession bid. But it will be helpful if we can trace whether member-country energy security considerations actually play any discernible role in their overall approach to the Turkish membership question.

In the first set of countries, Turkey's energy role is seen as yet another reason for why Turkish membership will contribute to the overall security of the Union. For instance, UK Foreign Minister Miliband's emphasis on Turkey as a bridge-country for ensuring energy exports helped him to justify why Turkey must be allowed to join the Union (EurActiv Network, 2009b).[7] Italy is another country strongly advocating Turkish membership (EurActiv Network, 2008). In Italian energy security strategy, infrastructure plays a central role and 'ENI is an important partner in the main infrastructural projects involving Turkey' (Pastori, 2008, p. 94). In addition, the future undersea leg of the TGII will not only link Italy directly to gas supply coming from Azerbaijan, but will also augment Italian influence in the South-East Europe Regional Energy Market (SEEREM).[8]

Greece has been supportive of Turkey's EU bid since the 1999 Helsinki Summit, altering its formerly adversarial diplomatic stance towards Turkey. It considers the Europeanisation of Turkish foreign policy as an opening to ensure peaceful relations in the region. In 2001, a memorandum of cooperation was signed between Turkish state-owned BOTAŞ and Greek state-owned DEPA to link the two countries' gas networks via the Turkey–Greece Interconnector. This was the first major joint project to bring together these two countries and an important development for Greek–Turkish relations overall (Ifantis, 2008, p. 79). The European Commission has accentuated the importance of such infrastructural development for completing the South East Gas Ring, a project in which Greece can realize its own potential 'to become a transit country to other European and Balkan area countries' (Tsombanopoulos, 2002).

Support for the Turkish inclusion in the Union is also relatively strong among Central and Eastern European EU member states. For instance, Poland has lent a strong support for Turkey that is closely tied to the issue of energy strategy:

> From the Polish point of view the most significant contribution that Turkey could make would concern European security in general and the security of energy supplies in particular. Turkey's future role as a transit country for crude oil and gas to 18 Central Europe will be crucial and of great strategic importance for Poland which seeks alternative sources of supply.
>
> (Forysinski and Osiewicz, 2006, p. 17)

In a similar fashion, Lithuania has asserted that 'EU energy cooperation with Turkey is also of strategic value. All alternative energy sources, which could reach Europe, go through Turkey' (Akdemir, 2008). Therefore, Lithuania considers the Turkish membership to be an asset for the entire EU.

Bulgaria, which has been a transit country for Russian supplies of natural gas to Turkey since 1987, and Romania are two additional EU member states that have adopted a positive view of Turkey's inclusion in the EU from an energy security angle. Indeed, both will become transit countries themselves for the Nabucco pipeline. For example, Ambassador Mihnea Constantinescu from the Romanian Foreign Ministry stated that, 'as a close partner to Turkey, Bucharest was interested in a successful conclusion of the energy chapter in the accession negotiations as Turkish EU membership would help to solve the EU's challenges' (Tuskon, 2009, p. 4). In this regard, the insertion of Turkey's relatively robust economy, a perception highlighted during the 2008 economic crisis, when Turkey consciously bucked its older tradition of seeking stand-by loans with the International Monetary Fund (IMF), could further stimulate regional economic interdependence, in which energy and transport cooperation will play the greatest role (Black Sea Economic Cooperation, 2010).

The second set of countries includes those who oppose the Turkish accession and tend to see Turkey's energy role for Europe as a matter of bilateral comity. Among them, Germany and France stand out as vehemently opposed to commingling Turkey's EU membership prospects with its energy-corridor role. German Chancellor Angela Merkel has been a hardline advocate of an extra-*acquis* status for Turkey – 'privileged partnership' – as opposed to full membership and French President Nicolas Sarkozy has basically seconded this proposal (Eurasia Daily Monitor, 2009). Luxembourg President Jean-Claude Juncker has also stressed that the EU needs to institute 'new forms of membership intensity in order to operate a union of more than 30 members' (EurActiv Network, 2005).

In their antagonism to the Turkish accession bid, the leaders of these countries did not seem to take into particular account the utility of Turkey in terms of European energy security. Their opposition to Turkey's full-membership is nonetheless multiply rooted. These roots include widespread judgement (or pre-judgement) of Turkish cultural codes as incompatible with 'European' features, apprehension of a shift in the balance of power within the EU, fear of mass immigration from Turkey and the economic burden entailed by such an enlargement on the EU (Tekin, 2005). As earlier chapters detailed, even on energy security, these countries seem to differ from the profile characteristic of Turkey's European supporters. Importing almost equal or even bigger supplies from Norway and Algeria, France enjoys a lower degree of dependence on Russian gas (Eoearth, 2008), while Germany seems to be less worried about Russia's capricious conduct, due in part to a strong history of bilateral cooperation dating back to Soviet times, but most recently exemplified by the Gazprom-piloted Nord Stream project (Umbach, 2008).

As opposed to the positive attitude of its strongest patron Greece, the Republic of Cyprus has steadfastly opposed Turkey's EU bid. Two historic adversaries of Turkey, Greece and the Greek Cypriots have nonetheless developed divergent attitudes.[9] Ker-Lindsay (2007) has argued that the divergence stems from how these countries viewed the influence of the EU on their relations with Turkey. While Greek governments have seen the EU accession process as vital to Turkey's internal and external transformation (Aydin and Acikmese, 2007), Greek Cypriots have perceived this process as a means to distance Cyprus from Greece's policy orientation and to utilise its membership as a bulwark against Turkey. The official Cypriot attitude towards Turkey's accession is backed by the use of its veto, exemplified on the energy chapter, in order to acquire concessions from Ankara regarding the settlement of the dispute over the island (Ker-Lindsay, 2007).

The Turkish view of energy cooperation with the EU

Turkey–EU relations are going through a problematic period. According to the latest Eurobarometer polls, two-thirds of Germans and French oppose any further enlargement of the EU (European Commission, 2009f). This negative attitude towards enlargement is likely to be even stronger in the case Turkish accession given the constantly voiced opposition by Sarkozy and Merkel to Turkish membership. Despite its relatively lesser impact on Turkey's economy, the ongoing financial crisis in Europe does not necessarily help matters. Significant adjustment problems in some of the new member states have compounded the unpopularity of new enlargements among EU15 constituencies. Turkey has also encountered more specific hurdles in the EU due to the unresolved Cyprus conflict. Therefore, the Turkish accession process is inching ahead very slowly, even imperceptibly. A total of 18 chapters of the EU *acquis* are closed for negotiations due to various EU and national vetoes, including those by France and the Republic of Cyprus (Barysch, 2010).

As expected, Turkish public support for the EU process has declined rapidly as a result of the negative signals emanating from EU member states. Although the majority of Turks still want to join the EU, their enthusiasm has dwindled since the negotiations began in 2005. While its relationship with the EU seems to have reached a dead end, Turkey's ties with countries in the Middle East and North Africa, the Caucasus and Central Asia and Russia and the Balkans have rapidly burgeoned. This emphasis on Turkey's immediate neighbourhood has stemmed not only from the Islamic policy orientation of the Justice and Development Party government (in power since November 2002), but also from the disappointment that most Turks have felt towards the West in recent years as well as an economic strategy to expand trade and investment with economies that boomed from an earlier wave of high energy prices. Yet, Turkish authorities deny that Turkey is changing course in its overall foreign policy orientation. They argue that Turkey's EU aspirations and deepening regional ties are less contradictory than complementary (Aras, 2009). As Turkey moves closer to the EU, its soft power in its neighbourhood increases, in turn making Turkey's increasing regional clout a more invaluable addition to the EU (Barysch, 2010).

Energy cooperation between Turkey and the EU has unfolded against this complex backdrop. Turkey, an accession country since 2005, has logically preferred to undertake joint work with the EU on the issues of energy and its transit within the context of these accession negotiations. Though the most relevant chapters (energy and TENs) are not open due to the vetoes by the Republic of Cyprus, screening activities indicate that Turkey has all but fully committed to harmonising its policies with the *acquis* by the time of its accession. Turkey has been gradually reforming its energy polices along EU lines. Yet, despite repeated entreaties by the EU, Ankara has resisted participation in the European initiatives that are also open to non-EU countries – the SEEECT, for instance – due to its wariness about accepting arrangements that fall short of full membership and might thus signal acceptance of such a status quo for the longer term.

Authorities in Ankara would like to use the emerging energy network involving Turkey and Europe as a lever to advance their country's eventual membership in the Union. Many believe that the energy overdependence of Europe on Russia and Europe's ensuing efforts to diversify energy supplies confer a significant geostrategic advantage on Turkey. The argument goes on to assert that the completion of certain pipeline projects, especially Nabucco, that cross Turkey would support European energy security in terms of diversifying both supply and transit routes (Domanic, 2007). Based on these assumptions, many Turkish leaders have hastened, perhaps unduly, to the conclusion that the EU needs Turkey as much as Turkey needs the EU. For example, at the signing ceremony of the Nabucco IGA on 13 July 2009 in Ankara, Turkish Prime Minister Recep Tayyip Erdogan openly opined that 'Turkey's partnership in energy justifies Turkey's EU membership' (EurActiv Network, 2009d).

Turkey has on several occasions shown that it views energy cooperation with the EU as an issue intimately linked to the question of its eventual EU membership. These instances include its reticence to join the SEEECT, its open linkage of progress on Nabucco to a lifting of the Cypriot veto on the energy chapter, its opposition to the participation of Gaz de France in the Nabucco consortium on the basis of staunch French opposition to Turkish membership and its assent to passage of the Gazprom-backed South Stream pipeline through Turkey's exclusive economic zone in the Black Sea.

Observer status in the SEEECT

In force since June 2006, the ECT aims 'to create a stable regulatory and market framework' to facilitate 'an integrated energy market allowing for cross-border energy trade' and to 'enhance the security of supply'. In order to reach these goals, the SEEECT requires 'the implementation of key sections of the EU acquis' (Energy Community Treaty, 2010). The SEEECT includes the Balkan countries that are potential candidates. Turkey has remained an observer. In order to facilitate its energy cooperation with Turkey, the EU has been encouraging Turkey to sign on to this treaty. The EU has argued that Turkey currently has limited alignment with the EU *acquis* in the electricity and gas sectors. The EU further contends that Turkey would benefit from membership in the community treaty 'through a more open and predictable investment climate in its energy sector; by gaining access to EU expertise and new funding options [...]; and by giving Turkey a say in the EU's external energy policy, so allowing the two to co-operate in the Caucasus and Central Asia' (Barysch, 2007a, p. 6).

Despite these arguments in favour of the SEEECT, the Turkish side has remained seemingly unmoved. Turkey has stated its intention of transposing the relevant EU acquis by the end of the accession process. The essence of its hesitancy was that Turkey did not like

> the idea of unilaterally signing up to a big chunk of the *acquis* without being able to ask anything in return. Turkish officials say that such an arrangement may suit countries that are not eligible for membership. But Turkey is already an EU candidate and it does not want to be fobbed off with what it sees as 'privileged partnership' in the energy field.
>
> (Ibid.)

Though EU officials do not see a functionalist link between the SEEECT and accession, officials in Ankara have insisted that Turkey will adopt the energy *acquis* as part of the accession process. The latter has therefore demanded the lifting of the Cypriot veto on the opening of the energy chapter.

As the Nabucco project gained momentum, EU criticism of Turkey intensified. In the aftermath of the signing of the Nabucco IGA in July 2009, Turkey finally accepted the start of the negotiations on joining the SEEECT in fall of the same year. Negotiations are ongoing, but the handling of this issue has led to the impression that energy cooperation between the EU and Turkey could remain problematic unless the Turkish accession process regains substantial momentum, which seems unlikely in the near future, partly due to the Cyprus problem.

Not even cooperation: the Cyprus veto on opening the energy chapter with Turkey

Resolution of the Cyprus problem has been a key challenge since the 1950s. In the post-Cold War era, the division of the island between the Turkish and Greek Cypriots has been found unacceptable and repeatedly addressed by the United Nations as well as the EU. When the Republic of Cyprus, which does not have jurisdiction over the Turkish-populated northern part but is recognised internationally, became a member of the EU in May 2004, the conflict was fully imported into the EU. Earlier in 2004, the UN-brokered Annan Plan was accepted by the Turkish community via referendum while the Greek side rejected it. At the December 2004 Copenhagen Summit that gave a green light to the start of the accession negotiations with Turkey, the EU demanded from Turkey to establish diplomatic relations with Cyprus by allowing Greek Cypriot vessels to use Turkish ports as part of its obligation to extend Customs Union rules to new EU member states. The decisions also included the international isolation of the northern (Turkish) part to be lifted. Turkey agreed to these conclusions.

Yet, Turkey has not done so largely because the EU could not deliver its promise to end the isolation of northern Cyprus. As the Republic of Cyprus became an EU member in 2004, it vetoed EU decisions to deliver on its promises to the Turkish Cypriots. This anticipated situation led to a diplomatic deadlock. The Cyprus conflict continues to poison EU–Turkey relations. Not only did it lead to instability in the Eastern Mediterranean between Turkey, Cyprus and Greece, but it also caused the partial freezing of the accession negotiations between the EU and Turkey. Out of 35 chapters, two of them have been set off limits in the negotiations because of Cyprus's veto on their opening. In addition, the EU froze eight chapters in December 2006 due to Turkey's refusal to open its ports to Greek Cypriot vessels. Thus, a total of ten chapters remained blocked due to the Cyprus conflict.

As mentioned already, one of the key chapters vetoed by Cyprus pertains to energy. The Cypriot position is that the energy chapter is validly related to offshore gas and oil exploration in the exclusive economic zone and therefore cannot be opened before Turkey desists in its claim that the Turkish Administration in the north 'also has rights and authority over the maritime areas around the island of Cyprus' (Skordos, 2007). The Turkish side, by contrast, has argued that the Cypriot embargo on the energy chapter is unacceptable and that the EU must exert pressure on Cyprus to lift its veto (EurActiv Network, 2009d). This has been one of the central animating reasons behind Ankara's reluctance to join the SEEECT. A few EU member states, such as France, have done little to discourage the unyielding Cypriot attitude.

Turkey's objection to Gaz de France's participation in Nabucco

As discussed in passing above, French President Sarkozy has opposed Turkish membership in the EU in favour of establishing a 'privileged partnership' between the two. Though it is not entirely clear what this partnership would entail, indications are that Turkey would be closely linked to the European policy structures without having a formal voice in them. Thus, France has effectively frozen the accession negotiations on five chapters on the basis of the assertion that these chapters lie too close to the heart of full membership and should therefore be excluded from negotiations (Barysch, 2010, p. 3).

Ankara has argued that the country already enjoys the fruits of a type of 'privileged partnership' with the EU. Turkey joined the Customs Union in 1996, it participates in many EU-led peacekeeping missions as a NATO member, it trades heavily with Europe, it has millions of citizens who work in various EU member countries and so on. In short, Ankara finds the French proposal unacceptable and amounting to nothing new. Combined with the occasional attempts of the French Parliament to adopt decisions on the Armenian 'genocide' question,[10] Ankara actually regards the French position as a manifestation of borderline hostility. When Gaz de France showed interest in joining the Nabucco consortium as its sixth partner, the Turkish government used its own veto in this sphere of activity to prevent its participation. This seems to be part of an unofficial policy of excluding French firms from state tenders, including in the coveted military sector. Under normal circumstances, the participation of Gaz de France would have been welcomed, as this could have ensured the support of an important EU member state for Nabucco. Interestingly, German firm RWE was accepted as the sixth partner to ensure German backing for the project. Though Chancellor Merkel's position on the Turkish accession differs little from that of French President Sarkozy, the official German position emphasises the honouring of EU decisions on Turkish accession negotiations by principle and thus does not countenance overt obstruction. Moreover, the active support by the German left for Turkish membership has qualified the otherwise negative Turkish perception of the current German position.

Allowing South Stream to cross the Turkish exclusive economic zone

As discussed at length in Chapter 4, Russia has been advocating pipeline projects that rival the Nabucco project, which by and large bypasses Russian controlled gas production as well as transit routes. One of these projects is the South Stream pipeline, which would connect Russia under the Black Sea to Bulgaria and to further points in Europe.

Leaving aside considerations of whether it is cost efficient and feasible, this pipeline would traverse the Turkish economic zone in the Black Sea, thus requiring Turkey's permission on its construction. Turkey granted this permission in August 2009. Considering the increasing economic interdependence between the two countries, this was not wholly unexpected, but many in the west took it as a symbol of Turkey's weak commitment to the Nabucco project. However, the Erdogan government argued that it does not see these two pipelines as incompatible alternatives to each other (Pronina and Meric, 2009). This accords with the official position of Austria's Reinhard Mitschek, head of the Nabucco Gas Pipeline International consortium, who has argued that the pipeline is open to Russian gas, and the cooperation of some of the very same EU consortium and member states, including Austria, in the rival South Stream Project (Pannier, 2008). It may also have been that the Turkish governments considered the South Stream project as infeasible and thus that its gesture would not hurt Nabucco's prospects in any real material sense. In addition, Ankara may see the South Stream project as a bargaining chip in the Nabucco negotiations, but some member states went even further in signing onto South Stream. There are 'split loyalties among the Nabucco consortium – the Bulgarian, Hungarian and Austrian governments all "flirted" with the proposed South Stream pipeline' (Tuskon, 2009, p. 5). But considering the potential gains in terms of gas and transit fees (and possibly EU membership) that it expects to reap from the Nabucco project, Ankara's motivation to support the project must not be underestimated.

The EU–Turkey energy nexus: step to full membership or bilateral cooperation?

The discussions above indicate that Turkey wants to use energy issue as leverage for getting into the EU. It prefers to deal with the energy issues within the framework of the accession negotiations, namely through negotiations on the chapters of energy and trans-European networks. It makes sense then for Turkey to push for the opening of these chapters to transpose the relevant EU *acquis*. Completion of negotiations in these chapters would amount to significant strides towards wrapping up its accession negotiations with the EU. Not surprisingly, the Turkish officials have pursued such a policy course while assiduously trying to avoid operating through diplomatic mechanisms that seem to fall outside the EU accession process. Thus, they have resisted proposals to discuss energy on a bilateral basis as well as on a wider regional basis involving a number of non-EU countries.

Then Turkish Minister of Energy Hilmi Guler had argued that the Nabucco and Baku–Tbilisi–Ceyhan (BTC) pipelines will be 'of considerable value to the EU, so should be discussed during Turkey's EU accession negotiations, but Ankara is still waiting for the energy chapter to be opened' (Tuskon, 2009). Turkish Premier Erdogan has continued to link the accession process in general and the lifting the Cypriot veto on the energy chapter to Turkish support for the Nabucco project (Corporate & Public Advisory Group, 2009). On the occasion of the signing ceremony of the Nabucco IGA in July 2009, Prime Minister Erdogan argued (Turkish Ministry of Energy and Natural Resources, 2010b, p. 1) that

> Turkey has become a reliable transit country gaining importance in terms of source and consumer countries. Meeting our objectives, complying with our energy strategy within the objectives of the EU, and the projects that we implement with our other partners, have further strengthened this reliability. [...] I hope that the NABUCCO Project will bring about a new dimension and breathe new life into our cooperation with the EU as we move along towards full membership.

Despite the fact that Turkey signed the Nabucco IGA and began accession negotiations on the SEEECT later in the year, the widespread impression is that 'energy co-operation has become hostage to the problems that besiege the accession process' (Barysch, 2010, p. 10).

On the other hand, motivated by an apprehension that inversely mirrors Turkey's, many actors within the EU prefer not to make any direct or overt linkages between the issue of energy cooperation and Turkey's accession for fear of reducing the latter to a goal that can be met by candidate countries on a single, albeit critical, material dimension. As they have done with Russia or Ukraine, they would like to utilise diplomatic mechanisms on energy cooperation that fall outside the scope of the accession process, such as bilateral cooperation or cooperation within the framework of the EU's external and neighbourhood policies. They see energy cooperation with Turkey in a similar vein.

Thus, both EU energy security and Turkey's EU accession have become mutually hostage to each partner's diametrically opposed perceptions of whether and how they should be linked. All in all, 'the fact that Turkey is a country negotiating for accession should facilitate co-operation in areas of common interest. Paradoxically, the opposite seems to be the case. Co-operation is blocked as long as the accession negotiations are not going as well as they should' (Ibid.). Nonetheless, the Nabucco project seems to have propelled the two sides beyond their inertia on energy cooperation. After the signing of the Nabucco IGA, Turkey and the EU Directorate General – Energy team met in September 2009 'for the first negotiation session in view of Turkey's accession to the Energy Community Treaty' (Europa, 2009a, p. 1). Energy Commissioner Andris Piebalgs stated that 'Turkey is well-prepared and has important role to play in the Energy Community. I hope that the negotiations will proceed swiftly and could be concluded in coming months' (Ibid.). Earlier, in July 2008, the Council of the EU had mandated the Commission to carry out SEEECT negotiations with Turkey (as well as Ukraine and Moldova). The EU's Second Strategic Energy Review, in November 2008, indicated that 'the accession of Ukraine, the Republic of Moldova and Turkey to the Energy Community would catalyse their energy sector reforms and result in a mutually beneficial enlarged energy market based on common rules' (Ibid.).

Some critics have warned that, although Turkey has some leverage in energy transit issues, it should not overplay its hand. They have emphasised that, 'as there is an alternative to using Turkey as a transit country, Ankara should not over-leverage its position: while EU Member States want to buy Caspian energy, the price will determine the energy routes' (Tuskon, 2009, p. 5). Turkey, in the same vein of thinking, should consider the Nabucco as a commercial project, not as a political tool to enter the EU (Ibid., p. 5).

Critics also argue that the accession framework is not robust enough to cover Turkey–EU relations in the energy field. The accession framework is limited in its capacity to provide Turkey and the EU with means to 'develop their foreign policy cooperation in a way that would make Turkey feel more valued and allow the EU to take advantage of Turkey's growing international clout. The EU faces similar dilemmas in energy and security policies' (Barysch, 2010, p. 2). Yet, Turkey needs to be assured that it will not be pulled outside the process towards ad hoc bilateralism. If the EU provides strong assurances that reinforced energy cooperation outside the accession framework does not substitute for eventual full membership, only then will Turkey overcome its anxiety about slipping down the slope of 'privileged partnership' and become more openly receptive to forms of cooperation that are open to non-EU countries. Such a course seems to require that EU leaders cease questioning the basic merit of Turkey's accession process, work to overturn national vetoes on various *acquis* chapters and persuade Turkey that the EU is sincere about the end game of its accession process (Ibid., p. 10).

Conclusion: energy security and belonging

Striking a balance between the opposing power relations shaping the dynamics of Turkish accession to the EU and regional energy politics remains complicated. Overdependence on Russia's energy exports brought the EU to consider the economic and security-related advantages to be gained by energy-supplier diversification. In this regard, the Caspian Basin's non-Russian Former Soviet Union (FSU) littoral states and their resources are particularly alluring, given their potential service as alternative energy suppliers to Russia. In this context, Turkey has undoubtedly assumed the key role as a means of transit for oil and gas coming not only from the Middle East and the Caspian but also from Russia.

The EU as a whole is well aware of Turkey's strategic relevance to meeting European objectives of supply security and diversification. Indeed, Turkey is the protagonist of several pipeline projects strongly supported by the EU and appears prominently in energy cooperation programs aiming to create an integrated, interdependent and functioning European energy space. However, in Turkey's process of accession, the role of energy-related considerations, although being thoroughly acknowledged either by some member states or the EU itself, has not yet sufficed to overcome pre-existing concerns on Turkish membership. Turkey's full membership, substantiated in terms of decision-making involvement and veto power in the EU, has become marginally more likely owing to the growing relevance of Turkey in European energy politics without meaning that it has become a cinch. In the end, Turkey's accession cannot be reduced to straightforward cost-benefit calculations and the logic of consequentiality. Rather, it is likely to become a matter of balancing among EU institutional priorities, member-state preferences, and Turkish foreign policy choices, the timing of which is a multivariate outcome not entirely reducible to Turkey's strategic position.

9
Conclusions

Introduction: EU energy security – more than a civil affair

Energy has been a vital element in the construction of the European integration project. The European Coal and Steel Community (ECSC) and European Coal and Steel Community (EURATOM) treaties not only ensured regular supply of coal and coordination in nuclear energy but also laid the seminal roots of European Community. However, despite the importance of energy in daily life, European Energy Policy has not served as a beacon illuminating a path towards tighter integration (Pointvogl, 2009, p. 5704). ECSC and EURATOM did not lead to a common energy policy, as starkly illustrated by the lack of energy chapters in the Maastricht and Amsterdam treaties. The Treaty on European Union (EU) relegated energy to an almost purely domestic affair equivalent in policy stature to 'civil protection' and 'tourism', with one lone article referring to energy infrastructure along with transport and telecommunications in the larger context of trans-European networks (European Union, 1992, pp. 6, 25). Nearly 15 years later, the 2007 Lisbon Treaty finally introduced a new legal basis for EU legislation in the field of energy as well as a clause recommending energy solidarity. Nonetheless, this treaty retains the EU's characteristically tepid language on cooperation in a field over which member states have traditionally guarded their sovereign prerogatives as jealously and zealously as they have in the realm of military and general security affairs. While greater unity of European thought and action in terms of dealing with outside energy suppliers could raise levels of energy security for all EU member states, real solidarity on energy affairs – especially in the external dimension – remains indeed an elusive collective good.

The EU: energy needy and challenged

For the past 25 years or so, EU demand for energy has been increasing at a rate of 1–2 per cent per year. While the EU is not necessarily bereft of any indigenous capacity to meet some of this rising need, its self-styled leadership on many environmental issues, most notably global warming, has placed certain supply options – not only coal but also nuclear power, literally the original raw materials of EU integration – beyond the bounds of acceptable-use criteria in most member states. The EU's commensurably constrained ability to service its energy consumption needs has thus made it ever more reliant on energy supplies originating from outside its territorial boundaries. Simply put, as it recedes further into history, EU energy self-sufficiency – if this refers to having enough intra-area resources to meet energy demand at its accustomed standard of living in environmentally sustainable ways – is even less feasible as a future option. At their present rate of growth, imported products will cover over two-thirds of the EU's energy requirements in the next 25 years. As strongly implied by the European Commission's (2000) warning at the beginning of this millennium, all economic sectors in the EU economy – from transport to industry – have thus become increasingly susceptible to events spanning a wide spectrum of possibilities and falling well outside of the EU's and its member-state governments' immediate scopes of jurisdictional control. These possibilities include direct confrontations with supplier states – which Europe first dealt with on a major scale during the 1973–74 Arab oil embargo – and other assorted disputes over terms of corporate economic access to the upstream sector in exporting countries. However, they also include halts in supplies caused by civil turmoil in producing regions, especially in Africa and the Middle East, as well as disputes between producing and transit states, as exemplified by the 2006 and 2009 Russian gas cuts.

Member-state economies are highly interconnected, even if not fully integrated, and the EU's interdependence with extra-EU27 supplier countries has grown as well, generally albeit not exclusively in favour of the Union. Consequently, purely national approaches to the energy issue and unilateral energy policy decisions taken to address the afore-mentioned challenges – both of which reflect the often uncomfortably expressed reality of disparate types and levels of energy consumption and importation across member states – tend to work at cross-purposes, even to the point of 'externalising' the larger social and political costs of actions and policies designed to benefit particular member states to other member states. Indeed, while these may reflect highly specific calculi consistent with conventional understandings of energy-centric *realpolitik*, national decisions on energy policy that lack any coordinative reference point seem patently unrealistic in terms of detracting from – or even crippling – the Union's collective ability to respond to external threats to the security of its energy inflow. To the extent that this collective response capacity in the face of energy-supply-related threats could function to safeguard the interests of the most at-risk EU member states, tacit permission given to uncoordinated national decision-making on energy policy contains a certain immoral (relative to EU norms and values) quality to it as well.

While garnering positive renown for its efforts to address the adverse environmental effects of fossil-fuels production, transportation and especially consumption, the EU has nonetheless achieved more success in obtaining its preferred results on energy efficiency and greater use of renewable resources by working closely with multilateral regulatory institutions, as well as with a range of producers, transit countries and energy importers. Nonetheless, regardless of whether or not they wish to confront this unpleasant reality facing the European economy, EU policy makers have been forced by circumstances and events to face head on the EU27's rising energy-import dependency and all of the potential for economic disruption that this entails. Institutions in Brussels and some member states have indeed begun to take steps, even if these seem highly conflicted, half-hearted and tentative, to deal with energy security by means of encouraging investments in diversifying the dominant mix of energy sources and foreign suppliers. Rising global energy consumption has also brought Europe into a situation of potentially greater conflict not only with many extra-EU27 suppliers but also with the world's fastest growing consumption-orientated countries. As suggested in Chapter 2, rising consumption in population behemoths India and especially China heralds a potentially bleaker scenario of competition and rivalry among *consumers* to acquire or maintain increasingly more restricted or otherwise scarcer hydrocarbon reserves.

The EU's energy-related agenda, which many would prefer the modern or post-industrial issues of climate change, efficiency and renewables to dominate, has been compelled to accommodate quintessentially traditional concerns for energy security raised by events generated by 'upstream' (and 'midstream') states that do not necessarily share the European worldview of the proper rank-ordering of these issues. As amply elaborated in earlier pages, while this did not constitute European countries' first encounter with politically motivated cuts in their energy supplies, the 2006 stoppage of Russian gas to Ukraine and then in succession to other European customers served by the main transit pipeline reverberated more intensely and widely – both in an economic and political sense – within the newly enlarged EU25 economy. In short, this cut-off and the second major one in 2009 provided telling if somewhat unwelcome reminders to the EU as a whole, not just a disparate collection of European states, of the crucial importance of supply security and member states' commensurable vulnerability to external sources of disruption in their inflows of energy that result from the deliberate decisions of non-EU states. The 2006 'wake-up call' and the next claxon that sounded 3 years later to the day signalled that the EU needed a more active and concerted energy policy to deter or manage this type of energy crisis. Augmenting its energy security has become an important real and symbolic test of the EU's strength and integrity, one that had already been subjected to heavy stress from the 2010 Greek financial meltdown and the attendant economic ramifications for the 16-state eurozone subset of the EU27.

Giving external face and voice to European Energy Policy

In fact, as this book has explicated, major efforts to develop the skeletons of a common EU energy policy have largely responded to events. These began just after the first oil shock in the early 1970s and reflected a range of motivations that various European countries had for developing better relations with Middle Eastern producers, even those same ones threatening them with selected boycotts, and, as a backup plan, safeguarding their economies by accepting European Council and IEA mandates to stockpile emergency petroleum reserves. At this time and extending into the 1980s, even after the oil market had turned downwards, Western Europe also proceeded, albeit inchoately, to diversify energy sources (namely, from coal and oil to gas) and supply regions (from the Persian Gulf to the Soviet Union). However, it was only later in the post-Cold War era, when the commodity seller's market made a fierce comeback, that more systematic EU energy policies and concomitant policy instruments began to take shape. While their name connotes the tighter entwinement of energy and environmental concerns, a series of European Commission-spearheaded green papers, first launched in 1994 (just 2 years after the UN Framework Convention on Climate Change and in the same year that the European Energy Charter was signed) to lay out the EU's sense of thinking on how to balance these two sets of concerns, actually evolved to serve as a concrete roadmap for a common EU approach to internal and external energy issues. Unmistakably after 2006, these green papers incorporated implicit or overt reference to problems associated with the supply and transportation of Russian gas. Thus, they seemed at least in part intended to coax member states out of their respective parochial policy ghettos and narrowly sovereign mindsets and push them onto the track of greater unity of action in addressing collective EU energy security issues.

Yet, given the highly disparate energy consumption and importation profiles associated with different states, with the EU12's relatively heavier reliance on Russian hydrocarbons distinguishing it as a bloc from the EU15, member states have clearly adopted *sui generis* and often clashing interpretations and approaches to 'their' energy security 'problem' and to that of the EU as a whole. Certain countries want the EU to base its policies on the principle of free markets internally and externally, via externalisation of the energy *acquis* to the EU 'neighbourhood'. The EU has indeed made certain inroads into institutionalising its relations with energy producing and transit regions and countries, such as Norway, the countries of Southeastern Europe and some in the Caucasus. However, others remain dismal about the end game of market liberalisation if it simply broadens the swath of new 'downstream' market territory for Gazprom or Transneft. Instead, they prefer a geostrategic approach based on bilateral or regional diplomatic initiatives. The EU has been forced to navigate between these polar positions. Its efforts have been stymied by the lack of a common European policy framework that could promote liberalisation, not just by hammering EU members and some non-EU states with the 'stick' of *acquis* directives, but also by offering the 'carrot' of wider choices of supplier, both domestically and internationally. In short, without a common energy policy, members act less concertedly, which results in outcomes that make this policy ever more necessary but even harder to attain.

Theories of international relations, closely affiliated with those of integration studies, help to illuminate the nature of the EU's collective dilemma with respect to energy security. Inspired by neo-functionalist logic, liberal approaches tend to emphasise the potential for internal market integration, which entails greater competition and institutionalised regulation, to generate pressure towards more efficacious EU-wide external policy, especially in terms of the EU's capacity to act in a unified manner to advance its member states' common interests vis-à-vis powerful external suppliers. On the other hand, realists focus on member states' abiding concern for retention of their remaining sovereign identity and prerogatives. Thus, they would be less surprised by the poor translation of EU market integration, which itself has developed fitfully in the energy field, into coherent EU external energy policy, the weakness of which in turn drives many individual member-state players to strike separate deals with these suppliers, thereby undercutting common energy policy even more.

Contentment and disquiet in the EU-Russian energy house

One of Europe's biggest energy suppliers, Russia is also one of the biggest sources of anxiety animating Europe's energy security considerations. Both exporters and importers operate in a global energy market characterised by pervasive competition and uncertainty (about supply and demand security). If each side could ensure the other that it could count on predictable supplies or stable demand, then the basis for an international regime might emerge. Economically speaking, Russia depends even more on the EU in terms of its energy market than the EU is reliant on Russian energy exports. Nonetheless, both sides have come to perceive that they cannot abandon their respective searches for diversity – Russia for a wider range of energy consumers (in East Asia for example) and the EU for greater multiples of supplies and suppliers (in Central Asia for example). Russia may even need demand diversity more than the EU requires supply diversity and many consumers in the latter feel that the Russian gas 'crises' of 2006 and 2009 originated not 'upstream', but in those 'midstream' transit states that lie outside the EU27's territorial ambit. To reiterate what was discussed up to this point, for consumers and importers lying further 'downstream' in the energy flow geography, diversification can be construed as relevant not only to the 'upstream' supply base but also to that of available transit routes. Indeed, diversity of transit routes can even promote greater diversity of suppliers, as trans-Turkey 'bridge' or 'hub' projects are expected to do, but this does not necessarily have to be the case, as exemplified by the Nord Stream and South Stream projects, designed to allow Gazprom gas to circumvent its 'troublesome' Soviet-origin passage through Belarus and Ukraine.

The morally untenable aspect of this 'great (energy) game' is that it is largely key EU15 players – namely, governments and firms in Germany and Italy – that have condoned or actively supported the pursuit of joint ventures with state-led Russian monopoly firms to construct these bypass pipelines. Conversely, some of the most ardent backers of EU-supported initiatives like the Nabucco Project (which would pass from Turkey into Bulgaria, Romania and Hungary before terminating in Austria) have been EU12 countries. However, the direct seaborne routes, by acquiring political life and momentum of their own, have posed threats to certain EU12 states, as well as smaller Russia-dependent EU15 member states like Finland and Greece, as well as forcing even Nabucco consortium members, including Turkey, to defensively conclude their own side deals (not all of which can simultaneously be honoured) with these Russian firms. Like any public good with collective long-term benefits but concentrated frontloaded costs, true diversification of suppliers via new pipeline routes is an expensive undertaking that can easily be thwarted by determined opposition from those who stand to lose the most. This dilemma requires all the more counter-effort on the part of EU institutions and its wealthiest member states (which admittedly became a tougher sell in 2010, as energy prices fell and European economies experienced ongoing difficulties). The latter countries may have to make larger immediate economic sacrifices, which in turn requires a higher level of confidence that new suppliers and independent supply routes (those not controlled or otherwise cooptable by a major interested supplier) can be brought into play. Turkey enters the picture here.

How can the EU get anything past Russia?

As opposed to real conflicts that have occurred over, or in the vicinity of, petroleum, 'war' might strike many observers as too strong a term to describe disputes that have occurred over the multinational flow of gas. Since most gas travels through pipeline networks, real physical and economic interdependencies develop that are costly to break. Yet, a gas-centric 'wide-area rent-seeking' strategy – gas 'w-a-r-s' – of which Gazprom has been an exemplary practitioner and master, can be applied in this realm without causing any obvious or prolonged disruptions to the flow of the energy source in question. In fact, this rent-seeking has been motivated more often by the prospect of capturing a larger fraction of the 'downstream' market than destroying the buyer's economy. Of course, as the end game revolves around obtaining a greater monopoly share of those markets, the supplier who attains that goal by crowding out, or gaining greater influence over, third-party rivals acquires a stronger potential position to demand and extract more onerous political concessions. This is especially troublesome when the target of these concessions – like Belarus or Ukraine – combines the roles of transit route and consumer.

The EU has certainly entertained the pursuit of and provided limited funding for a number of project options that involve tapping into non-Russian hydrocarbon supplies, saliently those from the Caspian region, without having to ship them through Belarus, Ukraine or even Turkey. However, moving gas and oil from the non-Russian Former Soviet Union (FSU) littorals of the Caspian Sea westward without first having to route these through extant 'transit' countries Russia and Iran (which posses conflicting interests associated with their 'upstream' status) has proven to be highly cumbersome without Turkey. Projects like the Odessa–Brody oil pipeline reversal and White Stream (for gas) would leave the EU even more dependent on Ukraine and may have thus failed to attract sufficient funding and support from Brussels. Thus, as we have devoted much of this book to analysing, perceptions have grown that a better road to EU energy security lies in Turkey. In that vein, it would be surprising if Moscow refrained from attempting to subvert Turkey's capacity to serve as a route for gas supplies that can bypass Russia altogether. First, Turkey's fast-growing energy consumption has made it resiliently dependent on Russian gas and the Turusgaz and sub-sea Blue Stream pipelines. Second, narrower interests in Turkey have sometimes appeared to cause the country to deviate from its potential role as an *acquis*-regulated conductor of Europe-bound gas supplies in favour of acting more like a self-interested merchant brokering deals in an energy bazaar. Thirdly, Turkey is not immune from the geopolitical calculations influencing government decision-making in other transit countries, most notably Ukraine, which has developed a growing reputation – even domestically – for its willingness to surrender energy assets and other symbols of national sovereignty in order to guarantee lower prices on Russian gas. Despite Ankara's hosting of the July 2009 Nabucco IGA, the Turkish government has also signed a raft of energy-related agreements with Moscow, most recently in August 2009, when it assented to allow the passage of the Gazprom-backed South Stream gas pipeline project through its exclusive economic zone in the Black Sea.

On the same side of the economic coin as the EU27, China, as a much faster growing consumer of all forms of energy, even gas, represents one of the greatest challenges to EU energy security policy. The People's Republic of China (PRC) has moved much more quickly than the EU, where member states seem to have dithered at their collective peril, to consolidate access to Caspian hydrocarbon reserves. As China has diverted some fraction of the potential energy supply pool away from the European economy in a way that also contradicts Russian

energy firms' rent-seeking interests, its energy consumption may constitute a truer long-term threat to Europe's supplier portfolio. Thus, while
the current operation of smaller trans-Turkey pipelines – namely, the
Iraq–Turkey (IT), Baku–Tbilisi–Ceyhan (BTC), South Caucasus Pipeline
(SCP) and Turkey–Greece–Italy Interconnector (TGII)– carrying flows of
energy originating in the Middle East and the Caspian has conferred
upon Turkey a certain advantageous 'incumbent' position, China has
inserted itself into the EU energy-supply equation as a competitor, thus
offsetting the otherwise positive impact of European firms' growing
trade with the PRC.

Turkey's EU membership through secure energy corridorship

Though the strategic nature of Turkey's energy transit role has grown
increasingly evident, multiple challenges to the viability of this role
have arisen from all nodes of the supply value chain, not least of which
in the putative transit country itself. However, many of the hurdles
facing the centrepiece Nabucco project, one that involves a candidate
country but has nonetheless managed to acquire major EU backing and
funding, would probably seem eminently more surmountable if some
of the unity of purpose that the EU needs to show on the issue of its
collective energy security were to include greater willingness to ensure
progress on Turkey's own accession bid.

It would be politically more palatable for the Union to treat Turkey's
ability and willingness to serve as a transit country, primarily in terms of
gas, within existing frameworks of cooperation, notably the earlier discussed SEEECT, which requires a number of non-EU signatories to accept
the energy *acquis*. This is precisely the slippery slope to acceptance of
one more form of 'privileged partnership' status (already enshrined in
Turkey's membership in the Customs Union) that Ankara has strenuously sought to evade for fear that it would prevent its attainment of
full membership, which certain EU member states oppose outright anyway. While certain short-sighted economic interests may have impelled
Ankara to overplay its energy cards in hopes of winning more narrowly
conceived economic gains, thus tarnishing Turkey's goal of serving
as a secure and independent and pro-EU energy corridor, this devi-
ation could have been checked more effectively – and may yet be
reversible – by greater and more sincere reassurances on the country's
much longer-running bid to join the EU (in its successive incarnations).

A number of member-state governments and their constituencies have undoubtedly adopted the more comfortable belief that even if Turkey's value were reducible to its energy corridor status, this functioning may be realised to its fullest fruition through simpler forms of bilateral cooperation, which many EU member states are already accustomed to engaging in with its existing producer and transit states. This might be true if the Commission preferred a mere proliferation of transit routes like those crossing Belarus and Ukraine. However, Turkey has already obtained EU-member candidacy status. Thus, it has been expected, in that capacity, to apply an array of measures compatible with the energy *acquis*, not as a final goal, but as part of the larger set of conditions imposed on it for full membership. Moreover, its 'incumbent' energy corridor status has not advanced to such a stage that it obviates the necessity and negates the utility of applying extra effort on the part of the Union to ensure that this corridor complies with EU regulatory standards. Yet, the ideal operation even of the existing SCP and TGII pipelines or the planned Nabucco pipeline, however, presupposes the wider scope and denser quality of the regulatory environment in a fully integrated political union. Thus, if the EU really embodies a collective dual desire for a new energy nexus that operates not only independently of the control of its major incumbent suppliers but also in conformity with the EU's higher standards of operation, then this bolsters the accession negotiation leverage possessed by Turkey. Conversely, the appearance of backpedalling on Turkey's accession bid may cause the latter not only to spurn further implementation of the energy *acquis* but even jeopardise the prospects of continued bilateral cooperation on energy security.

Admittedly, in Turkey's accession negotiations, the role of energy-related concerns has not become so critically urgent as to surmount countervailing reservations on Turkish membership. This lack of urgency is exemplified by Cyprus, which, lacking any dependence on Russian or any other gas and mired in a host of disputes with Turkey, has freely exercised its veto rights – and thus far sustained this exercise – on the energy chapter itself. So far, Turkey's accession has not become governed by straightforward interest-based calculations and a logic of consequentiality. Instead, it remains a matter reflecting a search for balance among national preferences, EU priorities and Turkish foreign policy choices (Tekin, 2005). While the timing and fate of Turkey's accession are subject to many variables that cannot be boiled down to its strategic position, enhancement of the value of this position by external events impinging on EU27 energy security cannot hurt Turkey's chances of getting into the club. While the ECSC was created to ensure peace via economic interdependence, the genuine possibility of belonging to the ECSC's organisational successor provides a crucial source of motivation animating Ankara's efforts to make its energy sector and pipeline network more EU-friendly.

Notes

2 Evolution of EU Energy Policy

1. See http://www.energy-regulators.eu/portal/page/portal/EER.

3 External Dimension of European Energy Policy

1. An Action Plan is prepared for every country included in the ENP (Algeria, Armenia, Azerbaijan, Belarus, Egypt, Georgia, Israel, Jordon, Lebanon, Libya, Moldova, Morocco, Occupied Palestinian Territory, Tunisia and Ukraine). Each Action Plan makes reference to energy, convergence of energy policies and energy networks.
2. See for example p. 4 of the MoU with Azerbaijan http://ec.europa.eu/energy/international/international_cooperation/doc/mou_azerbaijan_en.pdf.

4 EU Dependence on Russian Energy

1. Reasons for this discrepancy relate to the 'relative comparative advantage' of the extractive sector, broadly inclusive of mineral and energy sources, in heavily commodity-dependent economies, and the prevalence in the latter of the so-called Dutch Disease, the observed tendency of external demand to raise the value of the commodity-exporting country's local currency and thus draw labour and capital into the commodity and non-traded goods (typically construction and real estate) sectors at the expense of tradable manufactures (Sachs, 2007, pp. 173–93).
2. Per tonne of oil equivalent (toe) consumed, however, in 2007, oil emitted less carbon dioxide than coal (2.7 vs. 3.8 tonnes, respectively), and natural gas generated 2.3 tonnes, less than the other fossil fuels.
3. Until the price collapse in late 2008, Russia had been, over the previous 5 years, moving to curtail and restrict extant foreign direct investment (FDI) that had been made by US and European energy firms in the form of production sharing agreements (PSAs) initiated in the 1990s (Goldman, 2008, pp. 93–135). While access to additional fields has been used as a strategic bargaining chip, in 2008, the Medvedev government legally restricted development of offshore energy reserves to national state-controlled companies (Rodova, 2008b). This came just prior to the first liquefied natural gas (LNG) shipments from the Sakhalin Island projects to Japan.
4. It should be noted that Ukraine would have to satisfy the EU that all of its operating NPPs were assessed to be safe before it would be allowed to join the South East European Energy Community.
5. An earlier decision by Ukraine's National Energy Regulatory Committee to raise domestic gas tariffs by 35 per cent effective 1 December 2008 was

nonetheless assessed in the Fourth Joint EU–Ukraine Report on EU–Ukraine energy cooperation to have been insufficient to cover gas import costs.

6. By the latter half of the year, Russia's Gazprom, itself a major buyer of Turkmenistan gas, Ukraine's Naftogaz, a customer of Gazprom-bundled supplies, and even some EU member-state companies, like Germany's E.ON, Germany's biggest customer for Gazprom gas, were bucking (as buyers), or waiving (as sellers), the standard 'take-or-pay' provisions of pipeline-based gas contracts that mandate purchases of contracted quantities even if these are no longer demanded.

5   The EU Outreach to Non-Russian Energy

1. The physical immobility of reserves gives potential market power to 'upstream' states only after the resources in question become economically usable. Over the course of most of the twentieth century, until the 1960s–70s, Western multinationals, headquartered in typically consumption- and importation-orientated countries, were granted generous concessions, including generous rent and tax rates as well as ownership rights, to develop the 'upstream' sector in foreign territories, especially in Venezuela and numerous Middle Eastern countries. Once the reserves became income-generating assets, incentives as well as capabilities materialised for the governments of producing territories to exert greater ownership of those assets and control over their use, which, in most empirical cases, meant unilateral revision of concessions and even outright expropriation of multinationals' assets. This process, known as the 'obsolescing bargain', was originally conceptualized by Raymond Vernon (1971) and more recently expounded on by Gould and Winters (2007) and Williams (2008).

6   Roads to Europe for Caspian and Middle Eastern Energy Supplies

1. This statement contradicts the same report's assessment that this armed conflict had a more negative affect on the passage of oil through Georgia than on the transit of gas, which was halted 'only two days, from 12–14 August', as a precautionary measure (International Energy Agency, 2008b, p. 47).

2. EU27-area imports of Azerbaijan oil can be found in Eurostat (2010a). The given range of that country's exports was established by taking one set of Azerbaijan's oil exports from the Department of Energy's Energy Information Administration (EIA), available at http://tonto.eia.doe.gov/cfapps/ipdbproject/IEDIndex3.cfm, and another by subtracting consumption from production, based on data found in BP, 2009, pp. 9–10.

3. The cited figures from 1993 are derived from data found in BP, 2004, pp. 10, 26, 33–7, while 2008 figures are based on data found in BP, 2009, pp. 32, 40–1.

4. CO_2 emission figures are derived from International Energy Agency (2009b, pp. 623, 629, 633, 647).

5. The figures used in this section are based on data taken from International Energy Agency (2009c, pp. II. 92, II. 255, II. 257, II. 259, II. 261, II. 264; 2009d, pp. II. 503, II. 506; and 2009e, pp. II. 34–5, II. 38–9).

6. Calculations based on data given by the International Energy Agency (2009a, pp. II. 17, II. 20) indicate that China went from being a net exporter of 1.948 bcm in 2006 to being a net importer in 2007 and 2008 of 1.420 bcm and 1.485 bcm, respectively. However, data given by the same organisation (International Energy Agency, 2009c, pp. II. 91–II. 92, II. 259) equate to net exports of 1.809 bcm in 2006 and net imports of 1.319 bcm in 2007.

7 Turkey's Role as a 'Trans-European' Energy Corridor

1. The EU, as expressed in the European Commission's 2003 Directive for the Promotion of Biofuels, is endeavouring to comply with the 1997 Kyoto Protocol and other European Commission directives pertaining to fuel quality standards and energy taxation (Pahl, 2004, pp. 83–91).
2. See also, Mann (2003).

8 Turkey's Energy Role and Its Accession Process

1. For details, see Eralp (1998) and Muftuler-Bac (1997).
2. More details will follow on these issues.
3. For this and many other positions on Turkey, see, Spiegel Online International (2004).
4. The emphasis is added.
5. The emphasis is added.
6. The Energy Charter Treaty (ECT) Trade Amendment has not been ratified by Turkey as of April 2010.
7. The same justification was also offered by US President Barack Obama (EurActiv Network, 2009c).
8. The SEEREM was included in the framework of the Stability Pact for South Eastern Europe and previously envisaged by the Athens Memorandum, in which the parties (the EU and Albania, Bosnia and Herzegovina, Bulgaria, Croatia, Greece, Kosovo, Macedonia, Romania, Turkey, and Serbia and Montenegro) committed to liberalize, integrate and enhance gas and power markets on regional scale, as a part of the wider European energy market (SEEREM, 2010).
9. Ker-Lindsay (2007) has argued that 'There has in fact been a growing divergence between Greek and Greek Cypriots policy, both in terms of their respective approaches towards Turkey and regarding the question of Turkish membership in the European Union' (p. 71).
10. Geropoulos (2009) has stated that 'Turkey cut off talks in 2007 with GDF, which merged with Suez in 2008, over joining the project because of a French law that termed the killing of ethnic Armenians under the Turkey's former Ottoman Empire as genocide' (p. 1).

References

ABHaber, 2008. *AB ve Turkiye'den enerji icin ortak aciklama (Joint EU-Turkey Announcement on Energy)*, [internet] 5 May. Available at: http://www.abhaber. com/ozelhaber.php?id=772 [Accessed 20 April 2010].

Adams, T., 2004. *Caspian Hydrocarbons, the Politicisation of Regional Pipelines, and the Destabilisation of the Caucasus*, [internet] Available at: http://poli.vub.ac.be/ publi/crs/eng/Vol5/adams.htm [Accessed 10 March 2008].

AFP, 2008. Uzbekistan rules out direct gas exports to EU. *Agence France-Presse*, [internet] 6 November. Available at: http://www.eubusiness.com/news-eu/ 1225988235.99 [Accessed 30 March 2010].

Ahrend, R., 2005. Can Russia break the 'resource curse'? *Eurasian Geography and Economics*, 46(8), pp. 584–609.

Akdemir, E., 2008. Lithuanian Ambassador Pranckevičius: 'Lithuania supports Turkey's EU full membership'. *ABHaber*, [internet] 18 September. Available at: http://www.abhaber.com/english/haber.php?id=4253 [Accessed 10 April 2010].

Alekperov, G., 2004. Energy resources of the Caspian region and the significance of Turkey for Europe's energy security. *The Quarterly Journal*, 3(3), pp. 115–23.

Alexander's Gas and Oil Connections, 2007. Blue Stream-2 feasibility study to be ready by July, [internet] 27 February. Available at: http://www.gasandoil.com/ GOC/company/cne70924.htm [Accessed 20 April 2010].

Andoura, S., Hatcher, L. and van der Woude, M., 2010. *Towards a European Energy Community: A Policy Proposal*, [internet] Available at: http://www.notre-europe. edu/uploads/tx-publications/Etud76-Energy-en.pdf [Accessed 10 April 2010].

Andoura, S. and Vegh, C., 2009. *Background Paper: Energy Trends in Europe* [internet] Available at: http://www.notre-europe.eu/uploads/tx_publication/Energy_ project_Note.pdf [Accessed 10 April 2010].

Andrianopoulos, A., 2003. The economics and politics of Caspian oil. *Southeast Europe and Black Sea Studies*, 3(3), pp. 76–91.

APS, 2008. Egypt-export pipeline project. *APS Review Gas Market Trends* [internet] 14 January. Available at: http://www.entrepreneur.com/tradejournals/article/ 173385208.html [Accessed 10 March 2008].

Aras, B., 2009. The Davutoglu era in Turkish foreign policy. *SETA Policy Brief*, [internet] 32. Available at: http://www.ciaonet.org/pbei/seta/0016473/index. html [Accessed 15 April 2010].

Aras, B. and Iseri, E., 2009. The Nabucco natural gas pipeline: from opera to reality. *SETA Policy Brief*, [internet] 34. Available at: http://www.setav.org/ document/SETA_Policy_Brief_No_34_Bulent_Aras_Emre_Iseri_The_Nabucco_ Natural_Gas_Pipeline_From_Opera_to_Reality.pdf [Accessed 20 April 2010].

Aydın, M. and Acikmese, S.A., 2007. Europeanization through conditionality: understanding the new era in Turkish foreign policy. *Journal of Southern Europe and the Balkans*, 9(3), pp. 263–74.

Bacik, G., 2006. Turkey and pipeline politics. *Turkish Studies*, 7(2), pp. 293–306.

Bagis, E., 2010. Turkey's EU membership process: prospects and challenges. *EU Diplomacy Papers 5/2010*, [internet] College of Europe. Available
at: www.coleurop.be/file/content/studyprogrammes/.../EDP_5_2010_Bagis.pdf
[Accessed 12 April 2010].

Bahgat, G., 2002. Pipeline diplomacy: the geopolitics of the Caspian region.
International Studies Perspectives, 3(3), pp. 310–27.

———, 2005. Energy security: the Caspian Sea. *Minerals and Energy*, 20(2),
pp. 3–15.

———, 2006. Europe's energy security: challenges and opportunities. *International
Affairs*, 82(5), pp. 961–75.

Baran, Z., 2005. The Baku-Tbilisi-Ceyhan pipeline: implications for Turkey. In:
F. Starr and S.E. Cornell, eds. 2005. *The Baku-Tbilisi-Ceyhan Pipeline: Oil Window
to the West*, [internet] Washington, D.C: Central Asia-Caucasus Institute & Silk
Road Studies. Available at: http://www.silkroadstudies.org/BTC_6.pdf [Accessed
20 April 2010].

———, 2008. *Security Aspects of the South Stream Project*, [internet] Brussels:
European Parliament. Available at: http://www.hudson.org/files/publications/
Baran-South%20Stream%20for%20EP.pdf [Accessed 30 March 2010].

Barroso, J.M., 2006. In: O. Geden, M. Marcelis and A. Maurer, eds. Perspectives
for the European Union's external energy policy: discourses, ideas and interests
in Germany, the UK, Poland and France. Working Paper for German Institute
for International and Security Affairs.

———, 2008. *Speech/08/612, Press Conference on the Strategic Energy Review
Package*, [internet] Brussels. Available at: http://europa.eu/rapid/pressReleases
Action.do?reference=SPEECH/08/612&format=HTML&aged=0&language=EN
&guiLanguage=en [Accessed 30 March 2010].

Barry, E., 2010. Putin surprises Ukraine with energy-merger plan; Russian seeks to
exploit closer ties with Kiev to win control over pipelines. *International Herald
Tribune*, 3 May.

Barysch, K., 2007a. What Europeans think about Turkey and why. *Centre for
European Reform*, [internet] 24 August. Available at: http://www.cer.org.uk/pdf/
briefing_kb_turkey_24aug07.pdf [Accessed 20 April 2010].

———, 2007b. Turkey's role in European energy security. *Centre for European
Reform*, [internet] 12 December. Available at: http://www.cer.org.uk/pdf/essay_
turkey_energy_12dec07.pdf [Accessed 06 April 2010].

———, 2010. Can Turkey combine EU accession and regional leadership? *Centre
for European Reform*, [internet] 25 January. Available at: http://www.cer.org.uk/
pdf/pb_barysch_turkey_25jan10.pdf [Accessed 6 April 2010].

BBC, 2009. Russia's Gazprom reports on progress in talks with Turkmenistan,
Italy's Eni. *BBC Monitoring International Reports*, [internet] 24 June. Available at:
http://find.galegroup.com/itx/start.do?prodId=SPJ.SP00 [Accessed 30 March
2010].

Belkin, P., 2007. The European Union's energy security challenges, [internet]
Washington, DC: Congressional Research Service. Available at: http://www.
cnie.org/NLE/crs/abstract.cfm?NLEid=1743 [Accessed 30 March 2010].

Belton, C. and Crooks, E., 2007. Kazakhstan in threat over ENI oil licence. *The
Financial Times*, 22 August, p. 7.

Belton, C. and Dickie, M., 2009. Russia opens new front to supply energy to Asia.
The Financial Times, 19 February, p. 10.

Benford, J., 2006. Special report 1: EU energy policy: internal developments and external challenges. *European Policy Analyst*, 2nd Quarter, pp. 39–46.

Bildt, C. and D'Alema, M., 2007. It's time for a fresh effort. *International Herald Tribune*, 31 August.

Black Sea Economic Cooperation, 2010, [internet] Available at: www.bsec-organization.org/Pages/homepage.aspx [Accessed 10 March 2010].

Blank, S., 2010. The strategic implications of the Turkmenistan-China pipeline project. *China Brief*, [internet] 16 February. Available at: http://www.james town.org/programs/chinabrief/single/?tx_ttnews%5Btt_news%5D=36010&tx_ ttnews%5BbackPid%5D=414&no_cache=1 (Jamestown Foundation) [Accessed 30 March 2010].

Blagov, S., 2010. Russia mends energy ties with Turkmenistan and Azerbaijan. *Eurasia Daily Monitor*, [internet] 13 January. Available at: http://www. jamestown.org/programs/edm/single/?tx_ttnews[tt_news]=35904&tx_ttnews [backPid]=484&no_cache=1 [Accessed 30 March 2010].

Botas, 2010. [internet] Available at: http://www.botas.gov.tr [Accessed on 20 April 2010].

BP, 2004. *BP Statistical Review of World Energy June 2004*, [internet] Available at: http://www.bp.com/liveassets/bp_internet/switzerland/corporate_switzerland/ STAGING/local_assets/downloads_pdfs/s/statistical_review_of_world_energy_ 2004.pdf [Accessed 30 March 2010].

———, 2008. *BP Statistical Review of World Energy June 2008*, [internet] Available at: http://www.bp.com/multipleimagesection.do?categoryId=9023755& contentId=7044552 [Accessed 30 March 2010].

———, 2009. *BP Statistical Review of World Energy June 2009*, [internet] Available at: http://www.bp.com/productlanding.do?categoryId=6929&contentId= 7044622 [Accessed 30 March 2010].

Bryant, C., 2009. The struggle over Russia's 'energy weapon' beneath the Baltic. *The Financial Times*, 26 October, p. 11.

Central Intelligence Agency, 2009. *World Factbook*, [internet] Available at: https://www.cia.gov/library/publications/the-world-factbook/rankorder/2179 rank.html?countryName=Iraq&countryCode=iz&regionCode=me&rank=11 #iz [Accessed 25 April 2010].

Chaffin, J., 2009. Reverse flow takes the heat out of crisis. *The Financial Times*, 30 December, p. 8.

Chazan, G., 2007. Algeria–Russia split on gas helps Europe. *Wall Street Journal*, 10 December.

Checchi, A., 2009. *Gas Interconnectors in Europe: More Than a Funding Issue*, [internet] Brussels: Centre for European Policy Studies (CEPS). Available at: www. ceps.be/ceps/node/1651 [Accessed 30 March 2010].

Checchi, A., Behrens, A. and Egenhofer, C., 2009. *Long-Term Energy Security Risks for Europe: A Sector-Specific Approach*, [internet] Brussels: Centre for European Policy Studies (CEPS). Available at: http://www.ceps.be/node/1608 [Accessed 30 March 2010].

Chinaoilweb.com, 2010. *China's Crude Oil Imports Data for December*, [internet] Available at: http://www.chinaoilweb.com/UploadFile/docs/Attachment/2010- 3-172344936.pdf [Accessed 30 March 2010].

Clingendael International Energy Programme, 2004. *Study on Energy Supply Security and Geopolitics, Final Report*, [internet] Available at: http://www.clingendael.

nl/ciep/events/20040130/CIEP_Final_Report_Complete_Version_2004.pdf [Accessed 20 April 2010].

Clover, C., 2010. Russia stops oil shipments to Belarus. *The Financial Times*, 4 January, p. 2.

Colombo, S. and Lesser, I., 2010. The Mediterranean energy scene: What now? What next? *Instituto Affari Internazionali (IAI)* [internet], Document IAI 10 06. Available at: http://www.iai.it/pdf/DocIAI/IAI1006.pdf [Accessed 15 April 2010].

Corporate & Public Advisory Group, 2009. *EU Corridors*, [internet] Available at: http://www.cpsag.com/UserFiles/Documents//fa95014d-f703-4f6d-a196-84 dacb79cff1.pdf [Accessed 01 April 2010].

Correljé, A. and van der Linde, C., 2006. Energy supply security and geopolitics: a European perspective. *Energy Policy*, 34, pp. 532–43.

Crooks, E., 2007. Kashagan becomes a thorn in Eni's side. *The Financial Times*, 4 December, p. 26.

Crooks, E. and Olearchyk, R., 2007. Five states agree Caspian oil pipeline extension to reduce reliance on Russia. *The Financial Times*, 11 October, p. 8.

Dejevsky, M., 2009. Ukraine in new gas showdown with Russia. *The Independent*, 5 March, p. 44.

Dinmore, G. and Gorst, I., 2007. Row halts work on Kazakh oilfield. *The Financial Times*, 28 August, p. 5.

Directorate General for Energy and Transport, 2008. *The Euro-Mediterranean Energy Partnership – Latest Developments*, [internet] 21 March. Available at: http://www.medenergy.org/docs/The-EuroMediterranean-Energy-Partnership-(English).pdf [Accessed 15 April 2010].

———, 2009. *EU Energy and Trasnport in Figures*, [internet] Available at: http://ec.europa.eu/transport/publications/statistics/doc/2009_energy_transport_figures.pdf [Accessed 15 April 2010].

Directorate General for Trade, 2009a. *EU Bilateral Trade with Azerbaijan*, [internet] 22 September. Available at: http://trade.ec.europa.eu/doclib/docs/2006/september/tradoc_113347.pdf [Accessed 15 April 2010].

———, 2009b. *EU Bilateral Trade with Kazakhstan*, [internet] 9 October. Available at: http://trade.ec.europa.eu/doclib/docs/2006/september/tradoc_113406.pdf [Accessed 15 April 2010].

———, 2009c. *EU Bilateral Trade with Norway*, [internet] 22 September. Available at: http://trade.ec.europa.eu/doclib/docs/2006/september/tradoc_113429.pdf [Accessed 15 April 2010].

———, 2009d. *EU Bilateral Trade with Turkmenistan*, [internet] 22 September. Available at: http://trade.ec.europa.eu/doclib/docs/2006/september/tradoc_113457.pdf [Accessed 15 April 2010].

Domanic, S., 2007. The Turkish accession to the European Union: mutually beneficial? Mutually possible? In: The future of EU enlargement: on track or derailed? *Center for Public Policy – Providus*, [internet] Available at: http://www.providus.lv/upload_file/Projekti/Eiropas%20politika/The_Future_of_EU_enlargement.pdf [Accessed 10 April 2010].

Dover, R., 2007. The EU's foreign, security, and defence policies. In: M. Cini, ed. *European Union politics*. 2nd ed. Oxford: Oxford University Press, pp. 237–53.

Dyer, G. and Lau, J., 2009. PetroChina secures $30bn state loan to fund 'go global' strategy. *The Financial Times*, 10 September, p. 1.

Economist Intelligence Unit, 2008. Oil and gas: Iran. *Economist Intelligence Unit-Business Middle East*, [internet] 1 March. Available at: http://global.factiva.com/ha/default.aspx [Accessed 10 March 2008].

Egan, M., 2007. The single market. In: M. Cini, ed. *European Union politics*. 2nd ed. Oxford: Oxford University Press, pp. 253–71.

Energy Charter Secretariat, 2004. *The Energy Charter Treaty and Related Documents: A Legal Framework for International Energy Cooperation*, [internet] Brussels: Energy Charter Secretariat. Available at: http://www.encharter.org/fileadmin/user_upload/document/EN.pdf [Accessed 30 March 2010].

Energy Community Treaty, 2010, [internet] Available at: http://www.energy-community.org/portal/page/portal/ENC_HOME [Accessed 10 April 2010].

Energy Information Administration, 2007. *Country Analysis Briefs: Azerbaijan*, [internet] November. Available at: http://www.eia.doe.gov/emeu/cabs/Azerbaijan/pdf.pdf [Accessed 6 December 2007].

———, 2008a. *Country Analysis Briefs: Kazakhstan*, [internet] February. Available at: http://www.eia.doe.gov/emeu/cabs/Kazakhstan/pdf.pdf [Accessed 6 December].

———, 2008b. *Country Analysis Briefs: Russia*, [internet] May. Available at http://www.eia.doe.gov/cabs/Russia/pdf.pdf [Accessed 30 March 2010].

———, 2008c. *Country Analysis Briefs: World Oil Transit Chokepoints*, [internet] January. Available at: http://www.eia.doe.gov/cabs/World_Oil_Transit_Chokepoints/pdf.pdf [Accessed 30 March 2010].

———, 2009a. *Country Analysis Briefs: Azerbaijan*, [internet] October. Available at: http://www.eia.doe.gov/emeu/cabs/Azerbaijan/pdf.pdf [Accessed 24 February 2010].

———, 2009b. *Country Analysis Briefs: China*, [internet] July. Available at: http://www.eia.doe.gov/emeu/cabs/China/pdf.pdf [Accessed 4 March 2010].

———, 2009c. *Country Analysis Briefs: Norway*, [internet] August. Available at: http://www.eia.doe.gov/cabs/Norway/pdf.pdf [Accessed 30 March 2010].

———, 2009d. *Country Analysis Briefs: Turkey*, [internet] April. Available at: http://www.eia.doe.gov/emeu/cabs/Turkey/pdf.pdf [Accessed 20 April 2010].

———, 2010. *International Energy Statistics*, [internet] Available at: http://tonto.eia.doe.gov/cfapps/ipdbproject/IEDIndex3.cfm [Accessed 10 March 2010].

Enerji ve Tabii Kaynaklar Bakanligi (Turkish Ministry of Energy and Natural Resources), 2010. *Stratejik Plan 2010–2014*, [internet] Available at: http://www.enerji.gov.tr/yayinlar_raporlar/ETKB_2010_2014_Stratejik_Plani.pdf [Accessed 20 August 2010].

Eoerth (Encyclopedia of Earth), 2008. *Natural Gas in France*, [internet] Available at: http://www.eoearth.org/article/Energy_profile_of_France#Natural_Gas [Accessed 18 December 2009].

Eqbeli, A. and Shiryaevskaya, A., 2008. Iran, Gazprom ink MOU, to set up joint energy company. *Platts*, [internet] 13 July. Available at: http://www.platts.com/OIL/News/9088054.xml [Accessed 15 July 2008].

Eralp, A., 1998. Turkey and the European Union in the aftermath of the cold war. In: L. Rittenberg, ed. *The Political Economy of Turkey in the Post-Soviet Era*. Westport, Connecticut: Praeger, pp. 37–50.

EurActiv Network, 2005. *EU-Turkey Relations*, [internet] Available at: http://www.euractiv.com/en/enlargement/eu-turkey-relations/article-129678 [Accessed 20 December 2008].

————, 2008. *Italy Wants Fast-Track Turkey's EU Membership*, [internet] Available at: http://www.euractiv.com/en/enlargement/italy-wants-fast-track-turkey-eumembership/article-177146 [Accessed 14 April 2010].

————, 2009a. *France Joins South Stream Pipeline*, [internet] Available at:http://www.euractiv.com/en/energy/france-joins-south-stream-gas-pipeline/article-187830 [Accessed 30 March 2010].

————, 2009b. *Miliband: Turning Turkey away from EU 'Unconscionable'*, [internet] Available at: http://www.euractiv.com/en/enlargement/miliband-turning-turkey-away-euunconscionable/article-186790 [Accessed 10 April 2010].

————, 2009c. *Obama Backs Turkey's Strategic Energy Role*, [internet] Available at: http://www.euractiv.com/en/energy/obama-backs-turkey-strategic-energy-role/article-181090 [Accessed 10 April 2010].

————, 2009d. *Turkey Plays Energy Card in Stalled EU Accession Talks*, [internet] Available at: http://www.euractiv.com/en/enlargement/turkey-plays-energy-card-stalled-eu-accession-talks/article-178623 [Accessed 10 April 2010].

————, 2010. *Nord Stream "A Waste of Money," Poland Says*, [internet] Available at: http://www.euractiv.com/en/energy/nord-stream-waste-money-poland/article-188727 [Accessed 30 March 2010].

Eurasia Daily Monitor, 2009. *Merkel and Sarkozy Call for Privileged Partnership Angers Turkey*, [internet] 13 May. Available at: http://www.jamestown.org/single/?no_cache=1&tx_ttnews%5Btt_news%5D=34983 (Jamestown Foundation) [Accessed 14 April 2010].

Euro-Mediterranean Ministers of Foreign Affairs, 2008. *Final Statement of Marseille Meeting*, [internet] Available at: http://www.eu2008.fr/webdav/site/PFUE/shared/import/1103_ministerielle_Euromed/Final_Statement_Mediterranean_Union_EN.pdf [Accessed 06 April 2010].

Europa, 1997. Agreement on partnership and cooperation establishing a partnership between the European Communities and their Member States, of one part, and the Russian Federation, of the other part. *Official Journal of the European Union L327*, [internet] Available at: http://eur-lex.europa.eu/LexUriServ/LexUriServ.do?uri=CELEX:21997A1128(01):EN:HTML [Accessed 30 March 2010].

————, 2003. *Road Map for the Common Economic Space – Building Blocks for Sustained Economic Growth*, [internet] Available at: http://ec.europa.eu/external_relations/russia/docs/roadmap_economic_en.pdf [Accessed 30 March 2010].

————, 2007a. *EU Energy Policy and Turkey, MEMO 07/219*, [internet] Available at: http://europa.eu/rapid/pressReleasesAction.do?reference=MEMO/07/219&format=HTML&aged=0&language=EN [Accessed14 April 2010].

————, 2007b. *Screening Report Turkey, Chapter 1 – Energy*, [internet] Available at: http://ec.europa.eu/enlargement/pdf/turkey/screening_reports/screening_report_15_tr_internet_en.pdf [Accessed 1 April 2010].

————, 2007c. *Screening Report Turkey, Chapter 21 – Trans-European Networks*, [internet] Available at: http://ec.europa.eu/enlargement/pdf/turkey/screening_reports/screening_report_21_tr_internet_en.pdf [Accessed 1 April 2010].

————, 2009a. *European Commission Opens Negotiations with Turkey upon Accession to the Energy Community, IP/09/1299*, [internet] Available at: http://europa.eu/

rapid/pressReleasesAction.do?reference=IP/09/1299&format=HTML&aged=0
&language=EN&guiLanguage=fr [Accessed 7 April 2010].

———, 2009b. *High Level Investment Conference on Modernization of Ukraine's Gas Transit System, IP/09/451,* [internet] Available at: http://europa.eu/rapid/pressReleasesAction.do?reference=IP/09/451&format=HTML&aged=0& language=EN&guiLanguage=en [Accessed 30 March 2010].

European Commission, 1994a. *Green Paper: for a European Union Energy Policy,* [internet] Available at: http://aei.pitt.edu/1185/

———, 1994b. *Proposal for a Council and Commission Decision on the Conclusion of the Partnership and Cooperation Agreement between the European Communities and their Member States of the One Part, and Ukraine, of the Other Part, Com (94) 226 Final,* [internet] Brussels: COM. Available at: http://eur-lex.europa.eu/LexUriServ/LexUriServ.do?uri=COM:1994:0226:FIN:EN:PDF [Accessed 30 March 2010].

———, 1996. *Green Paper: Energy for the Future: Renewable Sources of Energy,* [internet] Available at: http://aei.pitt.edu/1280/01/renewalbe_energy_gp_COM_96_576.pdf.

———, 1997. *Agreement on Partnership and Cooperation Establishing a Partnership between the European Communities and their Member States, of one Part, and the Russian Federation, of the Other Part. Official Journal L 327,* [internet] 28 November. Available at: http://eur-lex.europa.eu/LexUriServ/LexUriServ.do?uri=CELEX:21997A 1128(01):EN:HTML [Accessed 30 March 2010].

———, 2000. *Green Paper: Towards a European Strategy for the Security of Energy Supply,* [internet] Brussels. Available at: http://aei.pitt.edu/1184/01/enegy_supply_security_gp_COM_2000_769.pdf [Accessed 30 March 2010].

———, 2001. *Green Paper: Towards a European Strategy for the Security of Energy Supply,* [internet] Available at: http://ec.europa.eu/energy/green-paper-energy supply/doc/green_paper_energy_supply_en.pdf [Accessed 30 March 2010].

———, 2002. *Communication from the Commission to the Council and the European Parliament: Energy Cooperation with the Developing Countries,* [internet] Available at: http://eur-lex.europa.eu/LexUriServ/LexUriServ.do?uri=COM:2002:0408:fin:en:pdf [Accessed 30 March 2010].

———, 2004a. *Communication from the Commission: European Neighbourhood Policy Strategy Paper,* [internet] Available at: http://ec.europa.eu/world/enp/pdf/strategy/strategy_paper_en.pdf [Accessed 30 March 2010].

———, 2004b. 2004 *Regular Report on Turkey's Progress Towards Accession,* [internet] Available at: http://ec.europa.eu/enlargement/archives/pdf/key_documents/2004/rr_tr_2004_en.pdf [Accessed 10 April 2010].

———, 2005a. *EU/Ukraine Action Plan,* [internet] Available at: http://ec.europa.eu/world/enp/pdf/action_plans/ukraine_enp_ap_final_en.pdf [Accessed 30 March 2010].

———, 2005b. *Green paper on Energy Efficiency or Doing More with Less,* [internet] Brussels. Available at: http://eur-lex.europa.eu/LexUriServ/site/en/com/2005/com2005_0265en01.pdf [Accessed 30 March 2010].

———, 2005c. *Memorandum of Understanding on Co-operation in the Field of Energy between the European Union and Ukraine,* [internet] Available at: http://ec.europa.eu/dgs/energy_transport/international/bilateral/ukraine/doc/mou_en_final_en.pdf [Accessed 30 March 2010].

————, 2005d. *Report on the Green Paper on Energy: Four Years of European Initiatives*, [internet] Available at: www.jet.efda.org/wp-content/uploads/2005-green-paper-report-en.pdf [Accessed 30 March 2010].

————, 2006a. *An External Energy Policy to Serve Europe's Energy Interests*, [internet] Available at: http://www.consilium.europa.eu/ueDocs/cms_Data/docs/pressData/en/reports/90082.pdf [Accessed 30 March 2010].

————, 2006b. *Green Paper: a European Strategy for Sustainable, Competitive and Secure Energy*, [internet] Brussels. Available at: http://ec.europe.eu/energy/green-paper-energy/doc/2006_03_08_gp_document_en.pdf [Accessed 30 March 2010].

————, 2006c. *2006 Regular Report on Turkey's Progress Towards Accession*, [internet] Available at: http://ec.europa.eu/enlargement/pdf/key_documents/2006/Nov/tr_sec_1390_en.pdf [Accessed 10 April 2010].

————, 2007a. *Communication from the Commission to the European Council and the European Parliament: an Energy Policy for Europe*, [internet] Available at: http://ec.europa.eu/energy/energy_policy/doc/01_energy_policy_for_europe_en.pdf [Accessed 30 March 2010].

————, 2007b. *2007 Regular Report on Turkey's Progress towards Accession*, [internet] Available at: http://ec.europa.eu/enlargement/pdf/key_documents/2007/nov/turkey_progress_reports_en.pdf [Accessed 10 April 2010].

————, 2008a. *Second Strategic Energy Review: An EU Energy Security and Solidarity Action Plan*, [internet] Available at: http://eurlex.europa.eu/LexUriServ/LexUriServ.do?uri =COM:2008:0781:FIN:EN:pdf [Accessed 30 March 2010].

————, 2008b. *2008 Regular Report on Turkey's Progress towards Accession*, [internet] Available at: http://ec.europa.eu/enlargement/pdf/press_corner/key-documents/reports_nov_2008/turkey_progress_report_en.pdf [Accessed 10 April 2010].

————, 2009a. *Community Financial Aid to Trans-European Networks*, [internet] Available at: http://ec.europa.eu/energy/infrastructure/tent_e/financial_aid_en.htm [Accessed 30 March 2010].

————, 2009b. *EU-Ukraine Energy Relations*, [internet] Available at: http://ec.europa.eu/external_relations/energy/docs/eu_ukraine_energy_en.pdf [Accessed 30 March 2010].

————, 2009c. *EU-Ukraine Relations: Political and Legal Foundations*, [internet] Available at: http://ec.europa.eu/external_relations/ukraine/pdf/political_and_legal_foundations.pdf [Accessed 30 March 2010].

————, 2009d. *Fourth EU-Ukraine Report: Implementation of the EU-Ukraine Memorandum of Understanding on Energy Cooperation During 2009*, [internet] Available at: http://ec.europa.eu/energy/international/bilateral_cooperation/doc/ukraine/2009_12_04_report.pdf [Accessed 30 March 2010].

————, 2009e. *Neighborhood and Partnership Instrument*, [internet] Available at: http://ec.europa.eu/europeaid/where/neighbourhood/overview/index_en.htm [Accessed 30 March 2010].

————, 2009f. *Standard Eurobarometer 71*, [internet] Available at: http://ec.europa.eu/public_opinion/archives/eb/eb71/eb71_en.htm [Accessed on 14 April 2010].

————, 2009g. *TEN-E Financed Projects 1995–2008*, [internet] Available at: http://ec.europa.eu/energy/infrastructure/tent_e/doc/2009_ten_e_financed_projects_1995_2008.pdf [Accessed 30 March 2010].

———, 2009h. *2009 Regular Report on Turkey's Progress towards Accession*, [internet] Available at: http://ec.europa.eu/enlargement/pdf/key_documents/2009/tr_rapport_2009_en.pdf [Accessed 10 April 2010].

———, 2010. *Promoting Investment through the Neighborhood Investment Facility (NIF)*. Available at: http://ec.europa.eu/europeaid/where/neighbourhood/regional-cooperation/irc/investment_en.htm [Accessed 30 March 2010].

European Commission et al., 2009. *Joint Declaration: Joint EU-Ukraine International Investment Conference on the Modernization of Ukraine's Gas Transit System*, [internet] Available at: http://ec.europa.eu/external_relations/energy/events/eu_ukraine_2009/joint_declaration_en.pdf [Accessed 30 March 2010].

European Council, 1968. *Council Directive 68/414/EEC Imposing An Obligation on Member States of the EEC to Maintain Minimum Stocks of Crude Oil and/or Petroleum Products*, [internet] Available at: http://eur-lex.europa.eu/LexUriServ/LexUriServ.do?uri=CELEX:31968L0414:EN:HTML [Accessed 30 March 2010].

———, 1973. *Council Directive 73/238/EEC on Measures to Mitigate the Effects of Difficulties in the Supply of Crude Oil and Petroleum Products*, [internet] Available at: http://eur-lex.europa.eu/LexUriServ/LexUriServ.do?uri=CELEX:31973L0238:EN:HTML [Accessed 30 March 2010].

———, 1977. *Council Decision 77/706/EEC on the Setting of a Community Target for a Reduction in the Consumption of Primary Sources of Energy in the Event of Difficulties in the Supply of Crude Oil and Petroleum Products*, [internet] Available at: http://eur-lex.europa.eu/LexUriServ/LexUriServ.do?uri=CELEX:31977D0706:EN:HTML [Accessed 30 March 2010].

———, 1995. *Barcelona Declaration*, [internet] Available at: http://ec.europa.eu/external_relations/euromed/docs/bd_en.pdf [Accessed 20 April 2010].

———, 1997. *Luxembourg European Council Conclusions*, [internet] 12–13 December. Available at: http://www.consilium.europa.eu/ueDocs/cms_Data/docs/pressData/en/ec/032a0008.htm [Accessed 10 April 2010].

———, 1999. *Helsinki European Council Conclusions*, [internet] 10–11 December. Available at: http://www.europarl.europa.eu/summits/hel1_en.htm [Accessed 14 April 2010].

———, 2005. *Negotiation Framework [for Turkey]*, [internet] Luxembourg. Available at: http://ec.europa.eu/enlargement/pdf/turkey/st20002_05_tr_framedoc_en.pdf [Accessed 10 April 2010].

———, 2006. *TEN Guidelines Specify a Europe-Wide Energy Transmission Network, MEMO/06/304*, [internet] 24 July. Available at: http://europa.eu/rapid/pressReleasesAction.do?reference=MEMO/06/304&format [Accessed 10 April 2010].

———, 2007. *Brussels European Council 8/9 March 2007 Presidency Conclusions*, [internet] Available at: http://www.consilium.europa.eu/ueDocs/cms_Data/docs/pressData/en/ec/93 35.pdf [Accessed 30 March 2010].

———, 2008. *Council Decision of 18 February 2008 on the Principles, Priorities and Conditions Contained in the Accession Partnership with the Republic of Turkey and Repealing Decision 2006/35/EC*, [internet] Available at: http://eur-lex.europa.eu/LexUriServ/LexUriServ.do?uri=OJ:L:2008:051:0004:01:EN:HTML [Accessed 10 April 2010].

European Energy Charter, 2010. [internet] Available at: http://www.encharter.org [Accessed 10 March 2010].

European Investment Bank, 2007. European energy policy and the EIB, [internet] European Investment Bank. Available at: http://www.energy.eu/publications/QY7807387ENC_002.pdf [Accessed 30 March 2010].

European Parliament-Directorate General External Policies, 2006. *EU-Turkey Relations in the Field of Energy*, [internet] 20 April. Available at: http://www.europarl.europa.eu/meetdocs/2004_2009/documents/fd/d-tr20060425_06/d-tr20060425_06en.pdf [Accessed14 April 2010].

European Parliament and European Council, 2006. Decision No 1364/2006/EC of the European Parliament and of the Council of 6 September 2006 laying down the guidelines for trans-European energy networks and repealing Decision 96/391/EC and Decision No 1229/2003/EC. *Official Journal of the European Union, L262/1*, [internet] Available at: http://eur-lex.europa.eu/JOHtml.do?uri=OJ:L:2006:262:SOM:EN:HTML [Accessed 30 March 2010].

European Union, 1992. Treaty on European Union. *Official Journal C 191*, 29 July.

———, 2003. *A secure Europe in A Better World – European Security Strategy*, [internet] 12 December. Available at: http://www.consilium.europa.eu/uedocs/cmsUpload/78367.pdf [Accessed 10 April 2010].

———, 2007. Treaty of Lisbon. *Official Journal of the European Union*, [internet] 17 December. Available at: http://europa.eu/lisbon_treaty/full_text/index_en.htm [Accessed 30 March 2010].

———, 2009. *Memorandum on An Early Warning Mechanism in the Energy Sector within the Framework of the EU-Russia Energy Dialogue*, [internet] 16 November. Available at: http://ec.europa.eu/energy/international/bilateral_cooperation/russia/doc/reports/2009_11_16_ewm_signed_en.pdf [Accessed 30 March 2010].

European Union Press Release, 2009a. *CCS, Market Liberalisation and Energy Security Dominate the Agenda of the EC – Norway Energy Dialogue. Reference IP/09/849*, [internet] 28 May. Available at: http://europa.eu/rapid/pressReleasesAction.do?reference=IP/09/849&format=HTML&aged=0&language=EN&guiLanguage=en [Accessed 24 April 2010].

———, 2009b. *EU-Russia Energy Dialogue. Reference MEMO/09/121*, [internet] 19 March. Brussels. Available at: http://europa.eu/rapid/pressReleasesAction.do?reference=MEMO/09/121&format=HTML&language=en [Accessed 30 March 2010].

———, 2009c. *EU-Russia Summit on 21–22 May in Khabarovsk. Reference IP/09/817*, [internet] 20 May. Available at: http://europa.eu/rapid/pressReleasesAction.do?reference=IP/09/817&language=en [Accessed 30 March 2010].

Eurostat, 2007. *Energy, Transport and Environment Indicators*, [internet] Available at: http://epp.eurostat.ec.europa.eu/cache/ITY_OFFPUB/KS-DK-07-001/EN/KS-DK-07-001-EN.PDF [Accessed 30 March 2010].

———, 2009a. *Eurostat Yearbook 2009*. Luxembourg: Office for Official Publications of the European Communities.

———, 2009b. *Panorama of Energy: Energy Statistics to Support EU Policies and Solutions*, [internet] Available at: http://epp.eurostat.ec.europa.eu/cache/ITY_OFFPUB /KS-GH-09-001/EN/KS-GH-09-001-EN.PDF [Accessed 30 March 2010].

———, 2010a. *Eurostat Statistics Database-Energy*, [internet] Available at: http://epp.eurostat.ec.europa.eu/portal/page/portal/energy/data/database [Accessed 30 March 2010].

———, 2010b. *Eurostat Statistics Database-External Trade*, [internet] Available at: http://epp.eurostat.ec.europa.eu/portal/page/portal/external_trade/data/database [Accessed 30 March 2010].

Ferrero-Waldner, B., 2006. The European Neighbourhood Policy: the EU's newest foreign policy instrument. *European Foreign Affairs Review*, 11(2), pp. 139–42.

Financial Times, 2008. 9 July. In: International Energy Agency, 2008b. *Perspectives on Caspian Oil and Gas Development*, [internet] December. OECD/IEA. Available at: http://www.iea.org/papers/2008/caspian_perspectives.pdf [Accessed 30 March 2010].

Fink, D., 2006. Assessing Turkey's future as an energy transit country. *Washington Institute for Near East Policy*, [internet] Available at: http://www.washingtoninstitute.org/pubPDFs/ResearchNote11.pdf [Accessed 20 April 2010].

Forster, A. and Wallace, W., 2000. Common foreign and security policy. In: H. Wallace and W. Wallace, eds. *Policy-Making in the European Union*. 4th ed. Oxford: Oxford University Press, pp. 461–92.

Forward Magazine, 2008. *Arab Gas Pipe-Line Now Ready to Pass Via Syria*, [internet] 15 April. Available at: http://www.fw-magazine.com/print/13 [Accessed 20 April 2010].

Forysinski, W. and Osiewicz, P., 2006. *The EU- Turkish Accession Negotiations from the Polish Perspective: Allies or Competitors?* [internet] Available at: http://www.jhubc.it/ecpr-istanbul/virtualpaperroom/038.pdf [Accessed 10 April 2010].

Fukuyama, F., 2006. *The End of History and the Last Man*. New York: Free Press.

Gault, J., 2007. European energy security: Balancing priorities. *FRIDE*, [internet] 17 May. Available at: http://www.fride.org/publication/213/european-energy-security-balancing priorities [Accessed 30 March 2010].

Gazprom, 2010. [internet] Available at: http://old.gazprom.ru/eng/articles/article8895.shtml [Accessed 20 April 2010].

Geden, O., Marcelis, C. and Maurer, A., 2006. Perspectives for the European Union's external energy policy: discources, ideas and interests in Germany, the UK, Poland and France. Working Paper for German Institute for International and Security Affairs.

Geropoulos, K., 2009. Gaz de France: Nabucco's lucky number seven. *Centre for European Studies*, [internet] 25 October. Available at: http://www.neurope.eu/articles/Gaz-de-France-Nabuccos–lucky-number-seven/97047.php [Accessed 10 April 2010].

Gillman, J.S. and Martin, W.F., 2009. Energy security: the steps Europe now needs to take. *Europe's World*, [Online] Autumn 2009. Available at: http://www.europesworld.org/NewEnglish/Home/Article/tabid/191/ArticleType/ArticleView/ArticleID/21496/Default.aspx [Accessed 30 March 2010].

Globe & Mail, 2009. Turkmenistan grants rights to Nabucco partner. *Globe & Mail*, 17 April, p. B6.

Goldman, M., 2008. *Petrostate: Putin, Power, and the New Russia*. Oxford: Oxford University Press.

Gorst, I., 2007. A Caspian halt shows oil giants face fresh political perils. *The Financial Times*, 4 September, p. 11.

———, 2008. Gazprom push with Eni into Libya fuels EU security fears. *The Financial Times*, 3 April, p. 25.

———, 2009. Kazakhs approve pipeline to Russia. *The Financial Times*, 14 May, p. 2.

Gorst, I. and Hoyos, C., 2009. Russia and Italy sign gas supply deal. *The Financial Times*, 16 May, p. 3.

Gould, J.A. and Winters, M.A., 2007. An obsolescing bargain in Chad: shifts in leverage between the government and the World Bank. *Business and Politics*, 9(2).

Gow, D., 2008. US tells Europe to stop dithering over pipeline. *The Guardian*, [internet] 23 February. Available at: http://www.guardian.co.uk/business/2008/feb/23/oil.euro [Accessed on 20 April 2010].

Green, M., 2009. Total eyes role in trans-Saharan gas pipeline. *The Financial Times*, 26 February, p. 5.

Grgic, B., 2009. Brussels is losing its grip on the Caspian gas corridor. *The Financial Times*, 16 February, p. 9.

Gulf Oil and Gas, 2003. *Inauguration of the First Phase of Arab Gas Pipeline*, [internet] Available at: http://www.gulfoilandgas.com/webpro1/MAIN/Mainnews.asp?id=35 [Accessed 20 April 2010].

Haas, E.B., 1958. *The Uniting of Europe: Political, Social and Economic Forces 1950–1957*. Stanford: Stanford University Press.

Hadfield, A., 2008. EU-Russia energy relations: aggregation and aggravation. *Journal of Contemporary European Studies*, 16(2), pp. 231–48.

Hagelund, C., 2009. Europe's chance to stand up to Russia's energy bullying. *Journal of Energy Security*, [internet] 18 June. Available at: http://www.ensec.org/index.php?option=com_content&view=article&id=200:europes-chance-to-face-up-to-russias-energy-bullying&catid=96:content&Itemid=345 [Accessed 20 April 2010].

Haghighi, S., 2007. *Energy Security*. Oxford and Portland: Hart Publishing.

Hoffmann, S., 1995. *The European Sisyphus: essays on Europe, 1964–1994*. Boulder: Westview Press.

Hoogeveen, F. and Perlot, W., 2007. The EU's policies of security of energy supply towards the Middle East and Caspian region: major power politics. *Perspectives on Global Development and Technology*, 6, pp. 485–507.

Hope, K. and Troev, T., 2009. Bulgaria taps into gas pipeline to end reliance on Russia. *The Financial Times*, 15 July, p. 2.

Hoyos, C., 2004. BG in Kazakh dollars 5.4m tax dispute. *The Financial Times*, 23 July, p. 26.

Hoyos, C., 2008. Oil price helps Libya extract better terms with Eni. *The Financial Times*, 13 June, p. 17.

Hulbert, M. and Arian, A., 2009. After the oil bubble: unlearned lessons & political back-sliding, *Journal of Energy Security*, [internet] 27 August. Available at: http://www.ensec.org/index.php?option=com_content&view=article&id=209: after-the-oil-bubble-unlearned-lessons-aamp-political-back-sliding&catid=98:issue content0809&Itemid=349 [Accessed 30 March 2010].

Ifantis, K., 2008. Greece's energy security policy: between energy needs and geopolitical imperatives. In A. Marquina, ed. *Energy Security: Visions from Asia and Europe*. New York: Palgrave Macmillan, pp. 69–84.

International Energy Agency, 2006. *Trans Anatolian Pipeline Project*, [internet] Available at: http://www.iea.org/work/2006/energy_security/Cavanna.pdf [Accessed 20 April 2010].

———, 2007a. *Oil Market Report*, [internet] 14 December. Paris: OECD/IEA. Available at: http://omrpublic.iea.org/omrarchive/14dec07full.pdf [Accessed 30 March 2010].

———, 2007b. *World Energy Outlook 2007*, [internet] Paris: OECD/IEA. Available at: http://www.iea.org/textbase/nppdf/free/2007/weo_2007.pdf [Accessed 30 March 2010].

———, 2008a. *Oil Market Report*, [internet] 13 February. Paris: OECD/IEA. Available at: http://omrpublic.iea.org/omrarchive/13feb08full.pdf [Accessed 30 March 2010].

———, 2008b. *Perspectives on Caspian oil and Gas Development*, [internet] December. OECD/IEA. Available at: http://www.iea.org/papers/2008/caspian_perspectives.pdf [Accessed 30 March 2010].

———, 2009a. *Energy Balances of Non-OECD Countries 2009*. Paris: OECD/IEA.

———, 2009b. *Energy Statistics of Non-OECD Countries 2009*. Paris: OECD/IEA.

———, 2009c. *Key world Energy Statistics*, [internet] Available at: http://www.iea.org/textbase/nppdf/free/2009/key_stats_2009.pdf [Accessed 30 March 2010].

———, 2009d. *Natural Gas Information 2009*. Paris: OECD/IEA.

———, 2009e. *Oil Information 2009*. Paris: OECD/IEA.

———, 2009f. *World Energy Outlook 2009*. Paris: OECD/IEA.

———, 2010. *Oil Market Report*, [internet] 15 January. Paris: OECD/IEA. Available at: http://omrpublic.iea.org/omrarchive/15jan10full.pdf [Accessed 30 March 2010].

Interstate Oil and Gas Transport to Europe, 2010. [internet] Available at: www.inogate.org [Accessed 10 April 2010].

ITAR-TASS, 2010. Turkmenistan resumes nat gas supplies to Russia. *ITAR-TASS*, [Online] 9 January. Available at: http://www.itar-tass.com/txt/eng/level2.html?NewsID=14705397&PageNum=1&fy=&fm=&fd= [Accessed 30 March 2010].

Jaffe, A.M. and Manning, R.A., 1998–99. The myth of the Caspian 'Great Game': the real geopolitics of energy. *Survival*, 40(4).

Joint Press Release, 2007. *Turkey and the EU: Together for a European Energy Policy. High Level Conference in Istanbul*, [internet] 5 June. Available at: http://europa.eu/rapid/pressReleasesAction.do [Accessed 10 March 2008].

Kanter, J., 2009. Iraq signs oil deal with European companies; firms accept thin profits to secure future access to country's vast reserves. *International Herald Tribune*, 30 December.

Kausch, K., 2007. Europe and Russia, beyond energy. *FRIDE*, [internet], March. Working paper. Available at: http://www.fride.org/publication/137/europe-and-russia,-beyond-energy.

Keohane, R., 1989. *International Institutions and State Power: Essays in International Relations Theory*. Boulder: Westview Press.

Keohane, R.O. and Nye, J.S., 2001. *Power and Interdependence: World Politics in Transition*. 3rd ed. New York: Longman.

Ker-Lindsay, J., 2007. The policies of Greece and Cyprus towards Turkey's EU accession. *Turkish Studies*, 8(1), pp. 71–83.

Kommersant, 2008. Ukraine surfaced in South Stream project. *Kommersant International*, [internet] 29 February. Available at: http://www.kommersant.com/p859205/r_500/South_Stream/ [Accessed 10 March 2008].

Kramer, A.E., 2009a. In Ukraine, missed debt payment signals strain; gas transport firm's woes add new complexity to relations with Russia. *International Herald Tribune*, 2 October.

———, 2009b. Russian pipeline raises fears in Eastern Europe; German link creates worry over new leverage in former Soviet bloc. *International Herald Tribune*, 14 October.

———, 2010a. Russia-Belarus dispute threatens Europe's supply. *New York Times*, 4 January, p. 9A.

———, 2010b. Oil feud reflects growing rift between Russia and Belarus, once close allies. *New York Times*, 5 January, p. 4A.

————, 2010c. Pipeline planned for Baltic passes final hurdle; Finnish agency issues permit needed to begin undersea construction. *International Herald Tribune*, 13 February.

Krueger, A.O., 1974. The political economy of the rent-seeking society. *The American Economic Review*, 64(3), pp. 291–303.

Kupchinsky, R., 2007. Ukraine: Odessa-Brody pipeline potential still unused. *RadioFreeEurope RadioLiberty*, [internet] 12 January. Available at: http://www.rferl.org/content/article/1073974.html [Accessed 30 March 2010].

Larsson, R.L., 2007. *Nord Stream, Sweden and Baltic Sea security – Base data report March 2007*. Stockholm: FOI-Swedish Defense Research Agency. Available at: http://www.ii.umich.edu/UMICH/ceseuc/Home/ACADEMICS/Research%20 Projects/Energy%20Security%20in%20Europe%20and%20Eurasia/Nord%20 Stream,%20Sweden%20and%20Baltic%20Sea%20Security.pdf.

Le Coq, C. and Paltseva, E., 2009. Measuring the security of external energy supply in the European Union. *Energy Policy*, 37, pp. 4474–81.

Linke, K. and Viëtor, M., 2010. Introduction. In: K. Linke and M. Viëtor, eds. 2010. *Prospects of a Triangular Relationship? Energy Relations between the EU, Russia and Turkey*. Berlin: Friedrich-Ebert-Stiftung, pp. 3–4. Available at: http://library.fes.de/pdf-files/id/07150.pdf [Accessed 19 April 2010].

Lobjakas, A., 2009. 'Strategic' Nabucco deal inked to help curb dependence on Russian gas. *European Dialogue*, [internet] Available at: http://eurodialogue.org/Strategic-Nabucco-Deal-Inked-To-Help-Curb-Dependence-On-Russian-Gas [Accessed 20 April 2010].

Lucas, E., 2008. *The New Cold War*. New York and Houndsmills, UK: Palgrave Macmillan.

Luciani, G., 2004. Security of Supply for Natural Gas Markets: What is it and what is it not. *INDES*, [internet] Working Papers 2. Available at: http://aei.pitt.edu/ 11083/01/1108%5B2%5D.pdf [Accessed 20 April 2010].

Lynch, D., 2006. Foreward. In: A. Monaghan and L. Montanaro-Jankovski, eds. EU-Russia energy relations: the need for active engagement. *European Policy Center Issue Paper*, 45, pp. 1–29.

Mane-Estrada, A., 2006. European energy policy: towards the creation of the geo-energy Space. *Energy Policy*, 34, pp. 3773–86.

Mann, S.R., 2003. *Remarks: Florence IEA Conference*, [internet] Available at: http://www.iea.org/Textbase/work/2003/caspian/Mann.pdf [Accessed 10 March 2008].

Market Observatory for Energy, 2009a. *Country File: Norway*, [internet] Available at: http://ec.europa.eu/energy/observatory/doc/country/2009_10_norway.pdf [Accessed 10 April 2010].

————, 2009b. *Country File: Turkey*. [internet] Available at: http://ec.europa.eu/energy/observatory/doc/country/2009_12_turkey.pdf [Accessed 20 April 2010].

Medetsky, A., 2009. Gas exporters choose Russian chief. *Moscow Times*, 10 December, p. 1.

Meister, S., 2010. The EU, Russia and Turkey – prospects of an energy triangle. In: K. Linke and M. Viëtor, eds. 2010. *Prospects of a Triangular Relationship? Energy Relations between the EU, Russia and Turkey*. Berlin: Friedrich-Ebert-Stiftung, pp. 22–7. Available at: http://library.fes.de/pdf-files/id/07150.pdf [Accessed 19 April 2010].

Moravcsik, A., 1993. Preferences and power in the European Community: a liberal intergovernmentalist approach. *Journal of Common Market Studies*, 31(4), pp. 473–524.

——, 1998. *The Choice for Europe: Social Purpose and State Power from Messina to Maastricht*. Ithaca: Cornell University Press.

Moravcsik, A. and Vachudova, M.A., 2003. National interests, state power, and EU enlargement. *East European Politics and Societies*, 17(1), pp. 42–57.

Mortished, C., 2009. European gas war looms as Ukraine seeks cash to pay Gazprom for July deliveries. *The Times*, 23 June, p. 42.

Moscow Times, 2009. Turkmen say Gazprom broke deal. *The Moscow Times*, 13 April, p. 3.

Muftuler-Bac, M., 1997. *Turkey's Relations with a Changing Europe*. Manchester: Manchester University Press.

Nabucco, 2010. [internet] Available at: www.nabucco-pipeline.com [Accessed 20 April 2010].

Nord Stream. 2008. The new gas supply route to Europe. *Nord Stream: Facts*, [internet] Available at: http://www.nordstream.com/fileadmin/Dokumente/ NORD_STREAM__FACTS/English/NORD_STREAM_FACTS_ISSUE_0_ENGLISH_ DOWNLOAD.pdf [Accessed 30 March 2010].

Nye, J.S., 2009. Get smart: combining hard and soft Power. *Foreign Affairs*, 88(9), pp. 160–3.

O'Byrne, D., 2007. Turkey, Iraq sign energy cooperation pact; to include Iraqi oil exploration, pipelines, power plant. *Platts*, [internet] 9 August. Available at: http://global.factiva.com.proxygw.wrlc.org/ha/default.aspx [Accessed 30 March 2010].

Olcott, M.B., 2006. International gas trade in Central Asia: Turkmenistan, Iran, Russia, and Afghanistan. In: D.G. Victor, A.M. Jaffe and M.H. Hayes, eds. *Natural Gas and Geopolitics – from 1970 to 2040*. Cambridge: Cambridge University Press, pp. 202–234.

Olearchyk, R., 2009a. Putin eases European gas supply fears in Yalta talks. *The Financial Times*, 21 November, p. 6.

——, 2009b. Ukraine's plea for $2bn loan refused by IMF. *The Financial Times*, 24 December, p. 5.

Onis, Z., 2000. Luxembourg, Helsinki and Beyond: towards an interpretation of recent Turkey-EU relations. *Government and Opposition*, 35(4), pp. 463–83.

Orekli, N.C., 2007. Turkey's energy strategy in a new era: time to re-look South, *TUSIAD*, [internet] 16 December. Available at: http://www.tusiad.us/Content/ uploaded/CEM%20OREKLI-TURKEY%27S%20ENERGY%20STRATEGY.PDF [Accessed 20 April 2010].

Oster, S., 2009. China's resource strategy gets boost with Brazil oil deal. *Globe & Mail*, 20 May, p. B8.

Pahl, G., 2004. *Biodiesel: Growing a New Energy Economy*. White River Junction: Chelsea Green Publishing Company.

Pancevski, B., Charter, D. and Womack, H., 2009. Nuclear fears as danger plant is reopened in gas war; Slovakia. *The Times*, 12 January, p. 31.

Pannier, B., 2008. Nabucco chief eyes Iranian and Russian gas despite US objections. *Radio Free Europe Radio Liberty*, [internet] 23 June. Available at: www.rferl. org/content/Nabucco [Accessed 20 April 2010].

Pastori, G., 2008. Between continuity and change: the Italian approach to energy security. In: A. Marquina, ed. *Energy Security: Visions from Asia and Europe.* New York: Palgrave Macmillan, pp. 84–101.

Petersen, A., 2009. China-Turkmenistan pipeline not a real threat to Nabucco. *Atlantic Council*, [internet] 24 December. Available at: http://www.acus. org/highlight/china-turkmenistan-pipeline-not-real-threat-nabucco [Accessed 30 March 2010].

Piebalgs, A., 2007. *Turkey and EU: together for a European Energy Policy*, [internet] Speech delivered at the conference 'Turkey and the EU', 5 June, Istanbul. Available at: http://europa.eu/rapid/pressReleasesAction.do [Accessed 10 March 2008].

Piebalgs, A. and Shmatko, S., 2009. *Energy dialogue EU-Russia, the tenth progress report*, [internet] Available at: http://ec.europa.eu/energy/international/ bilateral_cooperation/russia/doc/reports/progress10_en.pdf [Accessed 10 March 2010].

Platts, 2006. Iran cuts supply to Turkey. *Platts*, [internet] 12 December. Available at: http://global.factiva.com.proxygw.wrlc.org/ha/default.aspx [Accessed 16 December 2006].

Pointvogl, A., 2009. Perceptions, realities, concession – What is driving the integration of European energy policies? *Energy Policy*, 37, pp. 5704–16.

Pravda, 2005. BTC pipeline a loser? [internet] 6 February. Available at: http:// engforum.pravda.ru/showthread.php?131386-BTC-pipeline-a-loser [Accessed 20 April 2010].

Pronina, L. and Meric, A.B., 2009. Turkey Offers Route for Gazprom's South Stream Gas Pipeline. *Bloomberg*, [internet] 6 August. Available at: http://www. bloomberg.com/apps/news?pid=20601100&sid=a.TM4QijmIMk [Accessed on 14 April 2010].

Rabinowitz, P., Yusifov, M., Arnoldi, J. and Hakim, E., 2004. Geology, Oil, and Gas Potential, Pipelines, and the Geopolitics of the Caspian Sea Region. *Ocean Development & International Law*, 35(1), pp. 19–40.

Reuters, 2008. Factbox-Facts about Turkmenistan and its key projects. *Reuters*, [internet] 7 February. Available at: http://global.factiva.com.proxygw.wrlc.org/ ha/default.aspx [Accessed 10 March 2008].

———, 2009. Crescent eyes Iraqi gas routes beyond Nabucco. *Reuters*, [internet] 4 June. Available at: www.reuters.com/article/idUSTRE5535IH20090604 [Accessed 20 April 2010].

RIA Novosti, 2008. Libya signs oil deal with Gazprom on oil and gas production. *RIA Novosti*, [internet] 22 February. Available at: http://en.rian.ru/business/ 20080222/99883039.html [Accessed 10 March 2008].

Ritchie, M., 2008. Russia: the Putin doctrine. *Energy Compass*, [internet] 4 January. Available at: http://global.factiva.com.proxygw.wrlc.org/ha/default.aspx [Accessed 10 March 2008].

Roberts, J., 2004. The Turkish gate: energy transit and security issues. *Turkish Policy Quarterly*, 3(4), pp. 17–46.

Roberts, J.M., 2006. The Black Sea and European energy security. *Southeast Europe and Black Sea Studies*, 6(2), pp. 220–1.

Roberts, D., 2010. Russian energy group with the power to turn off lights in Europe. *The Guardian*, 11 January, p. 27.

Rodova, N., 2008a. Gazprom willing to cooperate on Caspian gas routes. *Platts*, [internet] 4 July. Available at: http://www.platts.com/Natural%20Gas/News/8856234.xml [Accessed 28 July 2008].

———, 2008b. Russia's Rosneft suggests joint Sakhalin development with Gazprom. *Platts*, [internet] Available at: http://www.platts.com/Natural%20Gas/News/8896557.xml [Accessed 28 July 2008].

Rosamond, B., 2000. *Theories of European Integration*. New York: St Martin's Press.

Sachs, J.D., 2007. How to handle the macroeconomics of oil wealth. In: M. Humphreys, J.D. Sachs and J.E. Stiglitz, eds. *Escaping the Resource Curse*. New York: Columbia University Press, pp. 173–93.

Schimmelfennig, F., 2004. Liberal intergovernmentalism. In: T. Diez and A. Wiener, eds. *European Integration Theory*. Oxford: Oxford University Press, pp. 75–93.

Schmitter, P., 2004. Neo-functionalism. In: T. Diez and A.Wiener, eds. *European Integration Theory*. Oxford: Oxford University Press, pp. 45–74.

SEEREM. (2010) [internet] Available at: https://devex.com/projects/38687?lang=es [Accessed 19 December 2009].

Shchedrov, O., 2008. Russia, Algeria talk energy, mum on gas OPEC. *Reuters*, 19 February.

Shiryaevskaya, A., 2008. Russia drafts charter for natural gas OPEC; Exporters' forum not expected to evolve into cartel. *Platts*, [internet] 22 April. Available at: http://global.factiva.com.proxygw.wrlc.org/ha/default.aspx [Accessed 6 May 2008].

———, 2010. Turkmens seek foreign bids for Caspian fields to expand market. *Business Week*, 11 February.

Sjursen, H., 2002. Why expand? The question of legitimacy and justification in the EU's enlargement policy. *Journal of Common Market Studies*, 40(3), pp. 491–513.

Skeet, I., 1988. *OPEC: Twenty-Five Years of Prices and Politics*. Cambridge: Cambridge University Press.

Skordos, A., 2007. Oil exploitation in the eastern Mediterranean: Cyprus, Turkey and international law. *Woodrow Wilson International Center for Scholars*, [internet], 29 March. Event summary. Available at: http://www.wilsoncenter.org/index.cfm?topic_id=109941&fuseaction=topics.event_summary&event_id=225758 [Accessed 10 April 2010].

Socor, V., 2006. Gazprom picks off one large German morsel, poised for another. *Eurasia Daily Monitor*, [internet] 3 May. Available at: http://www.jamestown.org/single/?no_cache=1&tx_ttnews[tt_news]=31644 [Accessed 10 March 2008].

———, 2007a. Kremlin energy strategy targets Western energy assets in Russia, Western supply sources in third countries. *Eurasia Daily Monitor*, [internet] 22 January. Available at: http://www.jamestown.org/programs/edm/single/?tx_ttnews[tt_news]=32413&tx_ttnews[backPid]=171&no_cache=1 [Accessed 10 March 2008].

———, 2007b. Western majors sign agreement on intent on trans-Caspian oil transport system. *Eurasia Daily Monitor*, [internet] 25 January. Available at: http://www.jamestown.org/single/?no_cache=1&tx_ttnews[tt_news]=32424 [Accessed 10 March 2008].

————, 2008. Gazprom on a shopping spree for gas. *Eurasia Daily Monitor*, [internet] 14 July. Available at: http://www.jamestown.org/single/?no_cache=1&tx_ttnews[tt_news]=33797 [Accessed 30 July 2008].

————, 2009. Strategic implications of the Central Asia-China gas pipeline. *Eurasia Daily Monitor*, [internet] 18 December. Available at: http://www.jamestown.org/single/?no_cache=1&tx_ttnews%5Btt_news%5D=35856&tx_ttnews%5BbackPid%5D=13&cHash=4b0f4138d8 [Accessed 30 March 2010].

Solana, J., 2006. *Towards an EU External Energy Policy*, [internet] 20 November. Available at: http://www.consilium.europa.eu/ueDocs/cms_Data/docs/pressdata/EN/discours/91788.pdf [Accessed 30 March 2010].

Spanjer, A., 2007. Russian gas price reform and the EU-Russia gas relationship: incentives, consequences and European security of supply. *Energy Policy*, 35, pp. 2889–98.

Spetschinsky, L., 2007. Russia and the EU: the challenge ahead. *Studia Diplomatica*, 60(1), pp. 151–70. In: A. Hadfield, 2008. EU-Russia energy relations: aggregation and aggravation. *Journal of Contemporary European Studies*, 16(2), pp. 231–48.

Spiegel Online International, 2004. Turkey and the EU – the pros and cons. *Spiegel*, [internet] 16 December. Available at: http://www.spiegel.de/international/0,1518,333126,00.html [Accessed 14 April 2010].

Steen, M., 2009. Gazprom to use Dutch gas storage. *The Financial Times*, 21 August, p. 16.

Stern, D.L., 2007. Kazakh leader suggests way to end oil standoff. *New York Times*, 8 December.

Tekin, A., 2005. Future of Turkey-EU Relations: a civilisational approach. *Futures*, 37(4), pp. 287–302.

Tekin, A. and Walterova, I., 2007. Turkey's geopolitical role: the energy angle. *Middle East Policy*, 14(1), pp. 84–94.

Tekin, A. and Williams, P.A., 2009a. EU-Russian relations and Turkey's role as an energy corridor. *Europe-Asia Studies*, 61(2), pp. 337–56.

————, 2009b. Turkey and EU energy security: the pipeline connection. *East European Quarterly*, 42(4), pp. 419–34.

Tobin, L., 2009. BG battles to claw back Kazakh duty. *London Evening Standard*, [internet] 22 September. Available at: http://www.thisislondon.co.uk/standard-business/article-23746995-bg-battles-to-claw-back-kazakh-duty.do [Accessed 30 March 2010].

Traynor, I., 2009. Russian gas begins to flow into wary Europe. *The Guardian*, 21 January, p. 26.

Tshkov, V., 2009. Bulgaria, Greece agree to link pipelines for delivery of Caspian Gas. *Los Angeles Times*, 14 July.

Tsombanopoulos, V., 2002. *The Turkey – Greece Gas Interconnection and the Arising Prospects*, [internet] Available at: http://www.iea.org/work/2002/seegas/NMCDEPA.PDF [Accessed 10 April 2010].

Tuna, C., 2010. Azerbaijan diversifies its energy routes. *Journal of Turkish Weekly*, [internet] 12 February. Available at: http://www.turkishweekly.net/op-ed/2635/azerbaijan-diversifies-its-energy-routes.html.

Turkish Daily News, 2007. Turkey and Iraq agree on trade and energy. *Turkish Daily News*, [internet], 9 August. Available at: http://www.hurriyetdaily

news.com/h.php?news=turkey-and-iraq-agree-on-trade-and-energy-2007-08-09 [Accessed 20 April 2010].

Turkish Ministry of Energy and Natural Resources, 2010a. *Intergovernmental Agreement for Nabucco Project Is Concluded*, [internet] Available at: www.enerji.gov.tr/BysWEB/DownloadBelgeServlet?read=db&fileId=62086 [Accessed 12 March 2010].

———, 2010b. *Untitled Document*, [internet] Available at: http//www.enerji.gov.tr/en/inc_enerji_EN.php [Accessed 12 March 2010].

Tuskon, 2009. *Turkey As an Energy Hub for Europe: Prospects and Challenges*, [internet] 14 March. Available at: http://www.tuskonus.org/tuskon.php?c=1&s=&e=113 [Accessed 16 March 2010].

Umbach, F., 2008. German debates on energy security and impacts on Germany's 2007 EU presidency. In: A. Marquina, ed. *Energy Security: Visions from Asia and Europe*. New York: Palgrave Macmillan, pp. 1–24.

United Nations, 2002. *International Trade Statistics Yearbook*. Volume I: trade by country. New York: United Nations. Available at: http://comtrade.un.org/pb/FileFetch.aspx?type=volumes&docID=3113 [Accessed 30 March 2010].

———, 2007. *International Trade Statistics Yearbook*. Country pages: Russia. New York: United Nations. Available at: http://comtrade.un.org/pb/FileFetch.aspx?docID=2520&type=country%20pages [Accessed 30 March 2010].

United Nations Commission for Europe, 2006. *Report on Global Energy Security and the Caspian Sea Region: Country Profiles*, [internet] Available at: http://www.unece.org/ie/se/pdfs/comm15/ECE.ENERGY.2006.3.Add.1_e.pdf [Accessed 10 March 2008].

United Nations Development Programme, 2001. *World Energy Assessment: Energy the Challenge of Sustainability*. New York: United Nations.

Valasek, T., 2009. Ukraine and the EU: A vicious circle? *Centre for European Reform Bulletin*, [internet] 69. Available at: http://www.cer.org.uk/articles/69_valasek.html [Accessed 30 March 2010].

van Aartsen, J., 2009. *Activity Report September 2007–February 2009*, [internet] Brussels: The European Commission. Available at: http://ec.europa.eu/energy/infrastructure/tent_e/doc/axis/2009_axis_linking_activity_report_2007_2009.pdf [Accessed 30 March 2010].

Vernon, R., 1971. *Sovereignty at Bay: The Multinational Spread of U.S. Enterprises*. New York: Basic Books.

Victor, N.M. and Victor, D.G., 2006. Bypassing Ukraine: exporting Russian gas to Poland and Germany. In: D.G. Victor, A.M. Jaffe and M.H. Hayes, eds. *Natural gas and Geopolitics – From 1970 to 2040*. Cambridge: Cambridge University Press, pp. 122–169.

Wagstyl, S. and Ward, A., 2010. Lithuania fears exposure as reactor shuts down. *The Financial Times*, 2 January, p. 8.

Waltz, K., 1979. *Theory of International Politics*. New York: McGraw-Hill; Reading: Addison-Wesley.

Weaver, S., 2009. Gazprom: the octopus in Europe's energy market. *European Affairs*, 10(1–2), pp. 48–52.

White, G., 2008. Gas-supply battle heats escalates between Russia and Ukraine. *Wall Street Journal Europe*, 5 March.

Wick, K. and Bulte, E.H., 2006. Contesting resources – rent-seeking, conflict and the natural resource curse. *Public Choice*, 128, pp. 457–76.

Williams, P.A., 2006. Projections for the geopolitical economy of oil after war in Iraq. *Futures*, 38(9), pp. 1074–88.

——, 2008. New configuration or reconfiguration? Conflict in North-South energy relations. In: R. Reuveny and W.R. Thompson, eds. *North and South in the World Political Economy*. Oxford: Blackwell, pp. 65–87.

Williams, P.A. and Tekin, A., 2008. The Iraq war, Turkey, and renewed Caspian energy prospects. *Middle East Journal*, 62, pp. 383–97.

Winrow, M.G., 2004. Turkey and the East–West gas transportation corridor. *Turkish Studies*, 5(2), pp. 23–42.

——, 2005. Energy security in the Black Sea-Caspian region. *Perceptions*, 10(3), pp. 85–98.

——, 2007. Geopolitics and energy security in the wider Black Sea region. *Southeast European and Black Sea Studies*, 5(2), pp. 23–42.

Woehrel, S., 2009. *Russian Energy Policy Toward Neighboring Countries*, [internet] Washington, DC: Congressional Research Service. Available at: http://fpc.state.gov/documents/organization/125528.pdf [Accessed 30 March 2010].

Wohlforth, W.C., 2004. Revisiting balance of power theory in central Eurasia. In: T.V. Paul, J.J. Wirtz and M. Fortmann, eds. *Balance of Power: Theory and Practice in the 21st century*. Stanford: Stanford University Press, pp. 214–239.

World Bank, 2007. *Russian Federation at a Glance*, [internet] Available at: http://devdata.worldbank.org/AAG/rus_aag.pdf [Accessed 30 July 2008].

——, 2009. *Global Economic Prospects: Commodities at the Crossroads*, [internet] Washington, DC: World Bank. Available at: http://siteresources.worldbank.org/INTGEP2009/Resources/10363_WebPDF-w47.pdf [Accessed 30 March 2010].

Xinhua, 2008. Russia, Uzbekistan reach agreement on new natural gas pipeline. *Xinhua News Agency*, [internet] 3 September. Available at: http://news.xinhuanet.com/english/2008-09/03/content_9761585.htm [Accessed 30 March 2010].

Yergin, D., 2006. Ensuring energy security. *Foreign Affairs*, 85(2), pp. 69–82.

Yigitguden, Y., 2010. Turkey – Turning the European periphery into an energy hub? In: K. Linke and M. Viëtor, eds. *Prospects of a Triangular Relationship? Energy Relations between the EU, Russia and Turkey*. Berlin: Friedrich-Ebert-Stiftung, pp. 12–18. Available at: http://library.fes.de/pdf-files/id/07150.pdf [Accessed 19 April 2010].

Young, A.R. and Wallace, H., 2000. The single market. In: H. Wallace and W. Wallace, eds. *Policy-Making in the European Union*. 4th ed. Oxford: Oxford University Press, pp. 85–114.

Youngs, R., 2007a. Europe's energy policy: economics, ethics, geopolitics. *FRIDE*, [internet] 10 January. Available at: http://www.fride.org/publication/54/europes-energy-policy-economics-ethicsgeopolitics [Accessed 30 March 2010].

——, 2007b. Europe's external energy policy: between geopolitics and the market. *Centre for European Policy Studies*, 278, November.

——, 2009. *Energy Security: Europe's New Foreign Policy Challenge*. London and New York: Routledge.

Zweig, D. and Jianhai, B., 2005. China's global hunt for energy. *Foreign Affairs*, 84(5), pp. 25–38.

Index